300 Tips to More Salmon & Steelhead   Scott Haugen

300 Tips to More Salmon & Steelhead

Scott Haugen

Acknowledgments

I would like to thank all the anglers in the world who enlightened me on the river throughout the years. Even as an adult I continue learning, which is one of the elements that makes our sport so rewarding. With the advent of new gear comes innovative tactical approaches that allow anglers to catch more fish. At the same time, creative minds and a willingness to succeed continually inspires anglers to reach the next level.

It is these anglers, the ones who are motivated to prevail yet are willing to share what they've learned with others, who have such an impact on the progression of our sport. Truth is, the more anglers we have actively participating in sport fishing, the better it is for ensuring the longevity of what we love to do, so future generations will be able to experience nature as we have, and all it has to offer.

Thank you all, and God bless!

Frank Amato Publications, Inc, P.O. Box 82112, Portland, Oregon 97282

503.653.8108 • www.amatobooks.com

Photographs by the author unless otherwise noted.
Cover photo by: Scott Haugen
Book and Cover Design: Kathy Johnson
Printed in Singapore
Softbound ISBN 10: 1-57188-409-2
Softbound ISBN-13: 978-1-57188-409-1
UPC: 0-81127-00243-6
1 3 5 7 9 10 8 6 4 2

Contents

Dedication

To every angler who ever wet a line, and the hard-working souls who do all in their power to promote and preserve sport fishing, thank you, and may you always strive to experience what the great world of fishing has to offer.

A special dedication goes out to my three favorite fishing partners: My dad, Jerry Haugen for introducing me into this great sport; and my sons, Braxton and Kazden who keep me going.

Jerry Haugen

The author's father.

Braxton Haugen

Kazden Haugen

Braxton Haugen, age six, with his first spring chinook.

Kazden Haugen, age four, and his first summer steelhead.

Fishing is a sport of perpetual change. New, innovative gear, from rods to reels to lines, terminal gear and even boats and clothing, make it possible for anglers to use their imaginations to apply new techniques in order to catch more fish. At the same time, storage systems, handy gadgets and simple forethought and organization go a long way in maximizing one's time on the water.

The purpose of this book is twofold: To increase your actual fishing time while on the river and to expand your arsenal of tactical approaches. The more time spent with the lines in the water, the greater the likelihood of catching more fish. Likewise, the more diverse your approaches, the more fish you will end up with. After all, no matter how much serious anglers claim to love just getting out and spending time on the river, the objective is to catch salmon and steelhead.

In my mind, a willingness to try new gear and apply unfamiliar tactical approaches are among the most critical elements in progressing one's fishing repertoire. Thanks to technological advancements, new gear is being designed at astounding rates. While some people may argue that the point of new gear production is to make money, fact is, if the gear doesn't catch fish, it won't create revenue over the long term. In other words, a great deal of thought and money goes into the creation and crafting of new gear, with the hopes that it will catch more fish.

As if the change in gear is not enough, the rivers and even fish themselves have a direct correlation to how we

Within these pages, the author offers insight as to how to catch more salmon and steelhead in river systems.

Introduction

fish. Rivers bottoms can change from year to year—especially in high-water seasons—meaning fish may move from traditional holding zones or that new techniques must be applied to reach target zones that were previously easy to access. Perhaps hatchery fish that have been introduced into a drainage run upstream a month or two prior to the wild fish we've become accustomed to pursuing; the river conditions in which we fish these early-run fish may be far different than when going after the wild fish, meaning different techniques may need to be applied in order to reach both. Bottom line, there are numerous factors that play a role in how we fish, and recognizing these factors, then adapting our approach, is wherein the success of salmon and steelhead fishing lies.

The fishing world carries a wide range of experience levels, and it is my ultimate hope that no matter what your range of expertise, you come away with a few key points that will enhance the way you fish, whereby allowing you to catch more fish. The words in this book come from more than 35 years of personal salmon and steelhead fishing experience. Many of the points are ones I learned through personal trial and error, while others I acquired from fellow anglers over the years.

Fishing is a great sport, and it lends itself nicely to the sharing of information which will help others. If this book helps you catch just a few more fish each season, then the time and effort spent writing it was worth it.

There is a great deal of preparation required to get a fish to this point.

The most successful fishing trips often begin days, weeks, sometimes even months prior to hitting the water. Knowing the behavior of salmon or steelhead being targeted is critical, for this will determine how to go about fishing for them. Being familiar with the water these fish inhabit under a wide range of scenarios also plays a large role in how anglers go about unraveling the complex decision of what to offer these fish to make them bite.

Not only do the fish themselves have an impact on how you fish, but so do fellow anglers. It may be a favorite hole is best fished by way of back-bouncing, but if boats have the prime slot tied up, drift-fishing may be the only option. At the same time, bank anglers may occupy an ideal boat-fishing position, or vice versa. Perhaps a half-dozen anglers are all throwing eggs into a salmon hole; maybe offering the fish something different is key to triggering the bite.

Another consideration must be a thorough physical assessment of the river being fished. Knowing what the bottom structure is like, if there are ledges, chutes or funnels the fish travel through, even water

Chapter 1 *Preparation*

temperatures, will all impact how an angler chooses to fish that particular system. What's the weather doing, and how is the river reacting? Is the target river fishable when running turbid or crystal-clear? Is the river on the rise or in recovery mode following a recent storm? What time of day are you fishing? All of these questions, and many more like them, will play a part in where you opt to fish in a river and what ploys will be used to draw that hit.

In this chapter you'll find 99 tips to consider when preparing for your next trip. These are steps to be done at home, before going to the river. While some of these tips can be taken care of several weeks in advance, others more aptly fit into the category of "last-minute" preparation. The keys to maximizing these points are forethought and organization. The more you can think ahead about the details surrounding an upcoming trip, and the more organized you can be at gearing-up accordingly, the greater your fish-catching percentages will be.

Being prepared is vital to consistent success, as proven here by salmon and steelhead legend, Buzz Ramsey.

1. Read Regulations

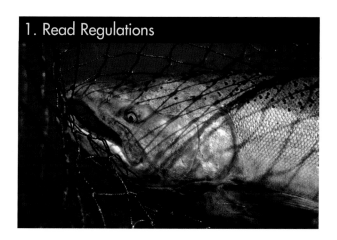

At the start of each year, or at appropriated times as established by fish and wildlife institutions, each state releases a booklet of fishing regulations. As soon as these regulations come out, pick up a copy and read through the parts which apply to the waters you fish. Look for changes which may have taken place, relating to both rivers and gear. Grabbing two or three copies is a good idea, keeping one at home, one in the truck and/or one in the boat.

Regulations are the written laws by which anglers must abide when on the water. It's our responsibility to know the information in them as well as apply what they say. Not only will this effort make your time on the water more enjoyable, knowing you're adhering to set laws, but it allows officials to make quick turn-arounds during checks, meaning you're fishing time increases.

In addition to the primary regulations, keep a watchful eye out for updated changes. As seasons progress in many rivers, catch rates, run numbers and escapements over dams are just some factors that may warrant a change in the regulations. Prior to launching the boat, check bulletin boards, signs or even fliers posted on trees updating anglers with the most relevant information and regulatory changes. Look in diners, gas stations, local sporting goods stores, even fish and wildlife websites for regulation updates. Radio and television spots are also good sources through which to monitor such changes.

Bottom line, it's the angler's responsibility to know the laws and any changes in the laws which may appear during the course of any given fishing season. There are few things that can taint a fishing trip as quickly as a citation, and as law-abiding sportsmen whose obligation it is to promote ethical practices and uphold the laws, the least we can do is take time to know these laws and how they apply to waters we're fishing.

2. Study Maps

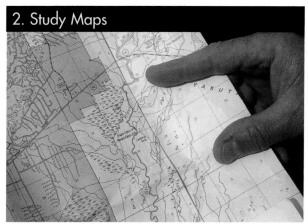

One of the best ways to learn a river prior to fishing it for the first time is by studying a map. Maps give an orientation to how a river lays in accordance with the surrounding landscape and even towns. Such basic information can greatly influence where you choose to fish, and how. For example, bank fishing near populated towns will often find you in tight quarters with fellow anglers; if this type of fishing is not what you're looking for, a map can save valuable time.

Good maps showing river details, including ramps, areas of caution, even prime fishing holes are available through various local and regional sporting goods stores. Books such as the *DeLorme Atlas & Gazetteer* series are good resources, and many states offer marine guides which are also beneficial. Many local stores carry maps made by independent companies, capturing outstanding details and offering local knowledge that's tough to get anywhere else.

But those books penned by fishing authors or publishers are likely the most beneficial. Frank Amato Publications publishes some excellent where-to books, capturing comprehensive details. Their *Oregon River Maps & Fishing Guide*, for example, is one of the premier books in terms of breaking-down rivers and providing valued fishing information.

Regional magazines are also good river resources, often running map stories to help point anglers in the right direction. Another option are websites, where some state agencies may keep up-to-date map information on rivers in their area. Think of it as planning a hunt; the more preparation that can be done prior to departure, the more time can be devoted to achieving the objective. Maps are a great investment.

3. Check River Levels

No matter what the time of year, checking river levels is a good idea. Several things can influence how much water is flowing in a river, thus impacting clarity levels and overall fishing. Rain storms, quick snow melt, emergency openings of dams, the operation of irrigation canals, even tributary activity impacts the level of a river. Not only can this effect if you'll fish, but how you'll fish.

During the rainy months it's especially important to inquire about river levels. This is the time of year when conditions can change overnight, and tracking storm systems can save many hours of frustration. There are many regional websites which lead to river level monitoring stations, and they are updated frequently which makes them a valuable information source. Radio, television and newspapers may also offer information worth knowing, depending on the rivers being sought. Some regions still offer telephone hotlines which can direct you to specific streams, though the shift is leading toward computer referencing. Typing in a simple search of river levels for the area you plan to fish can yield quick, informative results. State fish and wildlife agencies can also help point you in the right direction.

Knowing how much water is flowing through a system can dictate how you fish, thus, by being aware of what's happening, you'll be better prepared to use the most applicable approach which allows you to find fish. For instance, you may not be a plunking fan, but if the river is high and off-color, it's going to make for tough jig-fishing conditions. At the same time, if the river is low, those giant plugs may not be necessary. If a river is running exceptionally low and clear, it may be necessary to switch to fluorocarbon leader, so as not to risk spooking fish. Be aware of what the river is doing, and adjust accordingly.

4. Check Tides

Monitoring the tides paid off for Mike Perusse.

Some of the best salmon and steelhead fishing, no matter what time of year, can be directly correlated to tidal shifts. One of my best silver salmon days came while keying on a tide change; the same is true for fall chinook and winter steelhead. On one of my most memorable trips to Alaska, I even hit the head of an incoming tide to get into some of the most memorable spring steelheading action I've ever experienced.

The exact time a tidal shift occurs and the magnitude of that shift, are two important variables to consider when targeting tidewater fish. Another key point to weigh is how far upstream you intend on fishing once a tide change has taken place. A big tide may find you closer to the river's mouth if you want to get into those fish quickly, instead of waiting for them to come to you. On the other hand, if you don't want to battle crowds, you might want to wait for the fish to come to you, further upstream. While fishing an Alaskan stream one day, two buddies and I caught four fish in eight hours. That night a big storm blew in, and along with it one of the highest tides of the year which pushed in an estimated 40,000 kings. The next day we headed the jetboat downstream, to some of the lower holes, and ended up hooking and releasing over 100 kings.

If fishing tidal zones, be sure to reference the most up-to-date tide books. These are available for a nominal fee at local and regional sporting goods stores as well as area marinas. If fishing near a marina, the folks there are usually very helpful in terms of offering information as to when the fishing is best based on the given tidal conditions. When reading tide books, make certain to adjust for times as instructed, if necessary. By noting tidal fluctuation times, your fishing time can be spent in the best locale.

5. Call Resources

Some of the best information in terms of rivers, fishing reports and where to go are fellow anglers. Sporting goods store personnel, as well as tackle shop owners and hatchery staff members, are often dialed in to the hottest action. In rural areas, diners, gas stations and marinas can be a valuable aid. If you don't know someone who lives in or has been fishing the area you'd like to visit, give one of the aforementioned resources a call.

Ask about river conditions, the number of fish showing, what they're hitting on and where. One phone call can save hours of driving and an entire day of fishing in the wrong spot. These lines of communication can help direct you to where the best action is, and hopefully a productive day on the water. Local fish and wildlife agencies are also valued help.

Don't overlook fishing-related websites that often file timely reports, including the posting of river conditions. Chat rooms can also help direct you to the right destination; it's a great feeling knowing there are others out there wanting to help you succeed on the water.

6. No Cologne

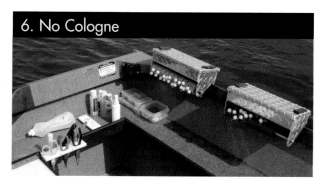

If planning on handling baits, plugs, lures or any other terminal gear during the course of the fishing day, keeping your hands clean is an essential, often-overlooked piece of the fish-catching puzzle. Unwanted scents can turn a salmon's nose quicker than anything, and taking the precautionary steps not to contaminate the water with foul odors can pay off.

Cologne, after shave, perfume and some lotions have a powerful odor that can remain on the hands for several hours. Even those spray-on colognes and perfumes that aren't touched by hand during the application process carry a strong enough odor that if contacted several hours later, will transfer pungent odors to the hand and potentially the bait. To avoid risk of contaminating fishing tackle, and turning off the bite, refrain from using these fragrant items up to 24 hours prior to the fishing trip. I've heard of guides who will phone their clients two days prior to a trip, reminding them to hold off on the smelly colognes and perfumes for fear of tainting the bait. It may seem trivial at times, but remember, a salmon and steelhead's sense of smell is measure in parts-per-billion, an incomprehensible number for the human nose. It's better to be safe than sorry, especially when the fishing action has been slow.

7. No Bananas

Sitting at the breakfast table, four of my buddies shot me a scathing glance when I picked up a banana, peeled and ate it, 30 minutes before we were going to be on the river. I baited my own hooks and ended up hooking five chinook and two coho by noon, far above the boat average. Granted, it was an experiment, one I've had mixed results with in differing situations.

The fear anglers have of bananas is the potassium they carry, and rightly so. Scientific testing has reportedly shown that fish don't like the smell of potassium. In fact, it's believed the odor of potassium drives fish away; some claim it can push a school of salmon clean out of a hole.

To be on the safe side, don't eat bananas for breakfast prior to a day on the river. And don't bother bringing them for lunch. Some guides, especially in Alaska, will sort through your lunch box prior to hitting the water, discarding any and all bananas they find. Others make it clear they don't want any bananas on board their boat. Again, it's a small piece of the puzzle, but can make a huge difference in success rates. After years of repeatedly testing the banana scenario in many situations, I'm a believer in leaving them home, and not eating them for breakfast.

8. Home Tackle Storage

Organization is one of the most critical elements to successful salmon and steelhead fishing. The best anglers I know are the ones who pay the most attention to detail, and it starts well before hitting the river. Believe it or not, how you store your tackle at home can have a direct correlation with overall fishing time, thus the ability to catch fish.

Storing gear in such a way that it can be readily accessed is not only a big time-saver, but it allows you to select the specific gear needed for a particular trip. For instance, if you're going to concentrate solely on side-drifting, there's no need for the jig, plugging or drift-fishing rods and gear. The space saved in the boat and extra gear that goes with these other methods makes things much more manageable when on the river.

There are many options when it comes to storing tackle at home. You may elect to have one big tackle box for each species, say one for spring chinook, one for fall chinook, one for summer steelhead, one for winter steelhead, and so one. This means when heading out for a particular species, you can grab one box and go. But what if you're hitting springers and summer steelhead in one trip, that's two bulky tackle boxes to take along?

For this scenario, many anglers choose to store their gear in manageable sized multi-compartment boxes. This means they can grab a box of Corkies and go, knowing the sizes and colors are there for targeting springers and/or summer-runs. The same holds true for plugs, sinkers, divers and other gear.

Another excellent set-up, if you have the wall space, is hanging all your tackle on pegboards. For smaller items, package them so they can be hung. This allows you to see exactly what gear you have in stock and more importantly, makes for easy selection when preparing for a trip. Simply grab an empty tackle box or similar type container and go down the wall, choosing the gear you'll be using on the next trip. This approach requires a bit more time in the preparation phase, but saves time on the water as you know exactly what you have available.

9. Break-down Gear

If storing gear in large tackle boxes at home, lugging them along in the boat can be cumbersome, especially if two or more buddies are joining you for the day. To save space, conserve weight and optimize overall efficiency, consider breaking down the gear into smaller tackle boxes. Rather than taking a hefty tackle box full of gear you won't use, sort through the tackle you know you'll be using and take only what you need.

For instance, if your big "salmon" tackle box contains weighted divers, an array of sinkers, flashers or big trolling spoons you only use on fall chinook, then leave this gear behind when targeting springers. The same holds true for winter versus summer steelhead. Though there is some gear crossover, that is, the same tackle is used for both spring and fall chinook, and for summer and winter steelhead, for the most part they are specialized species fished in specific water types that require precise approaches.

By taking along only the gear you know you'll be using on a particular trip, the amount of space saved and overall weight reduction is surprising. For bank anglers, keeping all the gear on your person allows for a great deal more water to be covered and dramatically increases your fishing time. It comes back to organization; the more organized you are, the more selective you can be, the greater your overall effectiveness when on the river.

10. Home Rod Storage

Believe it or not, how rods are stored at home can have a direct correlation to catching fish. It's not uncommon, for example, for people to break-down their springer rods at the end of the season and toss them in the corner of the garage until next year. Come the day before the season, they'll typically grab the rods, blow off the dust, remove the cobwebs and rig up. Never mind changing line, checking to make sure abrasions were not attained on the rod itself, or checking on the functions of the reel after a year of sitting.

Line ages, even when not being fished. The likelihood of breaking off that first fish is high with old line. At the same time, the odds of snapping a rod tip where it was scored as things were piled upon it in the garage, will not be realized until a fish is hooked. The same holds true for drags and springs in reels; not until it's too late do you realize something's wrong.

By storing rods in a safe, protected place, they'll receive more attention. Rod racks that can be screwed to the garage or shop wall, where rods can be safely stood upright in them, is a good way to go. If hurting for wall space, consider using some 2x2s hung from the ceiling, spaced apart so the rod butts rest on one end, the mid section on the other. Both storage systems keep the rods out of harms way, and allow for easy access.

The easier you can get to the rods, the greater the likelihood of changing out the line, coating the key parts with antirust spray and taking better care of them, overall. Reel covers can also be used to further increase the life of the reel. Having rods in view means they receive more attention, equating to better care which extends their life and performance level when it comes time to fish them.

11. Multiple Rods

In this age of specialization, it's easy getting tied to one particular piece of equipment, or one specific tactical approach. Years ago the craze was pulling plugs, then came jig fishing, followed by side-drifting. All are outstanding methods, and the creation of specialized gear allows anglers to carry out each approach with more efficiency than ever before. But don't limit yourself.

If fishing a river where water type varies widely, it opens the door for multiple approaches to be applied. For this reason, rigging multiple rods for a day on the river can be one of the best moves an angler can make. While the initial thought of setting yourself up to fish multiple rods can be a shock, don't let it overwhelm you. By chipping away at it over the course of a few years you'll have most of the rods and gear needed to pull off a multiple rod approach.

As a general rule, I like having six to seven rods in the boat, per angler. This allows for multiple riggings on specialized rods so each can be properly fished. It also lends itself to quick change-outs, which is a major timesaver. With multiple rods rigged and ready to fish, there's no time wasted tying on new terminal gear. Every hole you pull into, each riffle you pass through and all pockets you go by can now be fished with precision.

Take spring chinook, for instance. For each angler I like having a rod set-up with a diver-and-bait, Hot Shot, Kwikfish, bobber and jig/bait and two drift-fishing rods. I might also have a rod rigged with a prawn rig or spinner. You can do the same for every species being targeted, for the more you can throw at them, the better the results can be, especially on slow days.

I don't know how many days over the years I've pulled in behind boats who were having no luck pulling plugs, or side-drifting through a given stretch of water, only to offer the fish something different and come away with results. The same holds true with chinook; maybe drifting eggs isn't working, so switch to something different for results.

Bank anglers can also benefit from multiple rod set-ups, for the more varied the offering, the better the fish-catching opportunities. The key here is avoiding the tendency to bog yourself down, whereby limiting movement. Take only the gear you know will be fished, and cover water, applying specific techniques as you go. Be organized, invest in the gear and you'll put more meat in the freezer.

12. Spooling Line

It's a problem many anglers toil with, and that's how to best spool line on spinning and casting reels. Over the years I've seen numerous anglers waste valuable fishing time as they struggled to maintain line twist and bird's nests while on the river, especially on spinning reels.

Ideally, prior to spooling, it's best to know how the manufacturer of the line you're using puts it on the spool you're taking it off. On casting reels, for instance, the line I use comes off best over the top of the bulk spool, while it's turning. For spinning reels, one of the ends of the bulk spool should face the reel it's being added to, so that when line comes off, it's doing so in a clockwise motion while the main spool remains stationary.

If there's someone around, they can help you spool line with nothing more than a pencil. Slip the pencil through the large center holes on the bulk spool and turn the spool to the desired position for line to come off. Have whoever is holding the line apply tension to the spool with their hands. There are also line-spooling devices on the market, which make it even easier, especially when working alone. PLine's Spooling Assistant, for example, is ideal for this need. The tension springs are perfect for loading both spinning and casting reels.

On spinning reels, be careful not to overfill the spool, as this will cause a bird's nest. If, after proper spooling, the line does happen to twist, remove the terminal gear and let the line out, either trolled behind the boat or run downstream. This should remove any twist. If at home and noticing twists, tie a large barrel swivel to the end of the line, nail it to a fence post, let out the line and reel slowly but with tension; the twists should work out. Also, never reel against a fighting fish to the point where the drag sings, it causes twist.

13. Pour Your Own Sinkers

Other than specialized split-shots, in all my years of fishing I've never purchased a sinker. I don't have anything against them, in fact, there are some excellent ones on the market. It's just that I watch the pocketbook and figure I save at least $150 a year by pouring my own sinkers. Besides, it's easy and fun to do.

Today there are some very good, high-quality molds and melting pots on the market, making it even easier and much safer than it used to be to pour your own sinkers. Pouring your own lead allows you to not only craft an array of sinker types, but also a wide-range of weights. Instead of limiting yourself to a few 1-ounce bank sinkers, for example, pouring your own makes it more feasible to hit the river with a variety of sinkers ranging from 1/2 to 4 ounces. It's human nature that, because you're making them yourself, the likelihood of experimentation with a variety styles and weight ranges increases. The result is more precisely matching the design and amount of weight being used with the style of fishing being applied and the water type being worked.

Today, lead is fairly easy to get ahold of. In the past, metal shops sold their scrap lead to private companies, but with ever-tightening EPA regulations, many are forced to unwillingly stockpile the alloy and are happy to give it away. Keeping in mind that softer lead yields higher-quality sinkers, check out local plumbing and sheet-metal shops to see what they have available. Lead from these places typically comes in flattened sheets or rolls. Metal dealers, scrap-metal companies, roofing businesses and tire shops are also good sources to inquire about getting recycled lead. Typically, lead from tire shops is hard, resulting in brittle sinkers. If possible, it's ideal to mix brittle lead with soft.

A common mistake on any salmon and steelhead river is overlooking the importance of lead. If too much or too little weight is used, you're not fishing where you should be. Making your own sinkers allows for honing in on the precise amount of lead to be used, and isn't as painful when you've lost several at the end of a long day on the water.

14. Lead Processor

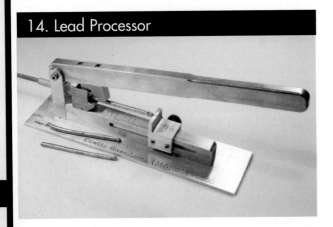

If you don't have the interest or time to pour your own sinkers, buying them is the next best option. When it comes to purchasing spools of pencil lead, be it 1/4 or 3/16 inches in diameter, there's a nifty device that can help you quickly cut, shape and punch those sinkers to the size you want. It's called the Lead Processor, and is available through Three Rivers Marine (www.3riversmarine.com).

The processor has a sliding ruler with a block to set the length (thus weight) of the sinker you want to create. Simply feed the roll of sinker through a tube, which channels it to the cutting block. Make the first cut at the very tip of the sinker. This will shape and punch a hole in the end, so a swivel can be snapped into place.

Once the initial cut is made, continue feeding the sinker through until it hits the stop block, which is preset to your desired length. Your next cut not only severs the lead to the target length, but it punches and shapes the next sinker, all in one, slick move. The rounded end which is created near the hole allows the sinker to swing freely on the wire, rather than getting jammed against the swivel. It may seem like a trivial thing, but it's a big benefit in terms of the sinker sliding more stealthily across the bottom during your presentation.

Rather than dealing with measuring spools of lead, cutting them with pliers, then punching a hole in the end, the Lead Processor does it all in one easy action. The design of this device can keep you cutting lead all day, without sore hands. It's a pricey product, but very ingenious, and well worth the investment if you go through lots of pencil lead. I wouldn't have one if I didn't think it saved so much time, which it does, and does well.

15. Gear Check List

I vividly recall the days as a kid when I'd hit the river with Dad and Grandpa. We had one glass rod each and all our tackle fit into one small box. If we wanted to drift fish, we'd use eggs, nothing else. If we wanted to pull plugs, we'd bite off the egg set-up and retie. Back then, fishing was simple. But now, with so many options available, keeping track of what you have is important.

It's a good idea to make a list of the gear you have, and it really doesn't take long. Make the list based on fishing style, i.e. side-drifting tackle, bobber and jig tackle, back-trolling tackle, and so on. When gearing up for a trip, figure out which tactical approach or approaches you'll be using, then go through the checklist to make sure you have everything on board.

It seems basic, but once you acquire a bunch of gear, it's worth taking a few minutes to check it off, making sure it's in the boat or vehicle, ready to go. Forgetting one simple thing, say that 1/8" hollow-core lead, or those silver-plated jigs, can ruin a day of side-drifting or jig fishing, respectively. By taking a few minutes to make sure all is in order, you're ensuring time on the water is well spent.

16. Boat Check List

Before hitting the river, double-check to see that you have everything.

As with gear, keeping track of everything in your boat is important to success and safety on the river. Before even wetting an oar, check state regulations to see what's required in the boat. Some states require a whistle, driftboat license, special licensing for kicker motors, lifejackets, and so forth.

Once prepared to hit the water, run through a basic checklist to make sure all is in order. Double-checking everything from anchor set-ups to ropes, clean towels, an extra oar, hand soap, heaters and whatever else you require to have a safe and productive day on the river is all-important.

The more you get out, the more automatic this checklist will become, but don't take it for granted. I know of several veterans who forget something important from time to time, myself included. It's a helpless feeling, planning a trip to the river, arriving and realizing you forgot a vital piece of equipment. Not only can this set back several hours of fishing time, it can ruin an entire day, especially if citations are issued.

17. Line Tamers

The more specialized tackle and fishing rods become, and the more you acquire over time, the more line you'll go through. From mainlines to leaders to droppers, the number of spools of line one can actually accumulate in a river boat or tackle box can be surprising. And the more line you acquire, the greater the likelihood for tangles, something which can cost valued time on the water or at home, when spooling reels.

To avoid wasting time snipping and untangling knotted lines, try installing Line Tamers on every spool of fishing line you own. These handy, inexpensive devices can save several minutes of time during the course of a trip, and save further headaches at home. No longer will time be wasted sifting through tangled messes, for the elastic band with a passthrough eye which makes up the Line Tamer keeps all lines in order and easily accessible.

Line Tamers come in an array of sizes to fit just about every spool on the market. I've picked up all mine through *www.ubfishin.com*. The time these little gems can save over the course of a season, both on the river and at home, will make you smile, and wonder what you ever did without them.

18. Line Check

Fishing line is not ageless. Over time it breaks down, even when sitting on the shelf unused. At the same time, the more you use line, the quicker it breaks down due to abrasion and exposure to sunlight and other elements.

When storing line at home, make sure it's in a dark, cool place, such as a cupboard, drawer or even in closed boxes. Protecting lines from exposure to light and heat will extend their life and overall effectiveness, so make the effort to properly store them.

If you go through lots of line, long-term storage is not a concern, but high-usage is. The more you fish, the more frequently

line should be changed. How often line should be changed depends on the situation. I've been on bedrock rivers chasing spring chinook where every run finds the mainline being dragged over ledges. As a result, I'll change line at the end of each day.

In other, boulder-strewn streams where hot summer steelhead abound, one may get away with changing line every three or four trips. If fishing salmon in deep holes with few hangups, line changes may be once every couple of weeks. If you don't get out as much as you'd like, line changes may be fewer, say every month or two.

The number one indicator that line should be changed is the presence of abrasions. Run a thumb and forefinger over the line, feeling for abrasions. If they exist, cut the line at that point and use what's left. If the abrasions run deep into the spool, strip it off and re-spool with fresh line. You don't want to leave yourself with too little line so as to impede casting distance and accuracy. Have an extra spool of mainline on hand, so complete change-outs can be made if necessary. If abrasions exist on the leader, retie.

Other indicators that it's time for a line change are fading, discoloration and the build-up of algae and other scum found on the surface of some waters. All of these indicate a probable breaking down of the line, and the result could be a busted line at the most inopportune time, costing you a fish. The best rule of thumb: If in doubt, change the line.

19. Pre-tie Leaders

One of the best time-savers in the fishing world, and one which will increase your catch rates, is having all the leaders pre-tied before hitting the river. Observe an angler who neglects to do this and keep track of how much time they actually spend fishing. For every rigging they break off, two to four minutes are spent tying up a leader. Over the course of the day, the amount of actual fishing time they lose will be a direct result of how many fish they catch, or didn't catch.

When on the river, the objective is to keep that line in the water as much as possible. By having leaders pre-tied, change-outs are quick when a leader is snapped off. It shouldn't take much more than 30 seconds to replace a broken leader, bait it and get it back in the water. Elaborate riggings may require a bit more time, but the key is having everything ready to go before that leader is broken. Be sure leaders, drift-bobbers and baits are all readily accessible for a quick turnaround time. When you're on the river, time is fish. Be certain there are enough leaders pre-tied for everyone who'll need them.

Some days on the river may find you going through a handful of leaders, while other days may see you rifling through four dozen or more. Know the river and conditions which you'll be fishing and pre-tie those leaders, accordingly.

20. Leader Keepers

Having a way to access your pre-tied leaders is as important as having them on hand. If you can't quickly get to the leaders, it defeats the purpose and negates the effort of having them ready for quick replacement. There are several options for storing leaders, but keep in mind the goal is to maximize storage and access efficiency.

There are a variety of tube-like leader keepers out there, and these can be handy devices. One key in selecting a good leader keeper is making sure you can quickly unwrap the leader. Check to see that there are no rubber or plastic nubbins in the middle on which leaders can hang-up; this makes unwinding a leader time-consuming. Likewise, make certain the hook will remain in place until you physically remove it.

There are a number of homemade leader-keeper possibilities, ranging from foam pipe insulation to cardboard. My preferred leader storage system, however, is the Pips Leader Caddy (www.mackslure.com). These round boxes fit in the palm of your hand, feature clear lids, hold multiple leaders and when used properly, will not tangle. I prefer having at least a half-dozen Pips boxes ready to go with different hook sizes and leader weights. They come in a mix of colors, the lids of which can also be labeled so you know exactly what you have on-hand. The more accessible the leaders, the quicker the change-out, the more time spent with your line in the water.

21. Masking Soaps

Smells play a big role in the world of salmon fishing. The author took this 70 pound king on the Kenai.

Even if you don't eat bananas or apply cologne, simply handling the many items which come your way during a day on the river can impact your fishing success. Rowing the boat on hot days leads to sweaty hands; touching a bacteria-infested towel or anchor rope transfers foul odors; working on a boat motor can contaminate fingers. The list goes on. That's why keeping hands clean when handling bait or lures is critical.

Remember, salmon and steelhead have an acute sense of smell, and the more foul odors we can eliminate, the better the chances of catching fish. There are several ways to go when it comes to masking foreign scents, and all are cost efficient and take only seconds. Mike's Ab-Scent Sportsman Soap, for instance, is a liquid soap that comes in a two-ounce squeeze bottle. It's compact size and easy-to-use design makes it quick and effective.

Perhaps the most famous cleansing soap is Joy, in lemon scent. Reports from the bass-fishing industry claim this soap is highly effective in cutting unwanted smells and human odors,

which explains why it's found in the boats of many top salmon and steelhead anglers. A couple drops applied every half-hour, or after handling objects with tainted odors, can make the difference between catching a fish or not.

Another effective option is masking scents. Rather than trying to rid the hands of unwanted smells, many anglers opt to apply scents they have available, using those to cover-up unwanted odors. There are several options out there made by various companies, but herring, anchovy, crawdad and anise scents seem to be among the most popular with salmon and steelheaders. Simply rub a few drops onto your hands during the course of the day; you'll know when it wears off and needs to be applied. Taking a few seconds to cover or eliminate unwanted odors can make a difference of whether or not you catch fish, especially when it comes to those fastidious springers.

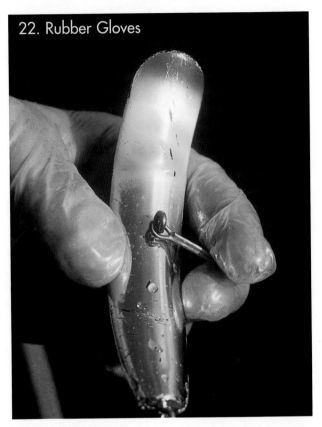

22. Rubber Gloves

As anglers grow more aware of the value of masking unwanted odors, more and more gloved hands are being seen on the river. Rubber gloves are likely the best way to inhibit human odor from being transferred to gear. The key is getting gloves that don't tear, or that are too thick. Thin, white latex gloves are fine when working with baits at home, but tear easily when on the river. At the same time, avoid gloves that are too thick, getting in the way of intricate jobs like tying knots or wrapping plugs.

What you want are the blue or purple gloves made with the substance called *nitrile*. Nitrile gloves won't react with skin like latex can, and are sturdy enough to withstand the rigors of everyday fishing while on the water. Nitrile-based gloves are ones used in hospitals, and the only difference between the purple and blue colors are the dyes used in each.

Buy these gloves in bulk, for not only is the long-term investment smart, but it allows you to have plenty on hand—no pun intended. Separate them into a few sealable baggies and store them in different places in the boat. This will allow for quick and easy access when fellow anglers join you.

In case you're skeptical about the effectiveness of rubber gloves, don't be. One summer I fished for kings with two buddies. We worked fresh eggs on the Nushagak, all day long, baiting our own hooks. In the morning, I didn't wear rubber gloves, my buddies did. They landed 22 fish between the two of them, I landed 3. In the afternoon I switched to masking scents and soaps, they still wore gloves and caught twice as many fish as me. In the evening, I went with gloves, as did they, and we were all within one fish of each other. Rubber gloves work, no question.

Nitrile gloves can be ordered over the phone from Nurnberg Scientific in Portland, Oregon. Call 1-800-826-3470, and the product will be delivered right to your doorstep. With an increased awareness in the effectiveness of these gloves, look for more fishing-related companies to start carrying them.

23. Scent Wipes

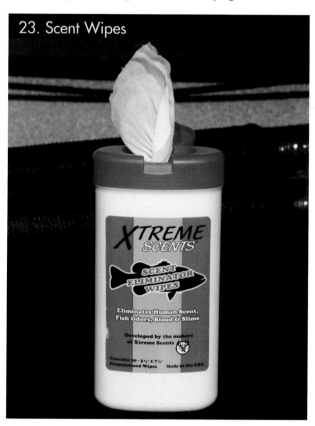

For those who don't like wearing rubber gloves all day long, or don't like applying masking soaps to their hands, there is an alternative. Xtreme Scents (www.xtremescents.com) has a disposable scent wipe that comes in a small container. The container itself is compact, taking up little space, and the wipes are easy to pull out. The purpose of the Scent Eliminator Wipes is to eliminate bacterial and other foreign odors which may be transferred by humans.

I've used these enough to believe they work. Simply wipe your hands prior to handling any baits, plugs or lures, then do your thing. When done, you can use the same wipe to clean your hands. They can also be used to wipe down plugs, lures, rod handles and more. You can get multiple uses with one wipe.

I was once doing some testing on handling baits with bare hands. My buddies wore rubber gloves and they got approximately four strikes to every one of mine. When I switched to using

these scent wipes, we were on nearly equal ground. It could be a confidence thing, but bottom line, it serves as an effective alternative to other methods of masking human odors, one that may appeal to some anglers who don't prefer other options.

24. Rubber Boots

In the hunting world, rubber boots are known to reduce the amount of human scent being laid on the ground. Fishing from a boat is no different. When working with baits, they often lay on or inadvertently fall to the bottom of the boat. Here, these baits come in contact with where we've been standing, or worse yet, get stepped on.

Rubber boots—versus leather boots or canvas tennis shoes—cut down on the amount of human and other unwanted odors picked up in a boat, and retard against further transferring these odors to the baits. Even in rain, where water runs down the pant leg, over leather boots and on to the floor boards, human scent and oils from waterproofing boots can be carried to the boat. If baits are then laid where we walk, they can become contaminated and decrease the chance of catching fish. Rubber boots help eliminate the transfer of unwanted odors.

25. Rod Wraps

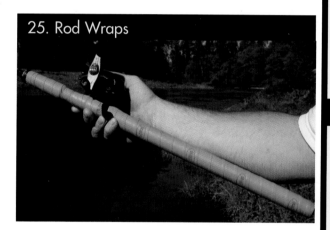

These innovative devices have made their mark in the bass-fishing world and are currently working their way into the salmon and steelhead industry. RodWraps (*www.rodwrap.com*) are an ingenious material that forms snugly around the rod handle. The wrap adheres to itself, and the quality of the material makes it appealing for wet-weather anglers.

In wet conditions, be it rain or simply river water contact, where cork or graphite handles can become slippery, RodWraps actually maintain a level of friction whereby allowing a firm grasp to be maintained at all times. At the same time, the wrap increases the actual surface area of the handle, and the material of which it's made transfers every subtle vibration to the hands of the angler, meaning each tick of the bottom and delicate bite can be detected.

RodWraps come in a variety of colors, and anglers who carry multiple rod set-ups find them valuable in color coding their rods. For instance, blue wraps may be put on back-bouncing rods, red wraps on plugging rods, green wraps on drift rods, and so on. This allows for quick transitions to be made, which increases fishing time. This is especially applicable when upwards of 15 to 20 rods are in the boat, with three or more anglers, as it allows for clear communication of rod selection to be made.

26. Load All Gear Early

Some anglers go so far as to have a check list of every item they want to have on board their boat or on their person prior to hitting the water. Those who have been fishing several years have in their mind what it is they want to take, but even at that, there are items which may be inadvertently left behind. Loading all your gear early, like the day before the trip, can help ensure you have everything in place and ready to fish.

The key is fitting all the gear to meet the needs of the water being fished. The last thing you want to have happen while on the river is pass by a section of water without fishing it because you didn't have the right gear. If wanting to focus on pulling plugs for springers, don't overlook drift-fishing gear that will allow you to access different types of water, where the fish may be holding on that particular day.

By loading your gear early, you can run down a mental or physical checklist to make certain all is in place. From lifejackets to wading shoes to terminal gear, leaders and baits, the more prepared you are, the lesser the chance of overlooking a valued item, the greater the likelihood of catching more fish.

27. Communicate Meeting Place

If fishing with a buddy, be it for the first time or the 50th, be sure to clearly communicate where you will meet and when. I've lost some valuable mornings due to an oversight in communication of when and/or where I was to meet someone. There's no one to blame, it's simply a matter of lost time, which can be valuable if you only have one day a week to fish.

Be certain to tell each other when and where you plan to meet, and at which time. Be so detailed that you even make clear on which side of the local market you will meet; you don't want to be sitting on the south end of the building while your buddy is waiting on the north end. The more information that can be communicated, the better for all parties involved.

In addition, be sure to have each other's home and/or cell phone numbers handy, so that if one person fails to show, a call could be made to figure out their whereabouts. This is also a good safety precaution, which could help save more than just time.

28. Be Early

Getting an early start paid off for the author and his son Braxton, then 4 years old, with his first steelhead.

There's no greater frustration than having to rush. The more hurried you are, the less fun the overall fishing experience. To relieve this level of undesirable and unnecessary stress, make it a

point to get an early start. This begins the minute you wake up, and sets the timing for the remainder of the entire day.

If you want to be on the river by 4:00 a.m., do all in your power to get there at that time. Whether it's making lunches the night prior, preparing all the gear the day before, or getting up 15 minutes earlier than you want to, do what's necessary to stay on that timeline.

Keep in mind that other factors may hinder your timeline as well. From road construction to weather to long lines at the boat launch, there are obstacles which may inadvertently pop up that you have not accounted for and have no control over. Manage what you have control of, and deal with hurdles as they come along. But remember, it's better to be early than late.

29. Set Two Alarms

My wife says I'm paranoid, but from the time I was a kid, Dad always taught me that you don't want to miss a day on the river by oversleeping. Usually, I'm so fired up to go, sleep comes tough, and I'm normally up before the alarm sounds. But that's not always the case.

Electrical outages and accidentally hitting the snooze button one too many times can lead to a late start, or worse yet, no start at all. Once you've had this happen, you likely need no further convincing that a backup alarm is essential. It may seem like overkill, but having two alarms can make the difference between a great day of fishing or no day of fishing at all.

Even when out camping, it's a good idea to bring multiple alarms. You bring one and have a buddy bring another, or if you're by yourself, set the alarm on your watch as a backup. It's a terrible feeling to be in a remote area, oversleep and wake-up to find someone has hiked in and beat you to your hole.

30. Pack Lunch Night Before

It may sound like a stretch, but once you've been late for a fishing trip because of food, you'll do all in your power to rectify the situation. If you make your own lunches, taking the time to do it the night before the trip can save valued time come morning, and it will afford you a few minutes of extra sleep.

At the same time, I'm not one to take the ingredients along in a cooler and make a sandwich on the river. When I'm on the water I want to be fishing, eating between holes. I don't want to waste time pulling over, making a sandwich and eating it when I could have been fishing. Conversely, if a buddy is rowing, then I'll gladly make lunches, or vice versa. Point is, don't spend time fixing food when you could be eating, or eating when you could be fishing.

If you stop by a deli to pick up your lunches, call in the day prior and have your order ready to go. Then all you have to do is pull up, pay your bill, grab your food and go. There's no waiting around, deciding on which items to include in your lunch. Get it all done before hand, so you can be on the go and focus on nothing but fishing.

My dad has always said, "There's no eating lunch until the first fish is in the boat." While this is a good adage to live by when the bite's hot, mom was never pleased when we returned home, not hungry for dinner because we starved ourselves during the day and harfed down lunch on our way home. Don't punish yourself by not eating, but at the same time, try to avoid loss of valued fishing time due to food.

31. Check Route To New Area

When heading to a new river, or a new stretch of river that's unfamiliar to you, do your homework to learn the most direct route. This may require making a few phone calls to local markets, fish hatcheries, service stations, tackle shops and even state highway departments, but the time is well spent. The series of River Map books published by Frank Amato Publications are also solid resources (www.amatobooks.com).

Such events as road closures, detours, holiday events and more can cause traffic flow problems that could impede your travel, thus time on the river. It's good to know what's going on prior to leaving home, especially during winter months where weather can factor in. If traveling over a pass, it's helpful to know snow and ice conditions, for example.

There are also excellent map programs on the Internet which can help direct you to a specific river, or nearby town. Additional sources include books and magazine articles which often have detailed maps to help point you in the right direction. Some of these resources even list local businesses you can call to help get up-to-date travel information as well as a fishing report. The more time you take to plan out your adventure into new territory, the smoother things will go, the more time you can devote to fishing.

32. Ice Ready For Coolers

This one falls in line with having a lunch prepared the night prior to leaving. Having ice ready to go will help you better manage your catch. On those hot summer days, I know of folks who were forced to cut their time on the water short because they forgot ice, and the fish they caught were literally cooking in their skins.

By having ice in the cooler, there's no rush to speed home to properly take care of fish and/or fish eggs. It can all be properly cooled in the boat. Ice in the cooler also helps keep lunches and baits cool on hot days, another reason to have it ready beforehand.

I prefer having large ice packs, or blocks of ice, pre-frozen at home that I can stick in the Coleman cooler and take with me. I know these will fit in my cooler, and block ice keeps longer than crushed or cubed ice. This also saves me from having to stop by the store on the way to the river, which is another early morning time-saver.

33. Fill Gas Tanks Early

No matter where it is you're going, when in a hurry, it can be very frustrating to take the time to fill up with gas. Nowhere does this hold more true than when heading out fishing, and you're in a mad rush. Worse yet is when you pull up to a gas station that doesn't open for an hour or more and the needle is on E, or at the very least, where a line of rigs are ahead of you, waiting for an open pump.

Think ahead, so the next time you're in town prior to going fishing, you can ensure the gas tank is full. It may even be worth the effort to fuel up the night prior, so as not to be caught by surprise the morning of the planned trip. This may require a bit of a drive, but can be time well spent.

I know of guides who actually keep fuel tanks at their house for the simple reason that the long hours they work does not always allow them to get to a gas station when needed. It's better to be safe than sorry, so think ahead on this one, and check that gas gauge prior to hopping into the truck and heading toward the river.

34. Carry Quality Raingear

No matter what time of year you fish for salmon and steelhead, you'll eventually encounter rain. There's no way to get around it, so you have to deal with it. Raingear has advanced so far in recent years, that there's no reason not to be in ultimate comfort on those wet days.

Be it in a continuous drizzle or a torrential downpour, you want to stay dry and warm. You can go the insulated route, and have rain and warm weather gear all in one, or you can go with layered warm clothing and an outer, waterproof shell. Which route you choose to take is of personal preference, and both are effective and applicable.

The key is finding raingear that performs all the functions you require. Tight-fitting cuffs on jacket sleeves, and a hood that keeps water from running down the back of your neck are essential. At the same time, a long jacket that goes over your rainpants is important, so water doesn't run-off to your waistline. This is where bibs come in handy, and add valued warmth. If spending time in the Pacific Northwest, Alaska or British Columbia, quality raingear is a must. The last thing you want is to have to leave the river because you're wet and cold. Don't let poor raingear keep you off the river; invest in what works best for you.

35. Hire A Guide

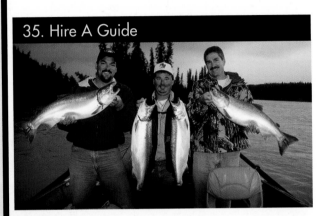

Many guides will scorn this section, while others will welcome it, but hiring a guide is one of the best ways to learn how to fish. You can learn valued information ranging from how they organize gear, to setting up tackle boxes and baits, to boat set-up and even how they use a certain technique. Some guides I know are happy to teach clients all they know, and view their time on the water as an opportunity to educate clients on many aspects of the sport.

The goal of many guides is to retain clients who return year after year. I know of guides who rebook clients simply due to the fact they are good teachers, meaning they have the ability to teach the clients new techniques they can then apply on their own, and they actually encourage them to do so.

When booking a guided trip, inquire as to whether or not the guide is willing to teach you a specific technique. Some guides are glad to, others wish to keep the information to themselves. Whatever it is you wish to learn, be up front with your guide. Convey to them what it is you wish to come away with from the trip, for then you both have a mutual understanding before hitting the river.

I actually know of some very proficient anglers who hire a guide every year or two to keep abreast of the latest techniques, or refine strategies they are struggling with. Again, some guides are for this, others may not be. Do your homework in advance, and you may come away with more information than you ever thought possible.

36. Sight-Fishing

For anglers new to the world of sight-fishing steelhead, it can be a frustrating experience until you learn what you're looking

for. Rarely will an entire bright-sided, blue-backed fish be seen. Instead, it's parts of fish that will be discerned. Perhaps the twitch of a tail or the outline of a back will catch the eye, which can make the game appear deceivingly easy.

Maybe it comes down to reading water, then trying to find the fish. No matter what the story, a good pair of spotting glasses is a must when sight-fishing. The key is finding a quality pair of glasses that fit snug to the face, blocking out incoming solar rays from all sides, while at the same time allowing ample room for air to circulate.

I once had a pair of shades that fogged so frequently, they made it tough to fish. Each time I wiped the fogged lenses, they smeared to the point where clarity was drastically minimized. Though these glasses were quite pricey, I couldn't replace them fast enough.

In many of the rivers, I've been most pleased with my Smith Action Optics fishing glasses. They fit nicely, can be worn all day long without eye or temple fatigue, come in a variety of lens colors to match existing stream conditions and they are durable. Amber, gray and copper colored lenses work well to meet the lighting conditions encountered in many western waters. Where sky conditions can vary, carrying three pairs of glasses afield with different tinted lenses can enhance your fish-sighting capability throughout the day. Once you have good, polarized glasses, the ability to spot fish boils down to simply spending time on the river.

37. Curing Ingredients On-Hand

Egg cures can be one of the most effective tools in the salmon-fisherman's repertoire, but it takes preparation to make it happen. Knowing what curing recipes you wish to use, and the ingredients needed to complete them, it's wise to have all items on hand prior to heading to the river. Typically, anglers get home too late, or are too pressed for time after a day of fishing to go out and round-up the ingredients necessary to achieve a given cure.

By having all of the ingredients on-hand prior to leaving home, the likelihood of actually trying those new cures increases. If it's multiple cures you wish to try, be sure and have all ingredients on-hand. On fishing trips where you know the chance of coming home with large amounts of eggs is good, this is a great opportunity to try multiple egg cures.

Even if you catch only one hen, the possibility to test new cures is still there. Cut the skeins in half and try a different cure with each section. The more willing you are to try new cures, the more likely you are to discover what ones work in which situations. It may be one cure works great one day, and a different cure the next, but you'll never know until you try.

Change is not always easy in the fishing world, and this is especially true when it comes to egg cures. People have a tendency to stick with what they know works, but whose to say a different cure won't work just as well, or better. By preparing yourself to test various cures, and then making the effort to use them on the river, you're on the way to becoming a tried-and-true egg fisherman.

38. Pre-cut Baits

When curing eggs, I like cutting them into bait-size clusters, then curing them. Not only does this maximize the surface area of the eggs which the cure and dies come into contact with, it saves valuable time on the river. Some people may point out that when curing their eggs, they may not be sure which fish they are intended for, thus don't like cutting them to bait-size at this stage.

Typically, I'll cut and cure my baits into species-specific sizes, i.e., big and juicy for fall chinook, smaller and more firm for springers and smaller yet for summer and winter steelhead. I'll label each package with the cure and what species they are intended for. If you acquire high volumes of eggs, this works great, and allows you the freedom to fish on the river rather than spend time cutting bait.

If you're not certain which species of fish you'll be using the eggs for at the time of curing, consider cutting each skein in half and curing that. Then, a day prior to heading out on river, thaw the eggs and cut them to bait sizes at home. This will minimize your time of cutting them on the river, then cleaning up the mess. Having your baits precut prior to leaving home can save you up to 10 minutes a day, maybe more, of what could be important fishing time and is just one more piece of the all-important timesaving puzzle.

39. Pre-tie Sinkers To Swivels

When you know the water level and specific holes you'll be fishing on a given river, taking the time to pre-tie your sinkers to the swivels can save one step on the river. Be it slinky sinkers threaded onto a snap swivel, bank sinkers tied to a dropper, or pencil sinkers slipped inside surgical tubing then stapled to a three-way swivel, taking the time to attach these set-ups before leaving home can save several minutes a day on the river.

Having sinkers and swivels pre-rigged is especially valuable in rivers where many hangups are inevitable. The more lost gear you encounter, the more time it takes to replace it, the less time you spend fishing. As with pretying leaders, sharpening hooks, precutting baits to proper size and so forth, setting up your sinkers ahead of time will no doubt increase your time in the water.

For sinkers to be fished off a dropper, there are two approaches to take. If using extra-strong mainline, like a braided line that rarely breaks, chances are the dropper will bust free of the swivel. In this case, having a sinker pre-tied to a dropper allows you to tie just one knot onto the swivel, then get back to fishing. If unsure how much lead you'll be using, tie a loop in the dropper,

to allow for quick sinker change-outs. These are just a couple suggestions that will help maximize fishing time.

40. Package And Label Baits

One of the biggest mistakes a bait fisherman can make is not properly labeling their baits. It sounds simple, and is, if you take a minute to mark the packages at the time of curing. What inadvertently happens is cures get moved to the back of the freezer, where they sit for who knows how long. The downfall comes when on the river, you open a container to find they are not the eggs you thought they were, or worse yet, burned beyond use.

When curing and packaging your eggs, label them with pertinent information that will help you manage them. Be sure to include what type of eggs they are, what cure was used, the date they were cured and which species they are intended for. Next, make it a point to go through your freezer every couple of months, and keep track of which eggs you have, which ones need to be used and which ones can wait.

Vacuum sealing your eggs, be they in jars or bags, will greatly extend their freezer life. If doing this in bags, prior to sealing them, first put the cured baits or skeins inside, then place them in the freezer for 20 minutes. This will allow the juices to set-up and not be sucked out during the sealing process, whereby preventing a tight seal. Next, take the bag and seal it. The firmed-up eggs will not burst under pressure and the juices will not seep, meaning you get an airtight seal that will keep the eggs for up to a year or longer.

41. Multiple Egg Cures

If you've ever busted your hind end to hit the river ahead of everyone else, then not touch a fish, the frustrations can be great. But it gets worse when you pull out thinking no fish were in the hole, only to see someone slip in behind you and start nailing springers. The fish were always there, and likely very little changed other than the presentation the fish were seeing. Chances are that change the fish liked was in the form of an egg cure.

One of the hardest things for an angler to do is experiment with something new, and this is especially true for egg fishermen. The mindset, "why fix it if it's not broken," has wide applications in the fishing world, yet can be an angler's worst enemy. How do you know the egg cure you use is the best? How do you know that on any given day another cure won't outfish your favorite? Answer is, you don't, and the only way to find out is by experimentation.

Yes, I have my favorite cure, and I take it with me every time out. But I also have a host of other cures I'm always trying. If I know fish are in a particular hole but not biting, I'll change out baits to try and find something they like. It doesn't always work, but often times it pays off. The last thing I want is to give up, pull out of the hole and watch someone else come in and catch fish that I'd been working so hard for. In this case, change is good.

42. Tuna Balls

Tuna carries lots of oil, and salmon love oils. While curing eggs in tuna oil, or adding drops of tuna oil into your egg cure can be very effective, there's another alternative bait that works very well, from Alaska to California and wherever chinook are found. Tuna balls are great baits, and can be fished alone or off the trailing end of a Kwikfish.

In either case, get the tuna in the can that is saturated in oil, not water. Next, get some spawn bags or mesh netting, in which the tuna will be wrapped. Make a ball about the size of an egg cluster you'd use. When drift fishing a tuna ball, thread it onto the hook, run it over the eye of the hook and pass the egg loop around it. This will hold it in place while casting and drifting along the bottom.

When fishing a tuna ball off a Kwikfish, turn the trailing treble hook so that the odd point is hanging down, with the other two points facing up toward the bottom of the plug. Simply thread the tuna ball on to the downward turned point, as this will keep the plug running true. These bait sizes can be slightly smaller than what you'd use while drift fishing. This is a great alternative to wrapping plugs with baitfish fillets, and can prove beneficial when nothing else seems to work. I know anglers who actually prefer this over herring or sardine-wrapped plugs when it comes to chasing spring chinook, and with good reason.

43. Pre-wrap Plugs

When it comes to wrapping your Kwikfish or Flatfish with baitfish fillets, be they herring, sardines or anchovies, doing it before heading to the river can save a great deal of time, especially if there are two or more people in the boat. The more people fishing, the more bait you'll go through, and the more baits you can have prepared, ready to fish, the greater the amount of time is spent with all the lines in the water.

If you cure your fillets, do it well ahead of time, and wrap up plenty of plugs the night prior to fishing. Simply wrap and store

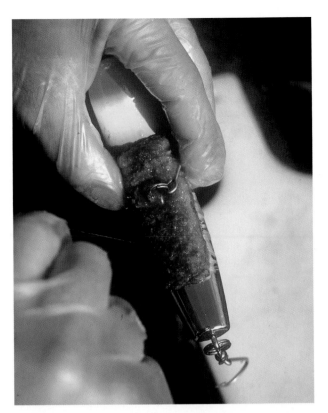

them in the refrigerator, so you can grab them and go in the morning. Of course, be sure and take extra baitfish along, in case you run short on prepared wraps and have to cut some more.

You can take it a step further and actually wrap then freeze the wraps with the plugs. If you have several consecutive days you'll be fishing, and ample plugs, you can get ahead of the game by wrapping a few dozen ahead of time, then keeping them in the freezer until needed. It takes some time at home, but it's better to spend the time at home doing it than wasting everyone's time doing it on the river. Believe me, it can be frustrating taking the time to cut and wrap plugs when the bite is hot.

44. Prawns And Shrimp

Prawns and bay shrimp are excellent steelhead baits, and work on salmon as well. But rather than fish these crustaceans raw, try curing them up and adding color and more scent to them. Both prawns and bay (aka, salad or popcorn) shrimp, can be purchased at the local market or seafood section of the grocery store. Bay shrimp usually come peeled, while prawn tails are still in the shell.

Prawns, being a thicker meat than bay shrimp, hold on the hook better, and are ideal when fishing fast-water settings. Bay shrimp are perfect for fishing beneath a float or side-drifting water, in less turbulent stretches. Both carry appealing, natural scent that steelhead and salmon thrive on. However, additional scent can be added, be it shrimp or anise oils, or perhaps powders like garlic or Slam-Ola.

In addition to scents, shrimp take dyes very nicely, and easily. Beau-Mac and Pro-Cure both make dyes which work great on shrimp, and TNT bait cure works well, too. In fact, dye takes so quickly on shrimp, you'll want to closely monitor the process. Bay shrimp take only seconds to dye, while prawn tails take just a bit longer. The longer they are left in the dye, the brighter or deeper the colors will be. Greens, reds and oranges are effective colors and make a great addition to the bait fisherman's arsenal, especially when it comes to summer steelhead and spring chinook.

45. Bait Dyes

When it comes to adding color to terminal gear presentations, most people employ the use of drift-bobbers, yarn or beads. Though these artificial add-ons can be highly effective, there may be times when you don't want the added size or buoyancy that can be associated with these items. If targeting a salmon or steelhead's sense of sight, consider utilizing bait dyes to help get the job done.

For decades anglers have called upon Jell-O dyes to add color to their bait. Today, there are several outstanding dyes on the market which are crafted solely for anglers. Dyes made by Pro-Cure and Beau-Mac are ones that have proven themselves time and again on a wide variety of baits, from eggs to shrimp, sardines, herring and more.

By dying baits, you're offering a dual opportunity for fish to bite by targeting their sense of sight and smell. This also eliminates the use of drift-bobbers, should you find yourself in a situation where such terminal will not work. Now, there's no reason to go without color, for dyes can be implemented, whereby offering an added edge.

If going to a river you know often finds fish biting on a specific color, be sure and include baits dyed in that color. Then again, it's a good idea to have a sampling of colors on-hand, should the fish be picky. Just as with switching plug or drift-bobber colors, changing bait colors can make a difference.

46. Crawdad Tails

One of the most overlooked baits, many anglers will agree is the crawdad tail. Years ago this used to be a common summer steelhead bait, but now it's seemingly forgotten. There are pockets of fisheries around the West where crawdad tails are still a mainstay of the bait-fisherman's plan of attack, but it doesn't have the wide-ranging level of application it once had.

Not only are crawdads a natural enemy of the summer steelhead, meaning the fish will readily attack them, but both salmon and steelhead find them appealing to eat. In fact, they make a great bait whether they are fished alone, on an egg hook, or wrapped on a Kwikfish or Flatfish.

Some anglers are so serious about their crawdad tails that they keep them in live wells year-round. Others will take their traps and capture crawdads to use seasonally, while still others will capture them while on the river in pursuit of fish. Either way, these are natural, very effective baits that will often draw a bite when other bait offerings don't seem to be producing. Crawdad scent is also growing in popularity among summer steelhead and springer anglers, be it applied on crawdad tails or plugs and lures.

47. Shrimp Cocktail

A great bait changeup which offers fish the best of both worlds is the shrimp cocktail. Rather than using eggs or sand shrimp alone, use them in tandem to give the fish something different to look at and smell. This set-up is nothing new, it's been around since the early 1970s, but it's still one of my favorite spring chinook set-ups and one of my top choices when it comes to running a diver and bait for summer steelhead.

There are many ways to arrange this set-up, but my preferred method is to run the hook through the shrimp tail first, sliding it over the eye of the hook, up the leader. Next, slip a cluster of eggs into the egg loop, then run the shrimp back down the leader. Run the point of the hook through the carapace of the shrimp, piercing it between the legs, exiting out the back. Slide the head end of the shrimp into the bend of the hook and you're set. This arrangement holds up well when drift-fishing fast water with a rocky bottom.

To keep this bait offering floating off the bottom, a drift-bobber can be placed on the leader. If using a spinning type drift-bobber, stack a few 3mm beads below it, so the spinning action does not cut into the tail end of the shrimp, weakening its holding strength. In terms of bait-fishing, this is one of the most visually appealing offerings I know of, and the level of scent it carries makes it an all-time favorite among springer anglers.

48. Dig Your Own Shrimp

Sand, or ghost, shrimp are one of the most revered baits among salmon and steelhead anglers. This natural food source constitutes part of the diet of these fish when at sea, but sand shrimp are very effective when fished in river settings. Due to their visual appeal and scent-carrying capacity, sand shrimp can draw strikes when nothing else seems to work.

Most Pacific Northwest coastal bays hold sand shrimp, meaning digging them on your own is easy. Hitting low tides provides good shrimping, but minus tides produce the best results. Search for pencil-sized holes in the sand—the more you can locate, the better. Clam, or better yet, shrimp guns are the way to go, as digging with a shovel is not efficient. Because it's common to extract multiple shrimp in one pull, upwards of 100 dozen shrimp can be obtained in one tide swing. Talk about a money saver.

If you live near the ocean, keeping shrimp alive in a large cooler of salt water is ideal. Changing the water each day assures they stay fresh and lively. They can be kept for several days, even weeks, if cared for properly. An aerator greatly extends the life of your shrimp.

If you don't live near the ocean, yet want to keep shrimp alive, you can transport them home in a cooler. Place blocks of ice in the bottom so no cracks exist, cover them with several layers of newspaper; this will keep the shrimp until you get home. The key is to keep the shrimp from coming into contact with

fresh water, which causes them to urinate on themselves and spoil. Atop the newspaper, lay a few layers of paper towels and dampen with salt water. Spread your shrimp over the toweling, covering with a few more layers of damp paper towels. This will keep them clean and cool. Once home, change out the paper towels for fresh, dry ones. I've kept shrimp alive for up to ten days in this way, but they do require a great deal of care. The water needs to be regularly drained from the cooler and the ice must be changed every two to three days to ensure the shrimp do not come into contact with fresh water. If they contact fresh water, they will die, discolor and turn soft.

Storing shrimp in the refrigerator is another option. Using the large kind of wood chips sold for dog or hamster bedding, place a few inches in a Styrofoam cup. Add a dozen or so shrimp and affix the lid. Many anglers prefer this method for keeping shrimp alive, as it requires less effort and if some die, at least the entire batch won't go bad, only what's in that carton. Keeping the shrimp cool, in the 40- to 45-degree range, will slow their metabolism and extend their life.

Because tending live shrimp can be time-consuming, many people choose to freeze them right away. If freezing shrimp, transport them home in a cooler of salt water, to keep them alive. Once home, remove the shrimp by hand, blot them dry and place in the containers in which they'll be frozen. Freezing a dozen or two per container is good, as many more than that will prolong the thawing process. You can also place a desired number of shrimp in baggies, cover them with salt water and freeze. Covering them with corn syrup, then freezing, is another proven method.

When thawing shrimp, do so at room temperature. The high water content inside a shrimp makes it an ideal scent chamber, while simultaneously retaining good color. Fished alone, in combination with drift bobbers or teamed with eggs, the presentation of shrimp can be tough to beat. If you go through a high volume of sand shrimp, purchasing them at $3.00 a dozen, it doesn't take long for your digging efforts to pay off.

49. Worms

When it comes to worm-fishing, anglers can choose between plastic or natural. While worms are primarily used for targeting steelhead, they have been known to catch salmon from time to time, though usually inadvertently.

Plastic worms come in a variety of sizes and colors, and can make the difference between a slow day or an exceptional day on the river. They can be fished alone, threaded onto the leader, or dangled beneath a jig or bait of choice. The idea is to stimulate a steelhead into biting by offering them something that's visually appealing and creates movement. Under the right lighting conditions, and in fast-water situations, bright pink and orange worms can be easy for steelhead to spot and react to. In slow water, the slightest water movement generates action of the artificial worm, often enticing a bite.

The use of plastic worms on steelhead is very popular in certain geographic regions, especially in Canada. It seems the further south you go, the less these baits are used. They've proven effective in most regions throughout the West, and should be in the tackle box of every serious angler. The key is using them.

As for natural worms, or nightcrawlers, these can be the steelheader's best friend. As a kid, I recall nightcrawlers often outfishing all other natural baits. But in recent years, the influx of so many trout have seen a lull in the use of night crawlers. They still work, in fact, I know of many guys who rate it their number one natural bait. One reason nightcrawlers are thought to be so effective today is because it's something different for the fish to look at, in other words, not everyone is using them.

To avoid trout pecking at your worm, thread them on whole. A whole worm is not too big, for an aggressive steelhead can inhale it surprisingly fast, and without hesitation. Nightcrawlers can also be dyed, something that's proving to be effective on steelhead.

50. Puff Balls

Puff balls serve a variety of purposes for the angler, perhaps more for the steelhead than the salmon crowd. When they first came on to the western fishing scene, the primary use of puff balls was as a drift-bobber. They are still widely used in this way, and with great success, but have since expanded their range of application.

Due to an ever-increasing expansion of color combinations, puff balls are great attractants for fish. Placed atop a cluster of eggs, or combined with a shrimp, crawdad tail or worm, they are a great way to not only add color, but buoyancy. The result is fewer hangups when drift fishing, meaning your time in the water is maximized.

Puff balls are also great for wrapping in spawn bags, with loose eggs or tuna. The purpose of using spawn bags is to hold loose baits together, whereby allowing them to be fished when it otherwise could not be done. Adding a few small-size puff balls will keep these baits off the bottom, and fishing more.

In the world of side-drifting, puff balls have one of their most effective applications. Threaded onto the end of the hook, and positioned in the bend of the hook, the puff ball makes the hook ride point-up. The result is fewer hangups, for the point of the hook will not dig into branches, moss and other debris. The best part is it allows anglers to cover much more water, and catch more fish. Because side-drifting is a presentation which matches the natural flow rate of the water, controlling the depth of the bait can be difficult, especially since such small baits are used. Puff balls help take some of the guesswork out of where your bait is, keeping it off the bottom and allowing it to be carried into slots and food funnels where steelhead often hold. Puff balls are cost efficient and highly effective in many scenarios.

51. Spider Set-up

I was introduced to spider sinkers in the mid-1970s, and have been religiously using them ever since. Once you learn how to make these nifty devices, the hard part is over and the fun begins. There are days on the river where I know I've increased my fishing time by over an hour, simply due to fewer hangups. The result is more fish being caught. At the same time, there are holes I simply would not be able to fish were it not for a spider, again increasing the catch rate.

When crafting spiders I prefer #12, 180-pound-test steel leader. Its pliable yet sturdy construction keeps your sinker active with minimal noise as it bounces over rocks. Cut two, 10"-long pieces of steel leader. Bend one in half, so a small loop forms at the midpoint. Twist the wire one time to secure the loop, approximately 1/4" in size. Bend the other wire in half and slide it through the loop. Cut a third piece of leader, this one about 11" long. Fold it in half and place it through the loop so the midway point rests on the bottom of the loop. Now you have six strands of steel leader suspended from one loop.

With a pair of heavy pliers and strong fingers, twist the longest hanging strand of steel around the lower part of the loop and each wire. The other end of the long strand will be bent inward in your final step, and is what the sinker is suspended from.

Bend the other remaining four strands out at 90-degree angles at the base of the loop. Half way down each leg make another 90-degree bend downward, toward the center. With all four legs complete, go back and make the sinker snap attachment.

The snap will be centered beneath and fairly close to the original loop, so it hangs straight when tied to your line. Be sure to make the snap so you can change sinkers as needed. You now have a four-legged "spider" that should stand alone.

All four legs and the sinker-snap should be firm, not collapsing on themselves at any point. If they tend to collapse at the loop, make another wrap with one of the existing legs. Be certain all legs stay spread equidistant and that nowhere does the sinker hang outside the perimeter of the legs.

The loop made in the first stage of the spider now becomes the point to where you tie your drop line. The mainline is tied to a three-way swivel, and the dropper and leader to the other ends. Sinker centered, all four legs spread, you're ready to fish. I prefer a dropper longer than my leader, sometimes twice as long when fishing deep swirl holes.

Once airborne the spider and bait separate, just like they do when on the river bottom. Once on the bottom, the spider holds upstream, while the bait travels downstream. Your bait now has the capability of covering a large swath as its moved along in the current, or shifted about in swirling holes.

Lead sticks to rocks, resulting in numerous hangups and, eventually, lost gear. Spiders keep the sinker from contacting the bottom, for the stiff steel leader deflects off rocks. It's not 100% failsafe—it will occasionally wedge between rocks or on a log—but I figure I lose about 1/10 the gear by using spiders.

52. Slider Sinker Set-up

There are various ways to rig a sliding sinker set-up, and different waters where such a system can be fished. Perhaps the biggest benefit of a sliding sinker is that it allows the fish to grab the bait and run with it, while not feeling the resistance of the sinker tugging on the other end.

One of the most common ways to rig a slider is simply running a barrel swivel up the mainline, to which a sinker is snapped into the other eye. The swivel slides freely up and down the line, which means it will come in contact with the mainline knot which is attached to another swivel. Because of this, be sure to thread a large bead between the sliding swivel and the mainline knot. This will ensure abrasion does not occur, whereby weakening the knot strength.

The other way a sliding sinker is commonly attached is with a commercial-made sliding rig. These plastic, tube-like devices come in a variety of sizes and thread onto the mainline, holding a sinker from the underside. They are easy to work with and allow for quick change-outs of different sized lead.

Where, exactly, a sliding sinker should be used is not agreed upon by all anglers. Some folks choose to use it most of the time, some only in select spots. Personally, I've learned that certain water constitutes better slider water than others. For example, if I'm anchored off to the side of a riffle, drift fishing fast water, it can be tough reading what the line is doing. Sometimes the hook will get hung while the sinker continues bouncing downstream, other times the sinker might get hung while the bait works down. When back-bouncing fast, deep water, I've found the same to be true, which not only results in more lost gear, but a loss of feel when the strike does come.

However, when back-bouncing slower water, or dragging behind a drifting boat, sliding sinkers are great. I like these scenarios in which to use sliders because it softens the bite. These are waters through which fish are often moving, meaning the strike may come from an upstream or downstream direction. When back-bouncing and there's a possibility of a slack-line bite, a slider is invaluable.

The key to using a slider is knowing when and where to apply it. Pay attention to the water, feel what the sinker is doing on the bottom and read how quickly your line is moving in relationship to the river flow and the speed the boat is moving. The more you can pinpoint the situations in which a slider can be used, the more effective they will be and the more fish you'll catch.

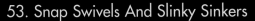
53. Snap Swivels And Slinky Sinkers

Often it's taken for granted, how to rig a slinky sinker to a snap swivel. But think about the objective and how the components work, and it makes sense that there is a right way and a wrong way to rig this basic set-up. Typically, the mainline is tied into the lone eye of the snap swivel, while the leader is tied to the eye which also houses the snap portion of the swivel. Next, the slinky sinker is slid on to the snap. The problem with this arrangement comes in the movement of the snap, which will rub against the leader knot. The result can be a lost fish on the hook-set or even during the fight, something that's often equated with a bad knot or weak line, when it was really the rubbing of the snap that caused it.

When the snap portion of the swivel—which holds the slinky sinker—is on the same eye as the leader, it naturally moves downstream. Whenever the line is reeled in, a fish is fought or the terminal gear hung up, the snap can shift downstream, rubbing against the knot. The result is abrasions in the leader knot, something that will eventually result in a snapped leader.

Instead, flip the snap swivel around, tying the mainline to the same eye the snap is in. Tie the leader to the lone eye of the snap swivel. This arrangement allows any resistance by the snap and sinker to work against the barrel end of the snap swivel, rather than rubbing against the knot. The result is fewer broken leaders and increased fishing time.

54. Caterpillar Sinkers

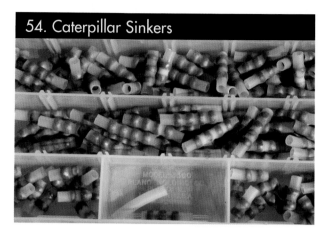

A unique alternative to slinky sinkers is one that carries the same concept in terms of performance, but is actually more efficient in some scenarios. It's called the caterpillar sinker, and consists of 1/4" surgical tubing and lead balls. Rather than seal the lead balls into the parachute cord, though, they are slipped into the surgical tubing. Not only can they be easily switched out, but they can be seen, so you know exactly how many lead balls you are fishing with. The result is precise weight specifications, something that can make a big difference when side-drifting or boondogging.

The section of surgical tubing can be as long as needed, typically between one to four inches, depending on the depth and speed of water being fished. From one end, slip the lead balls into the tubing and evenly space them apart. The other end of the tubing is attached to the snap portion of a snap swivel. A hole may need to be poked into the tubing to get the snap through it.

The beauty of a caterpillar sinker is that it allows for quick changes in weights—either by adding or subtracting lead balls—to meet the needs of the water being fished. When side-drifting big water, this sinker set-up allows everyone in the boat to efficiently match weights, allowing all the target water to be covered. With the caterpillar sinker, there is no guessing.

55. Barrel Vs. Three-Way Swivels

The more time you spend on the river, the more aware you become of just how many different types of water are out there, and the numerous ways they can be fished. In this age of gear specialization, the ways a hole can be fished have never been greater. There are specialty rods, reels, lines, drift-bobbers and more, that can allow a hole to be efficiently covered in various ways. Oh, and don't overlook the swivel.

For as long as I can remember, I've been using barrel and three-way swivels for salmon and steelhead. When drift fishing steelhead, I prefer running a half-inch section of 1/4" surgical tubing up my mainline. Inside this tubing I will slide a pencil sinker cut to desired length. Because the depth and speed of a single steelhead hole can greatly vary from top to

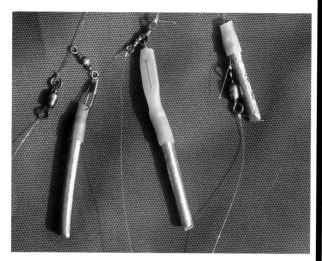

bottom, I'll often change out weights throughout a single hole. When the sinker does get hungup with this approach, it usually pops out, and the tubing slides over the size-7 barrel swivel, onto the leader. All I have to do to get back to fishing is slide the tubing back above the swivel, then slip a sinker into it.

I also prefer a barrel swivel when using a sliding sinker set-up, as there is less surface area for debris, moss and grass to get hung on as it drifts downstream. These swivels are also good for attaching a snap swivel and sinker to, or running a small dropper off of, as when side-drifting.

Three-way swivels are preferred when I want some separation among the terminal gear set-up. Anywhere I'm using a dropper measuring a few inches or longer—such as when back-bouncing, dragging, free-drifting or drift fishing—I like using a three-way swivel. The slight separation between the leader and dropper is all it takes to keep them from tangling amongst themselves when being fished. Choosing the right swivel will lead to fewer tangles, less hangups and increase your overall fishing time.

56. Make Your Own Spinners

Entire books have been written on this topic, and I'm not going to pretend to cover it all here. Suffice it to say, those anglers who make their own spinners typically outfish those who buy their hardware, at least, from what I've seen. The reasons are simple, as those who craft their own gear usually do so with a specific river in mind, even a specific hole.

The more you fish a river, or hole, the more you learn how the fish react under differing light conditions and water clarity levels. Go fishing with a serious spinner maker and you'll feel as if you're fishing in a tackle store. They carry lots of spinners, and with good reason, for they must be prepared to meet every need.

Once you get set-up with the equipment needed to start making your own spinners, a whole new world as to how you approach fishing will open up, as it forces you to think about what you're doing. You won't be making spinners simply because they look pretty, rather based on what color combinations you think will catch more fish. Experimenting with spinner making takes time, but in the end, what you'll learn from it will increase the number of fish you catch.

57. Spinner Blade Thickness

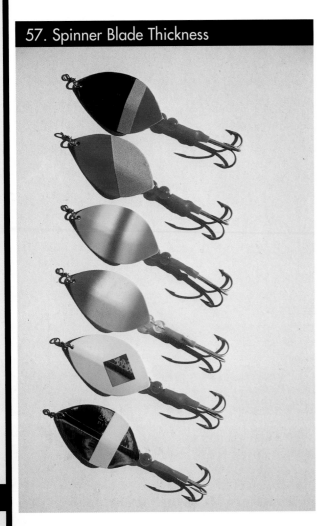

58. Match Drift-bobber To Hook Size

Perhaps making spinners isn't for you, that's okay. But when you buy spinners, be sure to look for specific characteristics that will fit your perceived fishing needs. Consider blade color, finish type and style as well as bead size, color and even hook size.

One overlooked aspect of lure-fishing is blade thickness, and this can really make a difference when trolling for fall chinook. This was first brought to my attention by Jeremy Toman, son of Bob Toman, the famed Pacific Northwest and Alaska father-son fishing team. We fished together on a slow day; slow for everyone but us. Some boats even called it quits, but Jeremy got us on to salmon well into the afternoon. The reason, I'm convinced, was due to spinner blade thickness.

We were using large blades, but they were thinner than what other people were using at the time. The reason this made a difference is because a thinner, lighter blade takes less force to turn it over. Because the fish were finicky, we could troll slower. We trolled just fast enough to barely kick the blade over. Each time the blade rolled over, the rod tip would twitch. Based on the twitch of the rod tip, Jeremy could monitor just how slow he could run the boat and still keep the lure fishing. The result was incredible, and is what kept Jeremy and Bob on this fishery after other guides sought new waters.

The Bob Toman spinners are world-renowned, and crafts-manship like this is why. This fishing duo even goes so far as to count the number of flips a blade makes per minute, whereby gauging the speed they troll. Talk about attention to detail; and it works! If gearing up for spinner fishing, include some thin blades, as they may work when others can't draw a strike.

As I unhooked a tangled mess of lines from the angler across the river, I couldn't help but inquire as to how he'd been doing. He just moved into the hole, and we got hungup together on the first cast. That didn't bother me in the least, but I was curious for a report. "Had two strikes so far, haven't hooked any-thing," he replied.

Plopping his line back in the water, I motioned for him to reel. When I saw the size-4 Corky perched atop a size-10 hook, it came as no surprise when I heard his response. The drift-bobber was too big for that size hook, or the hook too small, depending on your view. Actually, for the water he fished and the summer steelhead he was after, they were both mis-sized. But the problem was, when a fish did bite, it couldn't get hooked, for the large drift-bobber obscured the point of the hook.

I don't know how many riggings I've found like this over the years, and it surprises me, for it seems like a fairly common sense thing: If the drift-bobber is too large for the hook, make a change. If the hook is too small for the drift-bobber, make a change. It's simple.

Let the fish you pursue dictate what size hook is to be used, then match the drift-bobber accordingly. If you wish to up-size your drift-bobber, then up-size the hook, accordingly. This may be the case when arriving at the river and finding it high and off-color. Maybe you wish to go with a larger drift-bobber to increase visibility. That's a great idea, just be sure to switch the hook to match. The goal is to achieve more hookups, and taking the time to correlate hook and drift-bobber size is important in attaining this goal.

59. Extended Trailing Hook On Plugs

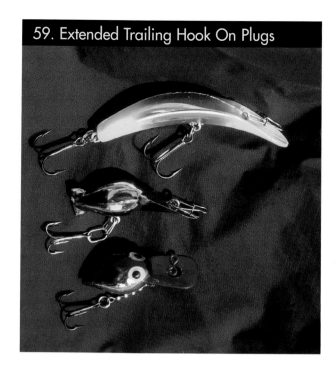

One of the most frustrating things a plug-angler faces is constant strikes with no hookup. "How in the world can a fish hit a plug so hard, and not get hooked?" I'd like to know myself sometimes. It's easy to see how effective a good plug really is, as can be evidenced by teeth marks on the body of the plug. Such marks reveal an aggressive strike, where the salmon or steelhead inhaled the entire plug into its mouth. On these tenacious strikes, getting a hook into the jaw is typically not a problem.

However, on short strikes—and there does seem to be many days of short strikes—the problem can be solved by dropping the trailing hook back a bit. This can be done by removing the hook, then running a D-ring or two, or even a large barrel swivel, off the back eye of the plug, then reattaching the hook. An added bonus when using a barrel swivel is that it rotates on itself, meaning there is less resistance on the hook and the plug when a fish is hooked, which is important when fishing two hooks on a plug.

When securing new hooks, the eyelets of both the hook and plug can be pried open and a barrel swivel slipped in. This seems to be a good rule-of-thumb distance in terms of a way to remedy the short strike dilemma. When using one or more D-rings, simply spread it apart and run it onto the eyelet.

Another option is running a Siwash hook off the trailing hook of a plug. This will also increase the distance between the hook and the plug, and results in a higher percentage of hookups. This is best done when a Siwash is already being fished, for attaching a Siwash to a treble hook can cause it to not run true. Simply open the eye of the Siwash to be attached, and run it over the point of the preexisting hook. Slide it into the bend of the hook and crimp the eye shut. The hook will naturally center itself.

After making any alterations to your plugs, be sure they run true, that is, are properly tuned. Oftentimes, tugging and tweaking on the eye of a plug will kick it out of line, and it's all but impossible to catch fish when this happens.

Because it's tough to predict when a short-strike day will occur, it's advised to have the items on-hand which will allow you to make a quick change of the plugs. Some anglers run extended hooks all the time. As with so much of fishing, what you choose to do comes down to personal preference, and altering your plugs is no different.

60. Siwash Hook On Plugs

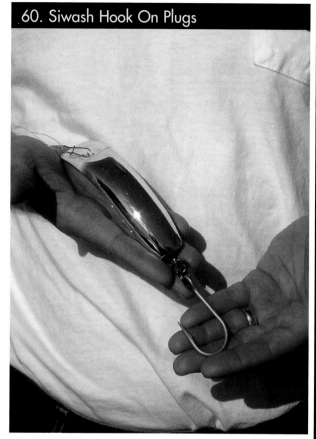

There are two main reasons I like using Siwash hooks on plugs. The first is a conservation-based explanation; that is, I know we'll be catching lots of fish that day and will only be practicing catch-and-release. The other is when I know the bite might be passive. This can be due to factors such as cold water temperatures, that fish may have been holding in a system for an extended period or because numerous anglers have been pressuring them.

Siwash, single-hooks designed for plug-fishing, are strong and offer a wide gap. The fact they lay flat when a fish hits them is also of vital importance. As a salmon or steelhead approaches a plug, then makes a timid strike, the less resistance they can detect, the better. A big treble hook might feel too cumbersome in the mouth, causing a fish to let go before it's even bit down. When a fish mouths a plug in this way, switch to a Siwash hook.

When a fish hits a Siwash hook, it almost always kicks the hook on its side, causing it to lay flat, and it does this under the least amount of pressure. Because the fish can't detect the resistance, it continues biting, burying the hook in the corner of its mouth as it turns on the plug. This is where the strong jawbones are located, and is one of the best places to hook and land a fish. Forget it's a single hook, if it's buried in the jaw, chances are the battle will be on.

Changing to a Siwash hook is easy, simply open the back eyelet on the plug and slip the eye of the hook into it, or vice versa. Crimp the eyelet closed, make sure the plug is tuned and you're ready to fish. This may seem like a subtle change, but can make the difference between catching fish or not.

61. Paint Divers Black

When it comes to back-trolling a diver and bait, there's a little trick which can help increase your strike rate. I've found this to be most applicable when fishing spring chinook, summer steelhead and winter steelhead in clear water conditions. Rather than working big, flashy divers, paint them black, so as to create a less intrusive presentation.

Under clear water conditions, presenting a big object to a fish can cause them to spook, and move out of the strike zone. Offering them a bait trailing behind a black, colorless plug which appears as nothing more than a shadow can often elicit a strike. Such an offering is more subtle, and when using bait, where the objective is to get that bait down deep and establish a scent trail fish can detect and hone in on, then it makes sense. A black diver allows a more natural, less intimidating way for bait to be presented, without spooking fish.

I've painted Mud Bugs, Hot Shots, Tad Pollys, Jet Divers and more, black, and am confident my catch rates shot up because of it. Mind you, the results aren't always fruitful, but I'm confident they have been higher because of the black diver.

On fall chinook, having the added color of a diver helps to attract them, and I don't typically paint them black during this season. In turbid water, especially when a river is running high, I won't be as apt to stick to the black divers, as I believe there are times when a colored diver will help capture the visual attention of fish. This is a case where the diver keys on the visual sense, while the bait hits the nose.

I always have a variety of colored divers on-hand, making sure there are various sizes and styles of black ones. On those clear rivers, especially when the sun is out, don't overlook the option of using a black diver, it may get the job done when all else fails.

62. Stinger Hook On Eggs

If you've ever experienced the frustration of short strikes when fishing bait, here's a simple solution. Drop a trailer beneath the bait. This free-hanging hook will not hold any bait, and in fact suspends below the bait, dangling freely in the current. It's called a stinger hook, and once you see how effective it really is, you'll find more applications under which it can be utilized.

The set-up is simple, as you're using snells to tie two hooks in tandem, much like a herring rig set-up. I like fixed hooks, not ones that can slide up and down the line; I don't want the top hook sliding on the leader, whereby it can possibly get hooked in a rolling fish, dislodging the stinger.

If fishing a river where regulations state only a single bend hook can be used, there's a way around this. Tie up two snelled hooks as normal. Once they are prepared and ready to store in the tackle box, take wire cutters and snip the upper hook off at the shank, between the knot and where the bend of the hook begins. This leaves the stinger hanging freely beneath the upper hook, which still has a loop in which bait can be affixed. This is how good friend, Brett Gesh, got us on to numerous big kings in past years on the Kenai.

The set-up can work well on sand shrimp and prawns, too, simply drop the stinger back a bit further than you would when fishing eggs. I've not found hook color to be a factor in spooking the fish, and there is no question in my mind that this slight change in hook positioning has accounted for many more fish over the years. It's just one more piece of the fish-catching puzzle.

63. Vary Yarn Color

Just as drift-bobber or spinner color can make a difference in drawing a strike, so too, can yarn color. The decision to utilize different yarn colors stems from personal preference, something that's usually developed over time spent on the water. Some people are fanatics about yarn color, others don't give it much thought. However, when you think of such things as water clarity, how fast a presentation moves through a drift, what the level of solar penetration is, as well as other factors, it becomes evident that yarn color can make a difference in catching fish. When you do use yarn, gear-up with multiple colors.

I have spent days on the river where green has been the hot color. The same stretch the next day may find red, or a combination of orange/green being the ticket. At the same time, pink may be hot for an entire season on one river; the next season it may be a different color. Then there are those rivers where one color seems to prove consistent year after year.

Knowing what yarn colors work on any given stream, or having the flexibility to change and find out for yourself what works, can make a difference in the number of fish you catch. However, the key is being prepared. If going to a new river, call local tackle shops or sporting goods stores to find out what the hot color has been. Try tracking down someone who has fished that river recently, and pick their brains for advice.

Before hitting the water, have an assortment of hooks pre-tied, with different yarn colors to choose from. I'll typically go with a half-dozen yarn colors on any given trip. This allows me to change colors should one not seem to be working. The color selection can vary, and the more time you spend tinkering with this, the more confident you'll become in terms of using specific yarn colors in different situations—at the very least, you'll develop a willingness to try new things. The outcome can be good.

64. Knot End Of Yarn

When steelhead fishing there's a nifty trick you can do to your yarn which will help hook more fish. With the yarn in place, either above the hook or within the egg loop, tie a knot at the tip of each tag end. To do this you'll want to make the tag ends a bit longer than normal, to allow room for your fingers to manipulate the yarn. Then, simply tie a knot in both ends of the yarn.

The purpose of this is so, in theory, when the steelhead bites the bait, the yarn will hang in it's mouth just a fraction longer, a result of the knot getting wedged between the pointed little teeth. That valuable fraction of a second longer the bait spends in its mouth can be critical in detecting a bite, for it's mind-boggling how quickly a steelhead can grab a bait in fast water, then spit it out without your ever knowing he was there.

Steelhead have small, very sharp teeth, and this ploy can work. I've found it most productive when drift fishing fast water, where the hook set comes straight out in front of me. As the line swings downstream ahead of the terminal gear which is bouncing along the bottom, it can be very difficult to detect exactly what's going on down there. A yarn knot can give you a valuable edge in such conditions, and allows you to hook fish you'd otherwise not feel.

65. Tie Good Knots

It sounds basic, but is one of the most overlooked steps in fishing, and that's tying good knots. As with other points in this book, knot tying is a subject on which books have been penned, so I'm not going to go over all the knot possibilities here. However, if you haven't already done so, and are in need of learning more on the subject, I strongly encourage you to get one of the basic knot tying books and learn a few of the basic ones.

A common error in knot tying comes in not properly matching the knot with the purpose for which it's being used. For example, if fishing big fall chinook, where the chances of hooking into a 60-pound fish are real, then be certain the knot strength can hold up to the test. At the same time, it's not an overkill to be conservative, and go with the highest percentage strength knots that you know will work.

Aside from which knot to tie, when working with copolymers and especially fluorocarbons, be sure to wet the line prior to cinching the knot down tight. This can be done with saliva, river water or rain. Wetting the line cuts down on friction which can weaken a knot once it's actually snugged down tight against a hook or swivel. The time to wet a knot is when it's still in its loose stage, not once it's been tightened.

Another helpful hint is to make sure there is plenty of tag end on the knot. You don't want it so short that as the line stretches, the tag end is pulled through, unraveling the knot. On the flip side, you don't want it too long to where it catches moss, grass or other debris floating downstream, whereby inhibiting the action of your presentation.

I've seen numerous fish lost over the years to inadequate knots and tag ends that have been clipped too short. Take a few minutes to master a selection of strong knots, then put them to use. The effort will pay off with an increased ratio of hooked-fish to landed-fish.

66. Copolymer Lines

Fishing lines have come a long ways, and can impact your efficiency.

With the multitude of lines on the market, choosing which one to use, when, can be a challenge. The more you fish, the more your thought process will develop—along with personal preference—as to which line you prefer to fish under various conditions and approaches. Based on my lifetime of fishing, I've found a definite fit with the lines available and the fishing styles I apply.

I prefer using copolymer lines when drift fishing, back-bouncing, free-drifting, dragging, side-drifting, spinner fishing and back-trolling baits. That's not to say that I only use copolys when applying these methods, but I like this line type for a three reasons. First, the line I use, PLine, is extremely tough and abrasion resistant for the true diameters in which they come. These are crucial requirements in the rocky, rough-running rivers I like fish. I once hooked a springer which took me under a ledge and badly frayed my CXX X-TRA Strong leader. Curious to see how the line would hold up, I caught another fish on it, then another. I caught 11 springers on the same frayed leader before finally changing it out. In my book, no pun intended, that's about the best test there is.

Second, in the forms of fishing listed above, hangups are inevitable, meaning lines will have to be broken. I much prefer breaking copolys over braided lines, especially on wet days when the line can slice into your hands.

Finally, I like copolys due to their memory levels. They are not as relaxed as say, a braided line, meaning they won't whip and wrap around the rod tip, costing valuable time, or worse yet, a fish. They are just stiff enough to maintain control over, and that's important when pinpointing where you want your line to be.

If you don't have confidence in the pound line you are using, then upgrade to a heavier pound test. It's better to go too heavy than too light, for what's the use in hooking a fish if there's not a prayer of landing it?

67. Braided Lines

Braided lines are valuable tools, and have revolutionized much of salmon and steelhead fishing. When it comes to bobber and jig fishing, I always use a braided line. For this approach, Berkley's FireLine is ideal, as it floats, allowing for mends to be made to ensure the bobber is being carried downstream at a natural rate.

I also like braided lines for running big plugs and trolling for fall chinook. These are methods where hangups are few, meaning you don't have to break the line. At the same time, these are approaches where a stronger line, with a smaller diameter, can allow you to better manage big fish, increasing the chance of landing them. These nonstretch lines also lead to a quicker hook-set.

I know of several guys who drift-fish braided line, but I personally find myself getting in too many tangles and not being able to control my terminal gear as I'd like. A lot of it comes down to fishing style, the gear, rods and reels you use, and the specific holes being fished. By making the line fit the situation, more fish can be hooked, and landed.

68. Fluorocarbon Lines

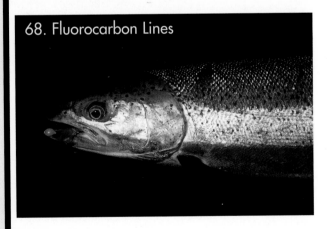

I once stood along a crystal-clear Alaskan stream, where steelhead into the 20-pound class were many. The man next to me was flustered at not landing any fish, so downsized from a 10-pound copolymer leader to 6-pound fluorocarbon. His reasoning was that the fluorocarbon would not spook the fish, and he was right, but where he made the mistake was in downsizing the line. If anything, he should have upgraded when switching to fluorocarbon. I preceded to watch him hook and break off

several fish, while I landed double-digit fish with 15-pound fluorocarbon leader, all in the same hole.

Fluorocarbon line is ideal in that it has a refraction index nearly identical to water. Translation: it's virtually invisible under water. Fishing fluorocarbon leaders makes the most sense in very clear water, where fish can possibly be spooked by a line passing near them. It's also valuable on extremely bright days, in slightly sediment-laden water, where light rays penetrate down to the leader. However, I routinely see it being used in off-colored water, which is fine, but not necessary.

Early in its developmental stages, fluorocarbon received a bad wrap, as there were some sub-par products on the market. Production and quality-control is more advanced now, as some companies stepped up their standards to compete with the higher-quality lines already on the shelf. The most dependable fluorocarbon line I've ever used is crafted by PLine, and I've caught big kings, countless steelhead and trophy trout on it.

Fluorocarbon is a hard line, and wetting the knot prior to cinching it down is a must. If the line is not wet, and a fish breaks at the knot, it's likely due to friction and loss of knot strength, something the angler can control.

Not always is there a time and a place for fluorocarbon. I use it only in very clear water, where fish may be spooked. The beauty of this line, however, is that it allows you to increase the size of line being fished, due to the refraction level, thus allowing you to land big fish. Nothing is sacrificed, in fact, you gain strength here. Experiment around with fluorocarbon, you won't be disappointed.

69. High-Visibility Plugging Line

Pulling plugs for salmon and steelhead has been around for decades, and really reached is zenith in the 1980s. Today, many anglers still apply this method, some even live and die by it. Some proponents of pulling plugs say they like it because it's easy; others say they prefer other methods because it's too easy. Pulling plugs is easy, but it's far from simple. There is a lot more to pulling plugs than tossing them in the water and backing it downstream.

Speed, position, depth, action and reading the water to see what's ahead are just a sampling of the factors plug pullers have to pay constant attention to in order to keep that plug-fishing. Just because the plugs are in the river doesn't mean a fish has a chance of biting it. I know of people who have pulled plugs for two and three years and never hooked a fish; and I can promise you, it's not the plug's fault.

Above all else, the oarsman must control where the plug is going, and know why it's going where it is. Plug positioning does not happen by chance. It's a deliberate movement put in place by the oarsman, and it relates to the factors mentioned above. But, in order to figure out where plugs should be positioned, you have to see where the lines are going.

This is where a high-visibility line comes in handy. I prefer a high-vis' green line (PLine's CXX X-TRA Strong in fluorescent green is my favorite), as I can see it in any conditions, be they dark mornings, against dark or bright water, in heavily shaded stretches, during tense rains and even in dwindling daylight where it might otherwise be difficult to detect a copolymer line. When running two or three rods, a high-vis' line is critical in allowing plugs to be maneuvered with pinpoint accuracy into the strike zone.

I'll simply tie a six- to nine-foot clear, copolymer leader on to a size-7 barrel swivel, to which the mainline is tied to the other end. If the swivel is picking up too much debris in the water, and the action of the plug becomes inhibited because of this, I'll join the two lines with a blood knot. Using a high-vis' mainline is a simple step, and by equipping your plugging rods with it, those plugs will be fishing for you a higher percentage of the time. Read the water, learn where the fish hold and travel and utilize the ability of this line to allow more water to be efficiently covered. Bottom line, you'll hook more fish.

70. Bobber Stop On Plugging Mainline

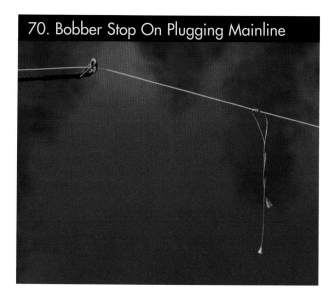

Line control is one important factor relating to plugging. That is, the oarsman controls where the line is at all times. While direction is just one facet of plug positioning, distance is another, often overlooked element. The more uniform the distance of the plugs in the water, the more precise the delivery will be, the better the chance of catching fish.

When it comes to plugging for steelhead, they can often be backed down a stretch of water, all the way to the tailout, where they must either escape over the break, swim by the plugs, or retaliate and attack. Given the attitude of steelhead, they'll often choose the latter option. That's one reason running plugs equidistant to one another is good.

Because the distance plugs are let out is essential to accurate delivery, there's a basic step which can be taken to ensure this happens. Prior to hitting the river, take all your plugging rods out into the yard or driveway. Now measure out 35 to 60 feet

from the rod tips. Next, pull all the lines out to the marked distance, then tie a bobber stop to the mainline at the tip of the rod. Snug it tight and nip the tag ends, so they don't get caught in the guides or reel parts.

What distance you choose to put the bobber stop depends on the water being fished. If it's shallow, run it a bit further ahead of the boat; if it's deep, run it closer, so the plugs pull hard, thus dig deeper. Many anglers choose to count the number or revolutions a line is let out on their casting reels, or to float all the plugs downstream on the surface before flipping the bail to send them down. Both of these methods work, but if a plug gets debris on it, is reeled in halfway and the stick pops off, then the angler has to reel it back in, then let it back out to try and match the proper distance. There are several such scenarios where this might happen, all of which eat up valued time.

A bobber stop positioned to mark preferred plugging distances takes out the guesswork as to how far the plugs are really let out. It also increases fishing time, by allowing anglers to leave their gear in the water longer, rather than reeling it in, then running it back out. It takes only a few minutes of set-up time, and believe me, it's time well spent.

71. Extra Line

Many streams occupied by salmon and steelhead are rough and either boulder-strewn or bedrock-laden. This means the habitat can be hard on line, especially when fish take you into such obstacles. When fishing these rivers—or any river for that matter—it's a wise idea to have an extra spool of fresh line on hand. I'll even have various spools of different line weights in order to match specific needs.

At the same time, when pursing big fish, there's the possibility of being spooled, that is, having every bit of line stripped off the reel, then snapping off at the spool. This is a helpless feeling when it happens, I know, I've had it happen twice with monster steelhead in ripping water. There's nothing worse than to be standing in the water with no more line on the reel, knowing full-well fish are there, and worse yet, biting.

Take a few minutes to replace damaged line, so the right water can be fished. Think ahead, be prepared and always carry an extra spool for emergency change-outs.

72. Fill Spools

With the development of so many high-quality reels, it's easy to get caught up in gear ratios and all that relates to it. For the drift-fisherman who is continually casting and retrieving the terminal gear, gear ratios can be a big plus; the higher the gear ratio, the faster the retrieve, the more time is spent with the gear in the water.

To maximize high gear ratio performance, however, the spools must be kept full of line. Take for example, a reel with a high gear ratio of 7:1. This means that with one complete turn of the reel handle, the spool itself rotates seven times. Of course, a 7:1 gear ratio takes up line faster than a 5:1, and is most efficient when the spool is kept full.

If a high gear ratio spool is only half-filled with line, it's actual performance level dramatically decreases. This means you have to crank the handle more times to take up the line, which contradicts the purpose of having a high gear ratio reel. To maximize reel performance, make sure the spool is full. If you break off a considerable amount of line, re-spool it as soon as possible to maximize the reel's capabilities. In addition to optimizing gear performance, a full spool will help you cast further and with much more accuracy. In reality, keeping a full spool of line can help you catch more fish in multiple ways.

73. Loop-Style Droppers

When fishing water where depth can vary from the head end to the lower end, it may require a quick change-out of lead to properly cover the target depth. If it's a deep, swirling salmon hole you're back-bouncing through, there might be big boulders at the head end, then a big dropoff. Such depth changes often alter the current flow, even on the subsurface level. If baits are getting away from you, then a quick sinker change may be all it takes to remedy the problem.

By tying a loop on the bottom of your dropper, it can be passed through the eye of a sinker, than the sinker can be threaded back through it. It's quick, easy and no knots are used. This allows for fast changes, and more importantly, for the target water to properly be fished. If your bait is moving too fast or too slow through the target zone, then it's not being fished with 100% efficiency. And in this game, attention to detail can make the difference between a good day or slow day on the river.

74. Dropper Set-up For Hollow Core

This tip was brought to my attention by good friend, Buzz Ramsey. It has to do with preventing line twist and allowing for quick sinker replacement when using hollow-core pencil lead, and the theory makes sense. When drift fishing or side-drifting, anglers commonly leave a tag end of either their mainline or leader, letting it hang from a barrel swivel. On this tag end is where the pencil lead is crimped on, but only do so when using very light lead. Attaching heavier lead to the tag end can impede line performance, thus inhibit natural presentation of the terminal gear.

If using heavier pencil lead, try tying a two- to three-inch dropper off the eye of the barrel swivel. It will either tie into the mainline eye or the leader eye, depending on what reels you're using, but the effect is the same; to allow freedom of movement between the line and dropper.

This is a very effective set-up which increases fishing time by allowing quick replacement of lead should you lose it, plus cuts down on retying leaders, as they untwist between every cast. When fishing with a spinning outfit, attach the lead to the same eye the leader is tied to; when using a casting reel, leave the tag end on the mainline end of the swivel. With the hollow-core leader attached to the proper dropper, you're ready to fish. This hollow-core sinker approach is especially effective in heavy water, as the sinker easily slips off the dropper, saving the primary terminal gear from having to be retied.

Another objective of this approach is to prevent line twist. When retrieved, line is spooled on to a spinning reel differently than it is a casting reel, thus the reasoning behind attaching the lead to differing ends of the barrel swivel. By doing so, the barrel swivel is allowed to work and rotate freely, rather than fighting line resistance. The ultimate result is less line twist, whereby allowing the line to maintain its strength and durability which is key when it comes to fighting fish.

75. Monitor Weather

No matter what time of year it is, or what species you're going after, monitoring the weather can make a big difference in your fishing success. It's no secret fish behavior can change along with approaching and waning weather systems. Even a cloudy or clear sky can impact how you fish on any given day. The key is knowing what to expect during your planned time on the water.

For instance, an approaching storm can turn off the bite in a certain river system, and may warrant delaying or postponing your fishing plans. At the same time, a big storm may mean lots of rain, which can cause river levels to rise, making it very tough to get fish to cooperate. Likewise, keeping track of how long it takes a storm to pass, then noting how long it takes a river to recover, can pay dividends, especially if you're on the river ahead of other anglers. Many anglers wait for a stream to fully recover prior to fishing it, when they could find results by applying high-water tactics a day or two ahead of perfect conditions, and before of fellow anglers hit the river.

Simple weather patterns like clouds or clear sky can influence what size and/or color of terminal gear you'll use. Tracking the weather ahead of time, and watching the barometer (both at home and on the water) ensures that you have all the proper gear you'll need to meet the demands of changing environmental conditions on the rivers you fish.

In many Pacific Northwest rivers, storms can cause a river to rise very rapidly. The result can be anglers stuck on the river, in a potentially dangerous situation. This happened to a buddy and I one day back in high school. It was spring, and a heavy rainstorm was nailing us all day long. But we weren't about to let a bit of rain cut into our fishing time. Bilge pump in hand, we hit the river. Over the course of the day the pump rarely rested, as it moved water from the driftboat into the river.

The river was obviously rising and turning turbid, in fact, visibility decreased to a matter of inches. The best part, we were catching fish, a rarity under these conditions. We were on to something and didn't want to give up, so we kept the bilge pumping as the fish kept biting. By late afternoon the river had come up more than two feet, and when logs started floating by us, we realized the predicament we were in.

Rowing the boat down to the take-out was not fun that day, battling logs, debris and heavy boils. We knew it was going to be a stormy day, and had we been smart and checked the predicted forecast, would have learned record-breaking rains were expected. Though the price paid was a bit scary, we did learn some high-water tricks that still catch salmon. Somehow our moms didn't think the tradeoff was a good one, as they were worried sick about us; but our dads were proud.

76. Monitor Water Temperature

Along the lines of monitoring weather patterns comes the tracking of water temperature in the rivers you fish. Water temperature and the bite is something that's followed very closely by ocean anglers, but overlooked by many river goers. In fact, when other variables are frequently blamed, too cold or too warm of water can often be the culprit of those days you go home empty-handed.

Though all salmon and steelhead bites can be impacted by both warm and cold water conditions, let's look at summer steelhead as a classic example. Summer steelhead begin making their way into many western rivers early in the spring, even in late winter, when water temperatures are still quite chilly. The result can be finicky fish that are reluctant to bite.

Once the sun starts warming the water, these steelhead not only begin holding and sometimes traveling in different areas of the river, but they grow more aggressive. As their metabolism is boosted, their aggressive nature kicks-in and they bite more frequently.

However, as the summer progresses and water temperatures escalate, the steelhead may take on a less active lifestyle in an effort to conserve energy and retain higher levels of oxygen. In this case the bite can greatly wane, almost come to a complete stop. But once early fall rains hit and nighttime temperatures decrease, it doesn't take long for water temperatures to drop. The result can be the best summer steelhead fishing of the year.

On many occasions we've had very good summer steelhead fishing in May and June, then it slows in July and August. Once the water temperatures drop in September, the fishing can be at its peak for the season. On through October double-digit days can often be expected, and at this time there is little pressure for these fish.

The species you pursue, the rivers in which you fish them and the time of year you're active, all factor in to water temperature monitoring and catching success. If you're not sure of the prime water temperatures in the river you intend to fish, ask local hatchery and fish and game experts, tackle shop owners, guides and fellow anglers. Those who consistently catch fish likely monitor water temperature; it's something not to be overlooked.

77. Call For Bait Availability

There's nothing more frustrating than being on the river without the right bite, or worse yet, no bait. Be it herring for fall chinook, eggs for springers or sand shrimp for summer steelies,

make sure you have access to bait, if you intend on using bait that day.

Herring, sardine and anchovy baits can be the toughest to come by, which is why calling local marinas or bait and tackle shops well ahead of your planned trip can be wise. The availability of seasonal baits can fluctuate from year to year, even from week to week. Just because bait availability was there last year, don't assume it will be the next. This is especially true if traveling any considerable distance, as it's frustrating to learn no bait is available at your final destination when, in fact, you could have acquired it at a tackle shop closer to home.

If you don't cure your own eggs and rely on store-bought selections, and the egg bite is on, the store may be out; the same holds true for sand shrimp. At the same time, it may be early or late in the season, and stores may not carry the bait you're looking for. Calling ahead of time can be critical to attaining bait, thus catching fish.

One fall day a buddy and I made a last-minute decision to go after some summer steelhead. Fish were everywhere, though we failed to hook a single one. We returned the next day with some fresh sand shrimp and Smelly Jelly. By 11:00 a.m. we landed 13 steelies, all on shrimp and scent. Had we called around to stores and checked on shrimp availability the first day, we wouldn't have been blanked, guaranteed.

78. PVC Rod Cases

Rod cases are available in countless styles and sizes from manufacturers across the nation. While some anglers invest in the best money can buy, others neglect to even use them. Not using a rod case is a personal choice, which is fine as long as it doesn't cost you a trip.

While traveling on planes, I've seen anglers carry on their rods, without any case. They stow the rods in the overhead compartments, sometimes with good results, sometimes not. On one occasion a man pulled out a pile of rods as we disembarked, only to discover the load had shifted during the flight, breaking the ends of every rod. Another time, a man yanked out his rods from the bulkheads and broke and bent several guides.

If traveling by plane, consider making your own rod case, especially if carrying multiple rods. In today's time of tightened flight regulations, fishing rods are now considered checked baggage; it didn't used to be that way for everyone, and hopefully it will change again some day. So, if rods count as checked baggage, then get your mileage out of it. I'll make rod cases out of 10-inch-diameter PVC pipe, gluing a cap on one end, slipping one on the other and taping it down for easy access.

To get the full value, that is space usage, from this magnum rod case, I'll wrap my clothes tightly around the rods, then slip them into the case. If room permits, I'll slip socks, underwear and other small items into the tubes. Not only does this pad the rods through the brutal baggage handling process, but it saves one piece of luggage that I'd normally put clothes in. My bigger, bulkier clothes, boots and tackle boxes go in the other checked bag. If traveling by vehicle, these rod cases also work well, and can be fashioned in smaller scale; they are great for rod protection when traveling any great distance. For modest dollars, a sturdy rod case can be constructed and potentially save a fishing trip that may have otherwise gone awry.

79. Hit Proven Holes

At the start of the season on any given river, for any given species, go to those places you know have held fish in previous years. Unless high water has changed the hole, that is filled it in with sand, rock or debris or removed structure that enticed fish to hold there in the first place, the action should yield results.

There are holes I've been fishing since the 1960s that I still catch fish in every season; these are the same holes that my father and grandfathers caught fish in well before my time. On the flip-side, one of my favorite steelhead holes of more than 10 years got filled-in with sand during a high-water winter. Steelhead don't like sand, and though I still flip a cast in there every time I pass by, I've not hooked a fish, nor seen one there, since it filled-in.

Note which holes produce during certain water levels, and hit those spots when the conditions match. Fish may occupy one hole when the river is at a specific level, then move to another hole, or a different location within the same hole, when the water rises or drops. Learning where these sweet spots are, and regularly fishing them will produce positive results.

If fishing a new river, mark where fellow anglers are spending time. Pay attention not only to how they fish the hole, but how they set-up to fish it and even how they approach it. The slightest change in anchor position can make a difference in where that terminal goes, and where that anchor falls can be dictated by how you slip into a hole. Stick to holes you know produce, but keep the eyes and mind open for new ones.

80. Rust Prevention Of Rods And Reels

Anglers along the West Coast and Great Lakes regions are accustomed to rain and getting gear wet. To prolong the life and proper functioning of this gear, it's a good idea to properly clean them at the end of each day. While wiping down rods and reels is a good place to start, spraying them down with a rust prevention product is even better.

Reels and reel seats can be sprayed with a light application of WD-40 or The Inhibitor. Both serve the purpose of retarding moisture build-up, thus rusting. The result is reels that work smoothly and efficiently. At the same time, metal reel seats are made to continue functioning well. This may not be noticed until it comes time to change reels, or spools, which often takes place on the water.

If proper care is taken, then you won't have to deal with rusty, non-working parts on the river. The end result is gear that works the way it's intended, whereby increasing your fishing time by not having to fiddle with gear that shouldn't be malfunctioning in the first place. Spraying down your gear can be done at home, or when pulling off the water. Many anglers choose to clean all their gear before the drive home, which means having a can of spray on-hand, either in the truck or boat. If you don't have the spray on-hand, then you can't use it. My best advice here is, buy it and use it, for it will save money and fishing time in the future.

81. The Inhibitor VCI Pro Chips

Another rainy-day tip we can all benefit from is that of rust prevention on hooks. Fact is, few of us will take the time at the end of the day to spray down the hooks of all the plugs, spinners and riggings we fished to prevent rust build-up. Often we put them away wet, or worse yet, leave them in a tackle box that has been rained on throughout the day.

There's a little device out there called The Inhibitor VCI Pro Chip, which is a cardboard-like wafer that has been treated on both sides with special VCI (Volatile Corrosion Inhibitors) that release a nontoxic vapor which blends with moisture and oxygen to stop rust and corrosion. The Inhibitor Chip has been used by bass anglers for some time, but is relatively unknown in the salmon and steelhead fishing world.

The Chip protects brass, bronze, copper, aluminum, steel and stainless steel. It leaves no scent and is not harmful on soft plastics or synthetic finishes. This means hooks no longer rust and grow dull, which cuts down on the time it requires to sharpen them or change them out for new replacements. How many times have you dug into a tackle box, pulled out a plug with rusty hooks, and thought nothing of it? Rust breaks down metal, thus inhibits its strength and durability. By incorporating these rust-prevention chips, hook quality will be retained, ultimately increasing the hookup-to-strike ratio and even increase the number of fish landed. It will also save you money by not having to purchase replacement hooks.

82. Leader Under 36 Inches

When drift fishing, leader length can play a large part of angler success. Leader length allows you to control such things as the depth at which you are fishing, swing-rates and terminal-gear position. However, there's a point where the distance exceeded can impede honest fishing practices.

Check applicable fishing regulations prior to tying-up a large number of leaders, for some rivers and states have leader length restrictions. On those that allow liberal leader length, however, be careful; you don't want to cross the line of ethical fishing to that of "lining" fish. Lining, or "flossing," is a term applied to the technique of using a long leader and dragging it through holding zones in hopes of passing it through the open mouth of a fish. The result is a hook that buries into the outer jaw of the fish, which is, frankly, snagging in the head.

Long leaders can result in the loss of line control, for there's simply too much line in the water to manage. Leaders of six to eight feet are not uncommon to see, especially when swinging drifts through fast, shallow steelhead water and narrow salmon chutes. Fish being hooked, or snagged, on the outside of the mouth are often the result of such long leaders.

Through decades of personal experience, I've found that leaders much beyond 30 inches are tough to control. The longest I'll typically go is 36 inches, when working deeper, slower-moving water where fish may be slightly suspended off the bottom. The fast rivers typically fished in the West make controlling the terminal gear a challenge. In order to efficiently control and manage each cast, conservative leader lengths will help get the job done. Leaders in the 18- to 30-inch range are easier to track the depth of, as well as move into position from an upstream or side-stream direction. The result is fewer hangups and more fish caught, as you're better able to direct the terminal gear to where fish are holding.

83. Rod Selection

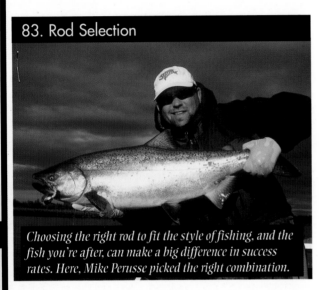

Choosing the right rod to fit the style of fishing, and the fish you're after, can make a big difference in success rates. Here, Mike Perusse picked the right combination.

When it comes to salmon and steelhead, the most significant advances in the fishing industry of recent times has been in the rods themselves. Never before have so many specialized rods been available to anglers, and with good reason. These rods are not introduced by accident; they are the result of in-depth, scientific study and often times, years of testing. Leading rod manufacturers won't put a product out there that's not proven, or that they feel won't hold up to its specifically designed purpose.

This is where anglers need the understanding support of a loving wife, for there are as many rods out there as there are ways to fish them. Be it side-drifting, drift-fishing, back-bouncing, plugging, casting spinners, floating jigs or any of a number of other techniques used to take salmon and steelhead, chances are there's a specialized rod to help get the job done. These rods are designed with the theory that each fishing approach can be maximized and efficiently applied by the angler, and that's exactly what happens. Have you ever tried running a bobber and jig with a stiff back-bouncing rod? It doesn't work, or at least not like it should. Such is the case with the majority of techniques, in that specialized rods now make it easier for anglers to learn and apply very specific fishing methods.

By matching the rods to the style being fished, many positive results happen. Increased line control, accurate casting, maximized sensitivity and feel, power, action and overall performance are just a sampling of what the right rod can do. The outcome is simple; you catch more fish. If you want to catch more

fish, one of the best investments you can make is in specialized rods that will help you master the technique being applied.

84. Reel Selection

As with rods, reels have experienced a great advancement in technology. The result is higher-performance reels that allow you to meet a wide range of fishing strategies and master specific requirements in order to properly apply specific techniques. I remember the days when, as a kid, the only reel I had was the old Mitchell 300, and I used it for everything.

Today, numerous spinning and casting reels allow anglers to choose a reel that best fits the method being fished. Ideally, having a reel for every rod is the way to go, for this saves time from having to changeover gear and dramatically increases the time your terminal tackle spends in the water.

When talking spinning reels and steelhead fishing for instance, a reel like the Shimano Symetre 2500 is a good choice when side-drifting. If fishing bobber and jigs, a larger capacity reel, like the 4000 series Symetre is necessary to allow more room for braided, floating line which will let you cover more water on each cast.

For bait-casting reels, or levelwinds, a larger capacity model may be a good choice, especially when targeting fall chinook in big water. At the same time, if drift-fishing for springers in a smaller section of river, downsizing the reel to one that comfortably fits in your hand will be beneficial. With so many specialized reels now available, and at affordable rates, there's no reason not to diversify and catch more fish.

85. Accurate Casting

It sounds basic, but is one of the most taken-for-granted approaches to salmon and steelhead fishing, and that's making each cast count. We see it every week on TV, bass fishermen making their living off accurate casting and fine-tuned presentations. It's no different for salmon and steelhead anglers. If the cast isn't in the right place, no matter how advanced the gear, the odds of catching fish dramatically drops.

In big rivers, it's easy to become overwhelmed with where to start casting. Read the water, determine where fish are either laying or traveling through, and start there. If fishing a new hole or section of river, it may take several trips, maybe even years, to pinpoint where fish are during certain water levels. At the same time, other factors like the amount of fishing pressure, time of day, water and air temperature, and more, can all correlate to where fish may be.

If fishing from a moving boat, you may only have one shot to place that bait precisely where it should be. If you miss it, no fish. I've seen this time and time again, where a group side-drifting winter steelheading failed to hit the sweet-spot, only to have a boat directly behind them find it and catch fish.

Practice casting at home, in the yard, with nothing more than a sinker tied to the line. Place certain objects like a can, paper plate, rock or hoop on the ground and cast with the intent of hitting them. You can even take sidewalk chalk and draw circles in the driveway, trying to hit those (my sons love doing this). Utilize every casting technique you'll apply in the river, with the same rods and reels you'll be fishing with. The more precisely placed each cast can be, the more fish you'll hook.

86. No Alcohol

This tip may offend some people, and that's not the intent. As a person who makes his living in the outdoors, I see alcohol use on the river to be one of the biggest detriments to the sport of fishing. Obviously alcohol is not to be consumed when running a motorized boat, but here, I'm talking about what's left behind.

When on the river I'll usually tote an extra garbage bag to pick up trash along the river banks when I can. By the end of the day, it's primarily filled with old line and Styrofoam containers, but a close third is often beer cans. Sportfishing has never been under so much scrutinization, and when anti-anglers see beer cans laying in the bottom of the river, or broken bottles littering

pristine river banks, who could blame them for their negative outlook on "all" anglers.

All I'm suggesting here is to monitor alcohol consumption, maybe save it for back at camp. How does this correlate to catching more fish? With anglers being under the watchful eye of many we owe it to the sport to do all within our power to preserve our great pastime and carry it on to future generations. At the same time, the intoxicated angler is the one who often loses focus and motivation while on the river, thus catching fewer fish.

When on the water, be mindful of the surroundings, and remember, you're representing all anglers. It's the goal of most anglers to fish for as many years as they can, and see that their children and grandchildren get the opportunity to do the same. This is one area we sportsmen can control.

87. Sunscreen

The awareness of skin cancer has greatly escalated in recent years, and anglers are prime candidates. Obviously, the summer steelheader, spring and early season fall chinook folks are the ones we're talking to here, but the point is, be aware. Not only should time be taken to apply sunscreen, but it should also be taken to clean the hands afterwards.

Nowhere is this more true than when fishing bait, where concern of passing lotion odors on to the bait often prevents us from applying the shield of protection we need to maintain healthy skin. On those sunny days, prior to launching that boat or hiking down to the river, take the time to apply sunscreen. As equally important, when done applying it, take time to clean your hands.

Wash any lotion residues from your hands prior to contacting any fishing gear, and I mean line, rod handles, reels, oars, plugs, baits...everything. When talking salmon, whose sensitive noses can decipher smells of synthetic lotions, taking a few seconds to wash your hands can mean the difference between a great day or coming up empty.

There are many hand soaps out there, even small squirt bottles of hand sanitizers get the job done. When in a boat, I'll frequently wash my hands with lemon-scented Joy, just to be sure no unwanted odors are being passed along to the terminal gear or key parts of the boat. Another option is the spray-on sunscreens, which don't taint hands.

88. Insect Repellent

The ThermaCELL is an effective deterrent of mosquitos and other biting insects.

In many of the places anglers journey to, biting insects can be a real problem. I recall days spent in Alaska's Arctic where mosquitos were so thick, a breath couldn't be taken without inhaling numerous bugs. It was so bad, people would not go outdoors, let alone spend the day fishing.

The more fishing you do, it's to be expected that, at one time or another, you'll experience a truly nasty biting bug trip. Once you make it through one of these ordeals, you'll forever remember the negative impact bugs can have on a trip.

But it doesn't take a pile of bugs to ruin a fishing trip, just a handful of persistent, biting ones can make things uncomfortable, even cost you fishing time. Know the bug situation prior to setting foot on the river. If traveling to a dream destination—like Alaska—in the middle of summer you don't want to sacrifice a quality trip due to tiny, biting bugs.

Lotions, sprays, sticks and wipes are available to help keep bugs at bay. If applying these products by hand, be sure to wash after application, especially if salmon are your target fish. Remember, salmon have an incredible sense of smell, and residues that are left on the hands and transferred to fishing gear can keep fish from biting.

If not wanting to risk bug-repellent contamination, bug suits are an option. Likewise a ThermaCELL unit (www.thermacell.com), an innovative mosquito-repellent contraption, works well and requires no handling of potential contaminants. Be prepared, guard against bugs, keep the hands clean and you will increase your fishing time.

89. Ice Chest

This point sounds obvious, but often goes overlooked, especially by anglers who intended to spend the morning on the river and be done by the time it gets warm. Often we get caught up in the moment, that is, we need one more fish to fill a limit, and aren't going home without it. In these instances, it's a shame to be in a hurry, whereby missing the point of fishing.

On hot days, I've seen fellow anglers—and been a victim myself—of having to call it a day earlier than desired because of neglect to bring a cooler with ice along. With fish in the box, and temperatures reaching the century mark, there's nothing more frustrating than having to catch one more fish, and having to call it quits for fear of losing already caught fish to spoilage.

Not only will having a cooler of ice ensure better-tasting meat, but it allows you to relax, not having to worry about getting off the water before you wish. For egg fishermen, after having caught a fat hen springer, extracting the eggs and getting them in a container then placing them on ice, leaves no question that they will be perfect for curing when you get home.

In addition, coolers allow for storage of cold drinks, snacks and lunches, which make for a more comfortable time on the river. And hey, the more comfortable you are, the more fun you'll have.

90. Heaters

On the flip side of the hot conditions is extreme cold weather, something that can ruin a winter steelhead fishing trip if you're not prepared. I remember the days as a kid, piling into Dad's boat with nothing more than several layers of clothes on and a bucket of briquettes. As ice formed in the guides of the rod, I hovered tighter to the bucket, trying to retain feeling in my hands so I could manipulate the reel.

Thankfully, like many aspects of this industry, boats have progressed, and now most are available with the option of installing multiple heaters for the purpose of keeping everyone warm and comfortable. For bank anglers, it's not always feasible to build a fire, and having a little portable heater can make those cold mornings more tolerable.

If toting a heater is not possible, hand warmers are an option. Even if you do have a heater along, hand warmers can still be placed inside gloves, boots, even wrapped on the body to maintain heat. On those biting cold mornings, you might want to take a couple hand warmers and place them on your back, where the kidneys are located. With an elastic athletic wrap they can be held in place. The result is increased body warmth that will make a considerable difference in your level of comfort throughout those cold, winter days.

Hand warmers have advanced a great deal and, themselves, can make an otherwise miserable day quite painless. No matter which heating device you chose, staying warm will keep you fishing, and the more that line is in the water, the higher the odds of catching fish.

91. Be Flexible

One of the greatest assets anglers can approach the sport of fishing with is that of an open mind. Having the ability to assess the situation and apply techniques or approaches that will best fit the immediate circumstances is often wherein the heart of success lies, and it often comes down to being flexible.

Many anglers are fixed in their ways. Mind you, that's not necessarily a bad thing, but it can be limiting at times. If, for example, upon hitting the river you find it to be high and off-color, a different approach may be necessary to get into fish.

Guide Bret Stuart adapted his approach to find this springer.

Maybe that bobber-and-jig presentation won't work well in these conditions, and opting for eggs rolled along the bottom, tight to shore, would be best. Maybe it's as simple as giving in to that favorite color drift-bobber and putting on something the fish have a better chance of seeing.

On the other hand, perhaps the fish simply aren't moving into a particular river, meaning a change of location, say to another river, may be necessary. The key is approaching each day with an open mind, letting the conditions dictate how and even where you fish. Some sections of river may fish better when the water is low. In this case, if the river is high, be willing to seek optimal water.

By being flexible in your approach, not only will your fishing repertoire increase, but you'll catch more fish. If willing to adapt to the situation at hand, you're opening the door to learning, and if there's one thing I've discovered in my many years of fishing, it's that there is always something to be learned. Bottom line, the more you learn, the more proficient an angler you will be, and that comes with being flexible.

92. Take Chances

Anglers have a level of mental comfort, that zone we don't like to deviate from because we have the confidence that what we know and how we do it, works. But how can we improve if we don't stray from the norm? Often, we can't, and the answer comes in taking chances. I'm not suggesting to broach danger, rather simply taking chances by delving into something new and unfamiliar.

One may argue that there's not enough time to take chances. "I only have one day a week to fish, and I'm not going to waste it trying new things." It's an understandable approach. So why not devote one or two hours of that day to trying something new.

I recall a buddy who traveled to fish with a group of friends. This guy loves back-bouncing plugs for springers. His friends like dropping anchor, letting out the plugs and waiting for the fish to come to them. After a few hours of having not so much as a bite, my buddy suggested going on the search for fish by way of back-bouncing plugs. It took some convincing, but the group gave in and over the course of the next two hours they landed six fat springers, and all because they took a chance. Now, this is one of the most-used techniques for these anglers.

Taking chances can apply to numerous variables, from techniques to gear to boat set-ups, clothing and much more. Point is, if you don't try something new in an effort to catch more fish, how will you ever know if you actually can improve catch rates? It's hard, but making the effort to take chances by implementing change can pay big dividends for years to come. But you never know unless you try.

93. Be Comfortable

When living in Alaska, I was the varsity boys and girls basketball coach. I always told my players, especially the girls, to do what made them confident. Whether it was putting on makeup or knotting their hair in a ponytail, the more comfortable they felt, the better they played. It comes down to confidence. In life, the more comfortable we are, the more optimism we have. The more optimistic we are, the more confidence we have in what we do, the more successful we will be. This also applies to fishing.

From proper footwear to clothing to rod and reel selection to boat designs and more, the more comfortable we can make ourselves, the more we'll want to fish. Maybe organizing the tackle box or arranging the boat to where everything is easily accessible is all it takes to instill a greater level of comfort. Do what it takes to make you comfortable.

And don't limit yourself to physical comfort, for there's the mental aspect of comfort, as well. Being stressed over certain situations can taint an otherwise great day to be on the river. If you don't beat the boat ahead of you to the hotspot, so what? If a flat tire caused you to be late, or if you forgot a piece of key gear, get over it. Fact is, having the luxury of just being on the river is a blessing in itself, and something we often lose sight of in our narrow-visioned quest to catch the most and the biggest fish as quickly as possible.

The overall fishing experience is much more than numbers and size. Be comfortable in what you do, and how you go about it. Make sure fellow anglers are doing the same, and the results will be positive and uplifting, whereby increasing confidence levels which will, in turn, impact how well you fish.

94. Educate Yourself

One of the greatest abilities we have as humans is the capacity to continually learn. Without a doubt, the best anglers

I know are the ones who are eager to learn new things. Some of the biggest names in this industry have gotten where they are due to the fact they are never content with where they are at. These folks are continually trying new techniques, doing something different in an effort to improve their skills.

The media is a good source of information from which to learn, be it radio, television, videos or printed matter—this book being a prime example. You bought this book with the intent of learning something that will help you catch more fish. Good for you, and hopefully your goal has been met. That's a step in the right direction to becoming a more proficient angler. Books, magazines and other media are largely designed with the mindset of teaching something. By referencing these resources, and applying what's been learned, you will improve your angling skills.

Sportshows, seminars, talking with fellow anglers and fishing on the river are also learning grounds for improving fishing knowledge and skills. When fishing, pay attention to what fellow anglers are doing and how they are doing it. If they are catching fish, evaluate why, even ask if they will take a moment to share with you. We are all in this fine sport because of our love of catching fish, and true advocates of the sport will not hesitate sharing information in an effort to help you succeed. Take advantage of the resources that are out there, for they are some of the best tools to help improve fishing skills and build overall knowledge.

95. Communicate Your Plans

One thing that was instilled at me at an early age, and something I still abide by today, is to always let someone know my plans—namely, where I'm going and when I'll be back. No matter where I'm going or how long I plan to be gone, I'll let someone know the details of my plans. Not only is this a good safety measure for you, but it puts the minds of other people involved at ease.

More specifically, I'll make an effort to tell someone, usually my wife, which run I'm planning on making on a particular river. I'll give the details of where we are launching the boat and taking out, or if bank fishing, what section or sections of river we'll be concentrating on.

If I change my plans in the middle of the day, and I'm in cell phone range, I'll try to call and communicate that to someone. Plans often change throughout the day, and in the unlikely event that an emergency were to occur, it's comforting knowing help is not far away.

One day on the river, a buddy slipped and cracked his hip on a rock. We were halfway through the run when it happened. We knew it was serious, and after piling into the boat, made a quick phone call and hightailed it downstream. It saved valuable time, for there was someone waiting at the ramp when we arrived.

Bottom line, by letting someone know where you are, minds are put at ease, making for a more enjoyable time on the water. In addition, communicating your plans will set your mind at ease should there be an emergency whereby someone needs to contact you. People with children know what I'm talking about here. It's not necessary, but communicating plans is something I've found to help the day go a little smoother.

96. Keep Your Camera Ready

One of the greatest things about fishing is the lifelong memories that are generated from it. Some of my fondest memories on the water are not necessarily when we caught big fish, rather those times spent with my boys, Dad and grandfathers. Nothing brings those memories back to life as quick and easily as photos, even the old, tattered ones.

The problem is many people take cameras along, but few actually get them out until the end of the day, or worse yet, forget to use them at all. Waiting until the end of the day to snap photos often fails to capture the mood at the time of the catch, that magic moment when the fish are in good shape and smiles span from ear to ear. Instead of getting shots of fish that have laid in the box all day, with peoples' faces having lost the luster of the moment, take a few minutes immediately after the catch and snap some shots.

The key is having everything ready. Make sure film, or a flash card, and batteries are in the camera, then put it in an accessible place. If bank fishing, carry it with you. If in a boat, have it where you or someone in the boat can reach it in a rush, this is especially true if in a rush to release a wild fish. Some of the digital cameras these days fit into a pocket, are inexpensive and take great photos.

Photos are also a good source of recording where you caught fish, when and on what gear. Note these facts—and others—on the back of the photo and you'll find yourself referencing them in the future, something that can lead to your catching more fish. You'll find that by having a camera ready, it only takes a brief moment to capture memories that will last forever.

97. Carry a Tape Measure

You've just caught the fish of your dreams. It's a wild fish and you want to release it, but at the same time, want to preserve memories of the experience. A photograph isn't enough, but it's a start. The best answer lies in a reproduction mount, and to help pull it off, you need to be ready.

If heading to a trophy fishery, one where you know the chance is there of landing a fish worthy of mounting, be sure to have a tape measure in your pocket. The flexible, fabric style tapes work great, as they can get wet and easily wrap around a fish without harming their slime layer or scales.

If caught by surprise, where you've just landed a monster fish and don't have a tape, use fishing line. Take some line, either off the rod you're fishing with or from a spare spool, and measure the length of the fish. Cut that piece to length. Take another piece of line and wrap it around the body, to get the girth, then cut that piece to length. Take care not to stretch the line when doing this.

After getting a quick measurement of the length and girth, snap some photos release the fish, and send it all off to a taxidermist. Months later you'll have the ultimate in memories, that dream fish in a place where you can admire it every day. Technically, this isn't something that will increase your fishing time on the water, but it's a way to reap the rewards of all the hard work you've put in to catching fish.

98. Have Fun

This may sound silly, but remember why we fish. The objective is to have fun. Too often I see anglers losing sight of why they are on the water; I'm guilty of it myself at times. Fishing is not a competition. It's not a race to see who can catch the biggest fish. It's not a contest to see who can get the most fish in the shortest period of time. While these little games can be fun from time to time, in the right situation, don't get caught up in the moment and lose sight of why you're on the river.

I've seen people get so frustrated when others are catching fish around them, they seem to forget what the sport is all about. Rather than supporting and being happy for fellow anglers, people often turn competitive, whereby tainting the moment. This can range from verbal abuse to negative comments to infringing on other anglers' territories in an effort to make something happen.

Be patient. Maintain confidence in how you're fishing. You're time will come. I've been blessed to fish with some of the best salmon and steelhead anglers in the world, and believe me, now and then everyone has a poor day of catching. Don't lose sight of how fortunate we are to simply be able to fish. Keep working, keep a smile on your face and have fun. Stay positive when fellow anglers are catching fish around you, as this will keep from ruining an otherwise fun day for you and those around you.

99. Open Your Mind

At the time this book was written, I'd been fishing for nearly 40 years. People often ask if I ever get tired of it. The obvious answer is, no! Besides being with my family, there's no place I'd rather be than outdoors, fishing or hunting. There are many reasons as to why this is so, and atop that list is that there is always something to be learned.

The sport of fishing and the technology that drives it is always growing. Not to mention are the human factors which impact fish runs and even how we fish. Elements are always changing in the world of fishing, and keeping an open mind will help you adjust and catch more fish.

Being receptive to trying new products, applying cutting-edge ideas and adopting new techniques go a long ways in helping catch more fish. The best anglers I know are those who are continually learning. Typically, these are the folks who have been fishing for decades, yet still get excited when a new approach is learned or a new product comes out that they can't wait to try. And you know what, they do catch more fish.

Keeping an open mind allows you to adapt to changes. It forces you to take a close look at what's going on around you, be it throughout the course of the day or over several seasons. It makes you stop and think, from an objective as well as a scientific point of view, about what's happening and what you can do to catch more fish.

Avoid getting boxed in, both in tactical approaches and mental strategies. Open the mind. Be willing to change. You'll find that your time on the water will be spent more wisely and in the end, you will catch more fish because of it.

When it comes to fishing for salmon and steelhead, there are more anglers who fish from the bank than out of boats. This fact comes down to several reasons, with time and money topping the list. Not everyone has the time to run the river, and not everyone has the revenue to invest in a drift boat and/or a sled. In the big scheme of things, it matters not, for we all share that common thread: the love of fishing.

Over the years I've spent a great deal of time bank fishing, and what I've learned is there's always something to learn. There's always something that can be done to increase your advantage over the fish, no matter where you are or what fish you're after.

My first memory of bank fishing for winter steelhead takes me way back to when I was six years old. Dad, and one of our fishing buddies, had dropped the drift boat in the water and were shuttling the rigs, so we'd have the trailer at the landing at the end of the day. The roads were icy, it was bitter cold and it took them a long time, forever it seemed to a chilled six year old.

A few boats put in behind us and pushed downstream. Standing on the bank, I grew colder and colder, to the point I was losing feeling in my fingers. In an

Chapter 2   Bank Fishing

By having all needed gear on your person, fishing time will be maximized.

effort to keep warm, I did what anyone would do (we didn't have hand warmers and electric heaters back then), I fished.

After only a few casts I hooked a nice steelhead and landed it. It was my first solo winter steelhead, and I was pumped. Sad thing was, there was no one around to share the moment with me. A couple minutes later I had my second fish. Suddenly, the ice that had formed in the guides of my rod didn't matter. I had feeling in my fingers and toes and a limit of fish before the oars hit the water. I'll never forget the look on Dad's face when he walked down to the ramp and asked if I was ready to start fishing.

Point is, I caught these fish from the bank, from a place where many anglers had passed by that morning without so much as wetting a line. To this day, whenever I make that run, I can't help but take a few casts, from the bank. Sometimes it pays off, but the best part is that each cast I make there takes me back to that fond morning back in 1970. Bank fishing does have its advantages.

From Alaska to California, the many rivers and varied conditions I've faced have taught me a lot over the years. Following are hints that have increased my success while bank fishing, hopefully they will do the same for you, too.

100. Have Gear On Your Person

For bank anglers, one of the keys to maximizing fishing time is to have all of the gear on your person. This applies whether covering large stretches of water throughout the course of the day, or wade-fishing in one spot for several hours. The closer the gear is to you, the less time wasted searching for it, the more time can be spent fishing.

I'm always amazed to see bank anglers who wade chest deep into a hole, make a cast, break off, wade back to shore, open the tackle box, tie up a leader, totally re-rig, wade back out and repeat the process all over again. When compared, the time they actually spend wading to and from the fishing hole and retying actually exceeds that which they spend fishing. This is easy to fix.

By making the effort to get organized ahead of time, fishing time will dramatically increase. Fly vests are great for this, even for drift fishermen, as their multi-pocket design allows ample gear to be carried. There's even room for food, a camera, toilet tissue, extra fishing glasses and other amenities which can be nice to have throughout the day. If the fly vest seems like an overkill, strap on a couple bait boxes to your belt. These can be loaded with sinkers, swivels, drift-bobbers, lures, jigs, floats, beads, a file, small scissors; just about everything you'll need to fish with for a day.

With the hooks placed in a pocket, you have all you need right there, readily accessible for a quick change-out. Doing this means there's no need to be tied to shore, for replacing lost gear can be done while standing in the stream. This result is maximized fishing time, while at the same time, a minimized risk of spooking fish due to excessive movement.

101. Backpack Benefits

If fishing multiple methods during the course of the day, carrying all the gear on your person can be a challenge. Add in a healthy lunch, something to drink, cameras, bug dope and other accessories that help make for a comfortable day on the river and quickly, room becomes a valued commodity. This is where backpacks can come in handy.

The size and style of backpack you choose to use comes down to personal preference. The most important thing is selecting one that's comfortable, something you can wear all day without suffering from shoulder or back aches. Personally, the best packs I've used fit tight to the body. They feature waist straps as well as chest straps which connect to the shoulder straps. The more compression straps a pack has, the better. All of this is important for the wading fisherman because as you move through challenging water, you don't want your load shifting. Should the load shift at the wrong time, the results could be serious, especially in raging waters.

I also like a bright-colored pack for the simple reason it's easier to see when I set it down. It's easy to set a pack down, forget about it and keep fishing, only to remember it when you're 200 yards downstream...or was that 300 yards? The last thing you want to do is waste time searching for your pack when you could be fishing.

If you're serious about packs and want to invest in a high-end model, you can spend big dollars rather quickly. Then again, a

good pack will last years and is a wise investment. One of my favorite packs for fishing can be slipped off the shoulder, still attached by the waist belt. The pack can then be rotated around the torso and accessed off your belly, from the part of the pack that normally sits against your back. This means you don't have to waste time hiking to shore to dig through your pack. If fanny packs and fly vests don't offer enough room, a big pack may be the way to go.

102. Wading Vest

Traveling light makes bank fishing less cumbersome. The less gear you can haul around, the more comfortable you'll be, thus the more rewarding the overall experience. If strapping on a pair of bait boxes is not enough to hold your gear for the day, and throwing a pack on your back is an overkill, there is a happy medium out there.

Wading vests feature multiple pockets and oversized pockets, both inside and out, that allow for a surprising amount of gear to be stowed. If wading into waist-deep water, the short cut style of wading vests are ideally designed, as they won't drag in the water and get gear wet.

However, if you know you're not going to be wading above your waist, perhaps a full-size fly vest is what you're looking for. Fly vests aren't just for fly-fishermen, they can be used by anyone. In fact, for some of my bank fishing, where I know I'm not going to be wading very deep, but will be covering lots of water and will be gone all day, I like a photographer's vest.

These vests are a bit more heavily constructed than fly vests, and they offer multiple pockets which are ideal for carrying fishing gear. Large back pockets are perfect for rolling up raingear, packing camera equipment, a lunch, drinks and more. The thing to watch out for when packing vests is overloading them. I actually have several vests of various sizes and pocket counts, so I can fit the tackle and gear I need for a certain trip specifically to a vest itself.

Whichever vest or vests you choose, make sure they are comfortable. You'll be wearing them all day and want something that lasts and fits well. You'll also want easy-access pockets, which ultimately helps increase your fishing time.

103. Be Mobile

Unless you're spending the day at a single hole waiting for fish to arrive, one of the biggest detriments a bank angler can have is being tied down. If you're not mobile enough to find fish, it can be tough catching them. Being mobile relates to many factors, from what gear you bring to water levels to how long you have to fish.

Oftentimes, bank anglers hit one or two spots before work, so don't have much time to devote to finding fish. Still, if you're not catching fish, and other anglers around you aren't catching fish, it may be in your best interest to move and search for them. That not only goes for one particular river or section of river, but for exploring other rivers. One day a buddy and I hit three different rivers before we found fish.

Having kept track over the years, I've found that the majority of fish I've caught from the bank, especially steelhead, have come in the first 15 minutes or so after the initial cast. This is usually the result of the fish being in the hole, then my showing up and offering them something they liked.

As for salmon, some of my best bank fishing results have come by being mobile enough to move within the same hole. Some of the classic salmon holes bank anglers can reach are large, often characterized by a riffle at the upper end, ledges below that and big swirl holes at the bottom. This means salmon can occupy a variety of places within one large area and oftentimes it takes moving around and trying different approaches to find them.

Bring what gear you need, no more. However, be ready to fish a different method should the need arise. You may need to be floating jigs at one hole, drift fishing eggs at another. Diversify, be willing to try various approaches and stay on the move. Equipping yourself to be mobile can pay off in the form of more fish.

104. No Big Tackle Box

I caught my first solo limit of summer steelhead at the age of four, and even then my dad was teaching me to travel light on the river. Never have I taken a tackle box when bank fishing. Tackle boxes are big and bulky, whereby limiting my mobility. Even small-profile tackle boxes can be confining.

Not only will tackle boxes keep you from moving up and down the river in search of fish, they will also tie you to the bank. This is especially true when wading, and the further you wade from shore, the more limiting having a tackle box on the bank really is. Every time you break off a rigging or need to rebait, and have to wade to shore to accomplish that, the more time you lose fishing.

Rather than return to shore and dig through the tackle box, downsize and keep all the gear on your person. Go through the big tackle box at home, pull what you need and take only that

gear. Knowing where you'll be fishing and for how long, you'll be able to accurately gauge what gear you'll need and how much of it.

On summer steelhead, for instance, I usually put everything I need in two bait boxes which are strapped to my waist. One box will hold baits, the other has sinkers, swivels, pliers and drift-bobbers. Pretied leaders are kept in a Pip's Leader Caddy and slipped into a pocket for quick and easy access. For salmon, which requires more gear, I'll often rely on a fishing vest with multiple pockets to hold everything. Once you grow confortable with carrying all the needed gear on you, you'll be surprised at how easy it is to do, but more importantly, how much more time you can devote to fishing.

105. No Net

In all my years of steelhead fishing from a bank, I've only netted one fish. Sad thing is, that one fell through a hole in the net and broke off. My buddy whom I was netting the fish for wasn't happy, and the guy I borrowed the net from apologized for not telling me about the hole. The bummer part, I could have tailed that fish, but it was my buddy's first steelie and he questioned my approach.

Nets are great, and do have their place in the bank-fishing world, especially when it comes to salmon. If fishing holes with deep ledges and steep drop-offs, nets are almost a necessity, for tailing fish in these situations is dangerous as well as tough to do. But when it comes to steelhead, and some salmon habitats, you can often get by without a net.

Nets, however, do have a tendency to limit a person's movement. They can keep you from moving from hole to hole, or even changing locations within a single hole. As with a tackle box, nets can confine you to one area, meaning you're sacrificing fishing in what could be a potentially better location than where you are at the time.

I don't know how many fish I've landed from the bank, without a net, but the process is fairly easy. First of all, be patient and play out the fish. Nothing stresses a fish more than horsing it into the shallows when it's full of vigor. You'll be able to tell the fish is played out as it will relax and its head will easily come to the surface. Once you get the fish headed your way, almost planing across the surface, keep its momentum going toward shore by lifting the rod tip. At the same time, slip in behind it, keeping it moving to shore, and grab its tail with the free hand. Continue sliding it all the way out of the water, onto the bank. There's no tossing, kicking or scooping the fish, just a nice, controlled boost forward, by way of the tail. It works, and works well.

106. Stay Put

In some situations it's better to stay put, waiting out the fish.

I t may be that the place you bank fish is one where you're awaiting the arrival of fish, or for the bite to turn on. No one rule applies to every situation, so it's important to assess the whole picture before making a decision of whether to hole-hop or stay put.

In one of my favorite summer steelheading holes, a person can spend the entire day there waiting for fish to arrive. As the sun breaks over the mountains, about 10:00 a.m., the fish move into the riffles. As the day passes by, boat traffic also pushes them over to one section of the channel. At the same time, if fish are on the move, they are continually funneling through the hole. In this situation, it's best to stay put and keep casting.

At one of my longtime favorite salmon holes, the fish are almost always there early in the morning, but oftentimes the bite doesn't turn on right away. Sometimes the bite comes around 7:00 a.m., other times not until 11:00. One never knows. But if the fish are in the hole, there's no sense in moving, for once a salmon bite turns on, it can trigger a chain reaction, and just that quickly everyone is catching fish.

Evaluate the situation at hand. Find where the best place is to be situated in a specific hole and stick with it. Keep optimism high, always believing that the next cast could be the one to produce fish. The only time you may want to move from such a hole is if no fish are showing or you're not feeling them with your line. Sticking to one hole can have its rewards, for the bite can come fast, making it worth the wait.

107. Grid The Water

I t's easy to get lost in the serenity of fishing on a tranquil stream, forgetting about anything other than just being out there. But taking a mental vacation from the task at hand can cost you fish. When on the river, pay attention and make each cast count.

It's not uncommon to lose focus of what you're doing, especially when the action is slow. But the mindset that you'd rather be lucky than good doesn't apply to salmon and steelhead fishing. If you rely on luck, you'll catch very few salmon and steelhead. Catching these fish does not come by chance; you are at a certain hole at a certain time, casting a specific bait to a precise spot in hopes of getting a fish to bite. The bite may or may not come, but when it does, it's because everything came together at that given moment.

Perhaps, nowhere does this ring more true than when casting. If you're not casting to a specific spot, you'll not achieve the perfect drift, and if you're not getting the ideal drift, you're not going to catch fish. It's simple.

When casting, it usually pays to grid the water. That is, break the water in front of you into specific sections, and start systematically covering it all. When you're done, if there hasn't been a bite, start over, maybe with a different presentation, or move on.

Begin by casting close to your position and let it drift all the way to the end. Starting close targets fish that may be holding near to you, and lessens the risk of spooking them with your line by casting over top where they may potentially be holding. Continue casting farther away with each successive cast, extending two to three feet every time. When done, start over with a new presentation or move downstream, gridding the water as you go. This systematic approach, though tedious, will result in more fish than haphazardly casting.

108. Change Presentations

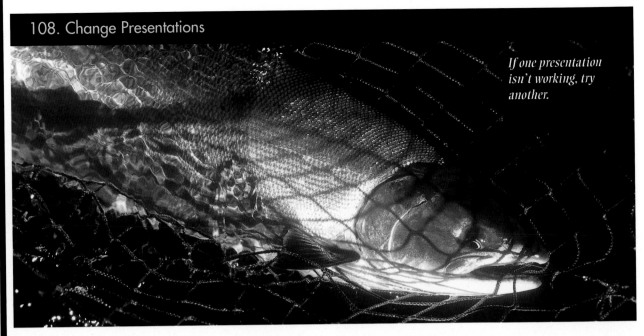

If one presentation isn't working, try another.

If you feel fish are out there, but not responding, oftentimes all it takes is a certain change in one tiny piece of gear to make something happen. Nothing can be more frustrating than knowing fish are in front of you—either seeing them jump or observing them with your polarized glasses—and not getting a bite. But rather than continuing to cast the same old thing at them time and time again, realize you're not left helpless.

The possibilities are many, and being cognizant of what changes can be made to solicit a bite is one of the factors that separates exceptional anglers from others. Maybe it's the size of a drift-bobber, the color of a lure or the length of leader. Perhaps a quarter-ounce more lead slows down the presentation, or a shift in your angle helps swing the bait into the sweet spot. Maybe scent should be added to the bait, or if you've been using a scent, maybe it's time to try another flavor.

Do hooks need to be downsized, or spinner blades tuned? Speaking of plugs, is the one you're using of the rattling variety? If not, try getting some vibration into the water. If the water is clear and the fish on edge, perhaps a fluorocarbon leader is necessary.

The point is, the number of changes an angler can introduce are many. So, the next time you feel frustrated or helpless, try changing some element of your gear to elicit that bite. You may just discover a new approach that will work for years to come, not only on that river, but other rivers you choose to fish as well.

109. Observe Others

One of the greatest resources from which to learn fishing skills is from other anglers. Unfortunately, not everyone is of the mindset that sharing information is a good thing. This is too bad, not only for the individuals who miss out on the rewards of sharing, but for the promotion and preservation of a sport we love.

However, there is another way to learn from fellow anglers, and it has to do with observation. When on the river, closely watch what other anglers are doing. It doesn't take long to figure out who the veterans of the area are. Even if they aren't catching fish at the time you're watching, you'll know who they are by the way they stand, fish, move about and by the gear they use.

If it's a big area, you might even want to bring binoculars along. Look to learn details, but don't overlook the obvious. Note where, exactly, an angler is standing and where they are casting too. Evaluate if they are casting to water to fish it, or if they are casting there so the terminal gear can be carried to the point they want it by the end of the drift. How much weight are they using? Are they moving through a hole quickly or slowly? Observe if they cast to different zones while standing in one place, and if so, read the water to figure out why.

Leader length, bait type and size are other factors to note. If everyone is using shrimp, and someone comes in and cleans up on eggs, make a mental note of it. If bait is being used, see if any scents are applied. Yarn color and drift-bobber size are another point to consider. You can even learn new techniques, like working jigs or spinners, through observation.

The possibilities of what can be learned through simple observation are many, and the more willing you are to open your mind and eyes, the more proficient the angling skills will become. It's also worth noting that what may be observed and learned on one river can often be applied elsewhere, with good success.

110. Note Where Fish Are Caught

In addition to learning the finer details of fishing by way of observation, don't overlook the obvious. Noting where fellow

anglers catch fish is among the most valuable piece of information out there. But once you see someone catch a fish, don't make the unethical move that too many anglers do, and close in on the other angler's fishing territory. There's no law against it, it's a common courtesy, and that's violated all too often. If you see someone catch a fish, keep your distance, your time will come.

When someone catches a fish, note where it came from. Look to see where the angler is standing, right down to their foot placement on a specific rock. Next, determine where the fish is holding during the fighting process. Chance are, if it's a salmon, it will hold in the deepest part, where other fish are likely present.

Once a fish is landed, don't stop observing quite yet. Watch to see where the next cast is made, for most of the time the subsequent cast made after landing a fish is right where the previous cast landed.

None of this is unethical, just a valuable way to learn where fish are. I've been picking summer and winter from the same exact spots for decades, and other anglers have done the same, in the same spots. Fact is, fish hold and travel in specific spots for a reason. Once they migrate through, other fish go to the same spot, filling the void. This is your time to slip in and catch fish.

111. Wear Drab-Colored Clothes

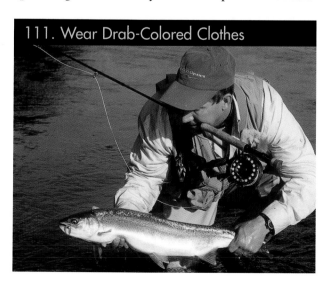

It's no secret that fish have incredible eyesight. As a result, anglers can take extra precaution to dress accordingly, so as to not spook fish. This is particularly true for wade-fishermen, who can move into and out of fish territories several times a day. The more stealth you can apply, the better chance you have of catching fish, and it all starts with wearing drab colors.

Take any lineman on the football team; they'd rather where black arm guards than white. Why? So the referee doesn't see them making an illegal block or get called for holding. The same mindset applies to bank anglers in that you want to do all within your means to keep from attracting attention to yourself.

Waders, themselves, are not a problem, for they already blend in well with the environment. Long-sleeve shirts, sweatshirts and jackets are the main concern, as are hats. Keep these colors toned down, for the brighter they are, the more likely fish are to see them. I know of guys who will even go so far as to wear camouflage when fishing, and they have good results.

Mind you, donning earth-tone colors is not a free ticket to haphazardly move about. You'll still want to keep movement, particularly of the arms and legs, to slow, deliberate motions, so as not to tip-off fish to your presence. When entering a hole for the first time, it's especially crucial to keep excess movement to a minimum. However, should you spook fish, note their location and return to the exact spot later, chances are another fish will fill the void, as there's something there they like. Bottom line: clothing can make a difference in the number of fish you catch.

112. Spot And Stalk

In clear-water conditions, pursuing salmon and steelhead can be a bit like hunting. That is, you're spotting the quarry, then making a move to close the deal. Spot-and-stalk fishing is one of the most rewarding, and effective ploys a bank angler can apply.

With drab clothes and quality polarized glasses, you're set. Quiet footwear, like felt soles, can also be beneficial. The next step is to practice stealth. Just as in hunting, when stalking fish, assume they will be there, and that it's up to you to see them before they see you.

Keep a low profile and move quietly, disrupting the water as little as possible. Avoid rolling over big, round river rocks, as this sound carries surprisingly far. When searching for fish, try seeking out angles that will take the glare off the surface and allow your glasses to penetrate. Look for parts of fish, rather than the whole thing. Oftentimes, all you'll see is the broken outline of something that doesn't match the bottom, maybe a gray, brown or blue line.

Sometimes you'll catch a moving tail, dorsal fin or the silver flash of a steelhead tossing on its side, but the vast majority of the time all you'll see is a faint hint of a fish. Practice is the best way to learn how to spot fish, and from there, learning the best ways to sneak within range will take place. When closing in for a cast, be sure to position yourself so you can move in and cast without being seen. Note the sun's position, making certain long shadows from your approaching body does not spook fish. A nervous fish is one that may not bite, and the objective should be to approach these fish and make the cast without them knowing you're there.

113. Quiet Wading

When approaching fish, keeping quiet is very important. Sound travels surprisingly far and fast through water, so be careful, take your time and think quiet. If fish are near, the simple task of moving your feet through water should be done with caution. Avoid kicking up water and creating excessive splashing. Such unnatural activity will alert fish to your presence, and either send them on to the next hole or potentially turn them off a bite.

Investing in a pair of felt-soled wading boots greatly helps reduce foot noise. If walking on slimy rocks, perhaps the cleat/felt combination sole is the way to go. If on bedrock, a rock that's less noisy to wade on, you'll likely be able to get away with strait spikes on the shoes. I've used old golf and baseball shoes for wading on soft bedrock, and they've worked great, just be sure to walk gingerly.

If you plan on doing much wade fishing, boots with interchangeable soles are a wise investment, for they allow you to meet the needs of whatever bottom type you're fishing. If you're fishing multiple rivers with a wide range of bottom types, these muti-soles pay for themselves on one road trip. The key to quiet wading is to do what you have to in order to make your way through the river, without sacrificing safety. Often it all starts with a comfortable pair of waders and quality boots.

Should you spook fish that you've made a move on, but they remain in the holding water, don't panic. Take your time, watch the fish, and hold still. After five to 10 minutes, sometimes as long as 15 minutes, the fish will often forget about what danger they saw and will respond to a bite. Patience is key and stealth is critical. When it all comes together, you will catch more fish.

114. No Waders

During the summer months, steelhead action as well as daytime temperatures can be sizzling. In such conditions, it might be worth foregoing the waders and simply wet-wading. I've been wet-wading for summer steelhead ever since I can recall and am a firm believer it makes me more mobile this time of year.

I know there are some lightweight, breathable, high-tech waders on the market—in fact I own a couple pairs—but when it comes to covering water in the heat of summer, I prefer getting wet. Not only does this keep a person cool on hot days, it can make a difference in your fishing.

Two of my favorite sections of summer steelhead water stretch over two miles on one river, nearly three miles on another.

Both fisheries require hiking through hills, thick brush, big gravel bars, willow patches, mountain creeks and more. This kind of terrain is brutal on waders, and overheats an angler rather quickly. These are the reasons wet wading is a favorite approach.

Personally, I simply would not cover as much water when fishing these stretches if I were wearing waders on hot days. Instead, a pair of old golf shoes and cutoff pants or swimming trunks allow for much more mobility. Sure the legs may get a little scratched going through brush, but I'd rather have a few scratches, cover more water and catch more fish than overheat.

It's about a mile hike to one of mine and Dad's favorite fishing holes, and upon getting there at daybreak one morning, a boater was surprised to see us pop out of the brush. "Wow, never seen anyone bank fish this before; are you landowners here?" he asked. Truth is, we waded and walked our way to the hole, on public land, and our effort paid off. Over the course of the summer we landed more than 80 steelhead from that one hole. Not once did we wear waders.

115. Walking Staff

Throughout the years of wade fishing, there has only been a handful of times I wish I had a walking stick for support. Not until I worked out to a casting station, walking stick in hand, however, did I realize the value of this tool.

The casting station consisted of a raised chunk of bedrock, about two feet under water, surrounded by deep cuts and a few narrow shelves of mixed gravel and bedrock. The water was rough and fast moving, always flirting with the tops of my waders. With only narrow paths to walk on, I knew that one missed step would find me swiftly being swept downstream. Gingerly working my way out to the casting station, the only thing I could think about was all the fishing I'd missed over the years because I failed to use a walking staff.

Without that staff I would not have been able to reach the platform, or make it back to shore when I was finished. The best part, I was able to get into position to work the fly rod and catch winter steelhead that I otherwise would not have been able to reach.

If you're serious about covering water, a walking staff can get you into places other bank fishermen likely won't be able to access. The stability this device provides is surprising, and the professionally constructed models are so superior to a stick, they shouldn't even be compared.

Mind you, when using a walking staff, be sure to proceed with caution. Know what you're getting yourself into, and make sure you can get yourself out of it. Safety is the most important factor, especially when wading in fast, deep water with waders on. One mistake can mean your life, so do not push it that far. Used wisely and safely however, a walking staff will help get you into waters you otherwise would not be able to reach and greatly boost the odds of catching fish.

116. Elevate To Spot Fish

Knowing what to look for when spotting fish and being able to move into safe casting position are two different things, but fish must first be located before a move can be made on them. To assist in initially locating fish, try getting to the highest vantage point around. This allows you to accomplish three things: Eliminate glare, spot fish from a safe distance with a less likely chance of spooking them, and being able to see more water. These are major advantages when sight-fishing, and it can make the difference in whether or not you catch fish.

I once sight-fished a summer steelhead stream and failed to locate fish in one of my favorite holes. I fished it blind, hoping fish were near. After 30 minutes and not a nibble, I hiked out of there. Some 300 yards up the hill, I looked down on the hole I'd been fishing. A dark streak then a silver flash caught my eye. I hiked back down to the river and on the second cast landed the fish, then another shortly thereafter. They were there the whole time, only about 10 yards upstream from where I was fishing. They were holding tight against some bedrock, but from my previous angle I failed to see them or get a cast to where they were. Once I saw them, I knew where to stand and cast to reach them, and it worked.

Hills, elevated roadsides and bridges are just a few examples of good vantage points from which to spot fish. Trees that hang over or overlook a stream are also good bets. I've had excellent results by standing on rootwads laying in the river, as well. Even partially submerged logs and big rocks can make a big difference. I've even had good success getting on the shoulders of a fishing buddy.

It doesn't take much of change in angle—oftentimes just a few inches—to open a viewing window into the river that could not be achieved at lower levels. Be creative, look around you and utilize what's there to help elevate you into a position to spot more fish. After all, the more you find, the more opportunity you have to catch them.

117. Ladder Fishing

Years ago I observed an angler fishing from a ladder. I thought he was nuts. "What advantage could he really be gaining over other anglers?" I thought. Not until a few years later did I see another angler doing the same thing. The more rivers I traveled to, the more often I saw this technique being applied. Of course, I had to try it for myself.

Fishing off a ladder definitely falls into the category of elevating yourself to find fish, but this approach deserves special attention. Interestingly, in the places I saw ladders being used, there were no other elevated vantage points around from which to spot fish. These anglers had the idea of lifting themselves above other anglers by way of a ladder, and they did see and catch more fish.

Not only are ladders used as a platform from which to locate fish, but also to cast from. This allows precise placement and monitoring of each cast, meaning the odds are greater of putting that terminal gear in the sweet spot.

Ladders are most safe when used on sandy or very small gravel bottoms. These substrates allow the foot of the ladder to securely hold, which is important when standing on the higher rungs of the ladder. Once fish have been located, simply cast from the ladder. When a fish is hooked, carefully step down and get to the action. When fishing from a ladder, it's a time-saver to have all your gear on you, for changeouts are done on the ladder.

The only drawback from using ladders is a lack of mobility. However, if fishing a hole where you're awaiting fish to come to you, these devices are quite handy. Fishing from ladders often requires a good bit of room, so if choosing to use one, pay attention to make sure it does not infringe on other anglers' waters. Used properly, ladders are a valuable tool that will enhance sight-fishing skills.

118. Rod Holster

Bank fishing, especially wade fishing, can be a challenge at times. Big rapids, brutal winter weather, slippery rocks and unstable river bottoms can all make bank-fishing conditions less than ideal. When the hands are free to work with, it often makes things more comfortable and secure. That's why many anglers prefer wading to the bank to retie lost rigging or get new bait, as this frees their hands. Such actions, however, correlate to lost fishing time, something we are trying to eliminate in this book.

If uncomfortable tucking the butt of the rod under an arm or between the legs, there is a nifty device called the Rod Holster. The Rod Holster (www.fullstrike.us) is just that, a holster which snugly holds the butt section of your rod. The holster itself is attached to a belt, and works under a spring-loaded system which is easy to manipulate with one hand.

It straps over waders and the belt is stiff enough to easily hold a pair of large bait boxes. The best part is the upward angle at which the Rod Holster secures your rod. Once placed in the holster, the rod will not move, and it's at the perfect, upward-facing angle so that the rod tip will not dip into the water or poke into shoreline brush while you're working.

The Rod Holster provides fishermen the opportunity to work on their terminal gear with two free hands. The result is quicker turnaround time, thus more time spent fishing. No matter what you're after, spring or fall salmon, summer or winter steelhead, if looking for a gadget that really will increase the amount of time spent with your line in the water, this one is worth looking into. The Rod Holster is already popular among surf anglers, which speaks of the durability of this device to operate in the salmon and steelheading world.

119. Hit Close To Shore

The next time you're on the river, observe fellow anglers and see where they are casting. You'll be amazed at the number of folks who make every single cast as far across stream as possible. They might even work the middle of the stream with vigor, but a surprisingly high percentage of anglers overlook the water at their feet; this is especially true for steelheaders. Plunkers can relate to this, as most of their fish come from within a few feet of the shoreline they're fishing.

Where each cast falls, or should fall, comes down to reading the water. When approaching any hole or stretch of water to be fished, especially new ones, study the water and breakdown what constitutes good holding or traveling water. By process of elimination, that is identifying what's not fishable water, then the water that is fishable can be pinpointed.

Such a process will increase your fishing time, for it eliminates the bad water from being fished. Interestingly, some of the most overlooked fishable water is right at your feet. I recall one day Dad and I were on the bank, looking for a place to fish. There were plenty of places to cast alright, but we wouldn't be fishing, just wasting time as none of it was holding water. Other anglers didn't see it that way, and newcomers stepped right in and started fishing, hooking nothing.

After nearly two hours of waiting, a spot opened up. Dad and I slipped in, stood shoulder-to-shoulder and started fishing. We knew the place we wanted to get, and waited. While waiting, we watched the angler fishing our target water, and every single cast he made was to the opposite shoreline. He didn't have fishing glasses on, either.

When we moved into position, glasses on, we could see seven steelhead laying within 15 feet of where we stood. In less than a half-hour we landed three of them. Similar scenarios have occurred many times over the years, proving how overlooked near-shore fishing really is. Read the river, figure out where fish will be and don't overlook the water right at your feet.

120. Retrace Steps

Fish move throughout the course of a day. Whether this is simply due to natural migratory movement, pressure from fellow fishermen, or changing weather conditions, the fact is that fish will move or at least change position. Because of this, it's a good idea to retrace your steps, fishing water you may have already covered.

Take the angler who fishes in one hole all morning long. That person is waiting for fish because they are confident something will move in. The same could be true for the traveling bank fisherman. Once you've fished a stretch of water, it often pays to cover that same water on your way back. Chances are, you have to walk by that water again anyway, so why not try a few casts to see if any fish have moved in? Oftentimes, boats passing over fish force them to change positions, and often these fish will bite where they didn't before.

In addition to fish shifting positions, new fish may have moved into the area. These are fish that may have slipped by you or had their mouths closed, initially, but now you can have another crack at them. Mind you, when retracing your steps, it's not necessary to devote the time to fishing it if you did earlier in the day. As you walk, make a few casts into the sweet spots, the ones where you know fish lay or have produced for you in the past. It only takes a few extra minutes and is worth the effort.

When reworking some of the water you've already covered, try offering the fish something new. Perhaps it's a different egg cure, maybe it's a different colored Corky, or maybe a combination of the two. Have any lures or jigs been fished? If not, these simple changes, offered in waters already fished, can make a difference in your catch rate.

121. Fish After Crowds

Fishing behind crowds is not always a bad thing.

An early start is not always the best answer for catching fish. In fact, a late start can often yield surprising results. Early morning pressure can be intense, especially when it comes to bank fishing. However, many folks are forced to head to work after only a couple hours of fishing, while others will usually call it good by mid-morning.

If looking to avoid crowds, try following them. That's to say, head to the river after the majority of anglers have left. Arriving around that 7:00 to 8:00 a.m. timeframe can work well, for the first shift of bankies will have left for work about then. Another good late-morning arrival time seems to be around 11:00 a.m., a time which some folks prefer as it gives the fish a little settling-down time from the early morning rush.

When fishing later in the morning, behind crowds, it often pays to offer the fish something they haven't seen. For salmon this may be a different egg cure, maybe a shrimp cocktail or tuna ball, maybe a strip of herring slipped on to the hook along with the eggs. For steelhead, it may mean offering jigs rather than shrimp tails, or a different color drift-bobber due to a change in lighting conditions.

Oftentimes, even pressured fish will respond to a different presentation. It may be a new smell that turns them on, or perhaps a different color of yarn or a drift-bobber with enhanced action. You never know unless you try, and it seems that the late-morning angler who follows the crowds and is willing to experiment with a variety of presentations will find results. For

anglers who are not afraid to follow the crowds, they may find just what they are looking for, a peaceful fishing experience and more fish.

122. Kick Up Water To Trigger Bite

When it comes to both summer- and winter-run steelhead, there are many theories and approaches about "triggering" a bite. Triggering a bite refers to agitating fish to the point they grow aggressive and bite. Mind you, I don't personally agree with all of these methods, but they are legal and applied by some anglers, thus I feel compelled to share them.

For bank anglers, one of the best ways to trigger a bite is by kicking up water. There's nothing more irritating then seeing fish stacked in a hole, and they are not biting, no matter what you offer them. As a last resort, try noisily wading around the edges of the hole, violently kicking up water. The idea is to agitate the fish, not drive them out of the hole. I've done this, and seen it done, with good success in many steelhead streams.

One morning a buddy and I fished a hole crammed full of winter steelhead. After three hours of fishing all we got was one bite. After numerous failed attempts of offering the fish something different, we stirred up the water. He kicked around in the lower end, me in the upper end. We then waited about 15 minutes for the fish to calm down. We ended up landing and releasing 11 bright steelhead before it was over.

When kicking up the water, assess where the fish are at and where they will likely flee to when disturbed. Don't push too hard for you want to avoid driving them out of the hole. Create just enough of a disturbance to get the fish moving, then settling down in a new location. It works, not all of the time, but it does work.

123. Toss Rocks To Trigger Bite

Another method of triggering a bite is throwing rocks. In places that are too steep to wade, rock tossing is a good alternative to stirring up things. When doing this, make sure fellow anglers aren't around, for they may not agree with the theory behind this approach.

I once observed a trio of anglers doing this on spring chinook. It was in a deep hole, and the salmon were holding tight against a ledge that the men could not get their terminal gear too because the boils were too violent. They hiked above the hole, dropping big rocks tight to the rock ledge. Their efforts worked, forcing the salmon out into the seam, where they could get a drift. Minutes later they were catching fish.

In holes that are too deep to wade in and disturb fish, tossing rocks is a good way to get them moving. Rock tossing is also a bit less intrusive than wading, for tree limbs, rocks and ospreys regularly fall or dive into rivers.

Start with small rocks, as these have a tendency to move fish without pushing them too hard. Hitting between the fish and the shoreline, so as to force fish into deeper water, seems to be a good approach when rock tossing. This is perfect for fish holding tight to shore, under fallen trees or limbs, as it can often force them into deeper, fishable water.

If fish aren't moving, progress to larger rocks. If that doesn't work, try tossing closer to the fish in order to get their attention. Even a smattering of a handful of small rocks can get the job done, for the surface disturbance is something these fish do not like. I've seen this work on suspended salmon, too.

Remember, the key with rock tossing is to try and spook the fish by being as natural as possible. It seems that fish spooked in this way don't take as long to recover, meaning the bite can come only minutes after they've moved.

124. Let Boats Pass Over Hole

Don't panic when a boat passes over your target water, it can move fish.

Bank anglers and boaters sometimes fail to see eye-to-eye. Unfortunately, all too often, one tries to fault the other for their lack of success. Whatever the reason, and there are many, the fact is a boat owner wouldn't own one if they thought they spooked fish to the point they couldn't catch them. That said, boaters can offer an advantage to bankies, not only benefiting their fishing, but cutting down on stress levels as well.

Whenever I'm in a driftboat and encounter bank anglers, I try avoiding their target water. Regrettably, what I interpret to be their target water is often not what they interpret it to be, so they throw a scornful look or soured words my way. "Sorry, but if you knew how to read the water you'd be thanking me," is what I think but never say.

Truth is, boats passing over a hole can spook fish into biting. This is more the case for steelhead than salmon, as salmon commonly occupy deep holes. With steelhead, boat traffic, especially heavy boat traffic, will often kick fish out of their main holding zones, causing them to seek water where passing boats won't bother them.

Oftentimes, the places these spooked fish move to are behind boulders, trees and tight to shore. These are the places bank anglers will want to concentrate their efforts on when boat traffic is high. I'll often motion oncoming boats to run down the middle of the river, right over where the fish are laying, in hopes of stirring things up. It doesn't work all the time, but it does work. In fact, some of the best success I've had with this method is on weekends, when angler pressure is high. The more boats there are, the less of a chance the steelhead have to retreat back into comfortable waters. This means the fish become more accessible to bank anglers, whereby actually increasing their opportunity to catch fish.

125. Plunking

Plunking shacks, like this one, are in place for a reason.

There's nothing new about the method of plunking. In fact, if there's one downfall to this approach, it's that it is so old not many young anglers are willing to give it a shot. Nonetheless, in the right conditions it's one of the most productive means of fishing there is. It's particularly effective on winter steelhead and spring chinook, when water levels run high and turbid. Under such conditions, fish often travel tight to shore and getting to them any other way besides plunking is nearly impossible. I can't keep track of the number of times we've lost steelhead in the brush, right after being hooked, because we were fishing so close to shore. We've even hooked springers within arm's length of the shoreline.

The principle behind plunking is that, given the conditions, the angler knows where the fish will be moving through. Pinpointing that slot, then anchoring a bait in the middle of it, is all it takes. In fact, it may not be a bait at all, rather a Spin-N-Glo, Kwikfish or other artificial lure that's being used. What you use depends on the species and water being fished. Use enough weight so the gear stays in one place, not moving downstream, and wait for the fish to arrive. It's simple and it works.

The biggest benefit of plunking is that it gets anglers on the river when no one else can fish. The water is too high and muddy to boat or use other methods from shore. Plunkers will often gain several more days of fishing during the course of a season, simply because they're not waiting for conditions to be perfect in order to apply other techniques. If you want to increase your fishing time, plunking is a good way to achieve that.

126. Bank-Ease Planer

The use of planers, or side-planers, is another approach that has been around for years, and used properly, can be highly effective. The theory behind planers is that they allow you to fish places you otherwise could not reach from shore. Most notably, planers allow plugs to be run through various sections of the river. Other presentations can also be made from a planer, just be sure you're not infringing on water other anglers are fishing.

At the time of this writing, there was a new planer that just hit the market, one I was impressed with and hope stays around. It's called the Bank-Ease Planer (www.moulder-llc.com) and what's great about this planer is that it does not attach to your line. The planer is actually attached to shore with a separate tow line.

The Bank-Ease Planer can be fished one of two ways: Line can be let out from shore each time the planer itself is let out, or it can be casted to. One of the biggest benefits of this planer is that once the line is tripped, it's not necessary to bring it back to shore to reposition the terminal gear. The Bank-Ease Planer stays in place, in the river. It features a flip-up style guide wire that, when casted over, hooks your line and snaps it in place so the terminal gear can work off the planer. Should a missed strike occur, simply real in the line, cast 10 or so feet upstream and beyond the planer and maneuver the line into the guide wire.

Once you get the hang of this device you'll see how easy it really is. Furthermore, it allows you to fish methods and reach waters from the bank that otherwise could not be accomplished. Another great feature, because this planer is not attached to your line, you don't have to fight it when fighting a fish. If searching for a new device that will increase your fishing repertoire from shore, try this planer.

127. Identify Holding Water

In order to maximize fishing time while on the river, it's best to know where the fish are. This sounds easy, but it's not always the case. The objective is to make every cast count, avoiding the tendency to get caught in a rut, hoping a bite will come by chance. This is where reading the water comes in handy, and identifying holding water tops the list.

Both salmon and steelhead will hold in certain sections of any given river. Over the years, most of these holding waters that are accessible to bank fishermen have already been identified as is evidenced by the beaten-down pathways leading to them. Once you find yourself in such a location, or even if it's that magic, undiscovered hole, knowing what to look for is key.

Keep in mind that river bottoms are continually changing, especially during years where flooding has occurred. Some of the best steelhead holes will fill in, and no longer be used by fish. Some traditional salmon holes will get laden with brush or a massive rootwad, and the fish will avoid it.

Search for water that will be less taxing on the fish, a place where they can rest and save energy for the spawning cycle. For salmon, deep holes are best. These may be against rock ledges, cut banks, amid holes carved into the middle of a river over time, or where gravel washouts occur. Swirling conditions on the surface often indicate good salmon water below. These may be drift fished or covered with bobber and bait.

For steelhead, their holding water can range from a couple feet on down to where salmon are found. A tailout where water pushes upwards, riffles, behind rocks and logs and on the edges of fast water are just a few of the prime holding waters used by steelhead. Open your eyes and your mind, evaluate the water and decipher where fish will hold. Once you learn such places, it will be easier to identify them in unfamiliar waters, and you'll catch more fish wherever you are.

128. Identify Seams

Locating seams would be next in the line of importance when it comes to reading water. For a bank angler, seams identify where fish move, and oftentimes that's precisely the type of water bank anglers want to target. In fact, many bank anglers would argue that seams are more important than holding water, and they'd likely be right.

For salmon, the prototypical seams they occupy are normally on the edge of big, heavy water. Often, large boils pop up along these seams, making them tough to fish. In this case, try increasing your lead to keep the terminal gear in the seam. One of my favorite boiling seams to fish will find me pumping five or six ounces of lead, when elsewhere in the hole two ounces is plenty.

In some waters and certain situations, salmon and steelhead will both travel close to shore; salmon choosing the deepest part of the seam, steelhead often being less finicky as to what path they take. In this case, cover the entire seam, that is, the inside and outside edges of the seam and even the middle of it. Once you discover where fish choose to move, carefully note it, for as long as the flow rate and bottom structure stays the same, fish will continue to use it.

If water levels do change, so too may the seams or the pathways through which fish choose to travel. In this case, note the water level and where fish are caught. It's a good idea to take it one step further and record the cubic-feet-per-second (CFS) flow. You'll be amazed out how accurate this one number can be in helping you figure out where to fish when the water is at a certain level, and how many more fish you can catch because of it.

129. Mid-Day Steelhead Riffles

Bret Stuart found success in the middle of a shallow riffle at high noon.

When the sun is directly overhead, many anglers choose to call it a day, concluding that the beating rays will drive fish down or turn off the bite. Though this may hold some relevance, it's not a reason to stop fishing. Fact is, this is a time when steelhead seek out riffles.

For summer steelhead, some of my favorite fishing takes place during the hottest part of the day. At this time, steelhead will often move into shaded holding water and deeper sections, but my favorite place to pursue them is in riffles. Especially when water temperatures begin to warm, steelhead will often lay in riffles to let the faster-moving water carry dissolved oxygen over their gills. In a sense, this helps the fish conserve energy by allowing the current to aide in gill ventilation. Biologists have concluded that the levels of dissolved oxygen are not greater in

riffles. So why are steelhead attracted to them? It comes down to protection.

Riffles break up the incoming solar rays, meaning less light directly penetrates the water. This correlates to riffles, no matter how shallow, serving as safe hideaways for steelhead to hold in. The more choppy the surface, the more broken the incoming light, the more safe the fish feel. Ever try sighting steelhead in riffles? It's tough, almost impossible.

When fishing these mid-day riffles, make an effort to cover every inch of water. I like starting from the bottom of the riffle, working upstream so as not to spook fish. My favorite places to find steelhead are right in front of big rocks and behind and to the either side of big rocks. These zones offer slack water and protection, they are also the avenue through which food is funneled. Once you feel the water has been covered, do it all over again with a different presentation. Maybe it's a different colored drift-bobber, adding a scent or offering hardware rather than bait that will turn on the bite. It may also be wise to use a bobber with a white bottom, to match the sky, so fish can't see it from below.

Once you discover what the fish like, note the time of day, date, sky conditions, what you caught it on and exactly where. This information will become a good resource base on future outings. Final word, when fishing riffles, it's never too shallow to try. I've pulled fish out of less than a foot of water, all the way down to 14 feet deep. The fish are there, it's up to you to find them.

130. Mid-Day Salmon Holes

As with steelhead, many salmon anglers call it quits when the sun stays on the water too long. Obviously, this does not apply to tidal fisheries, rather salmon that are being targeted further upstream. However, mid-day salmon fishing on hot days can be highly productive. As water temperatures warm and sunlight penetrates the surface, salmon are forced to seek cooler, darker areas of protection.

By nature, salmon already prefer deeper holes due to their protection value and cooler temperatures. But on hot, middle-of-the-day outings, anglers can concentrate efforts solely on such habitats to find fish. The biggest reward about this approach is that once you find salmon, there are often many of them stacked in there. At the same time, once a bite turns on in such holes, a chain-like reaction can take place, meaning a lot of fish can be caught in a short period of time. The challenging part is getting them to bite.

Because salmon are tight to the bottom in these situations, getting that terminal down there and keeping it there is crucial. Back-bouncing and drift fishing are the best approaches, and which one you use will likely depend on your position on the bank. This is where egg-cure fanatics lose their hair, for nothing's more frustrating than knowing salmon are there, but won't cooperate. Try various cures, scents, dyes and even other baits.

Prior to hitting the water on these days, know the conditions you'll be fishing in and gear-up accordingly. Be prepared to offer the salmon a multitude of baits, and make sure plenty of different weights are on-board so you're able to control the position of the terminal gear. By being ready, then spending time in these deep holes, more salmon will be caught.

One of the reasons fishermen enjoy the sport is because they can escape crowds and have time alone, in the outdoors. Then again, if the fish are in and people know about it, there will be crowds to deal with. If this frustrates you, stay home for you don't want to ruin it for others. But if catching fish is your objective, get out there with the rest of the crowd and have fun.

One of my most memorable bank-fishing moments took place in Alaska. It was a well-known stream and the kings were in. Everyone on the gravel bar was catching fish, up to 40 pounds. There were over 20 anglers there, spread out over 75 yards or so; not combat fishing by any means, but not the "Alaskan experience," either. With just the people I talked with that afternoon, six nationalities were represented, and it was fishing that brought us all together at this place and time.

Any of us could have moved upstream, escaping the crowds. Instead, we chose one another's company. Why? Because that's where the fish were. If you want to catch fish badly enough, go where the fish are and don't worry about crowds. Check out local fishing reports and see what they have to offer. Talk to tackle shop owners, fish and wildlife agents, gas-station attendants, fellow anglers, listen to radio reports and read the paper; all of these can point to fish.

Not only can these crowded places actually turn into a fun day of fishing, but there's a lot to be learned here. Veteran anglers often flock to such sites, because that's where the hot bite is. This is a good place to sit back and see how other anglers approach things; you may come away with something more than just fish.

There's nothing more miserable than being on the river, unable to feel your hands while vainly attempting to tie a knot. This is not to mention the task of trying to maintain a warm body on a cold day. Boaters have the luxury of heaters to keep them warm. Bankies often resort to building fires.

Shoreline fires are great if plunking, where you can cast, set the rod down and wait for fish to come to you. But if you have to take time away from fishing to build a fire, then you're decreasing the chance of catching fish. The goal is to catch fish, not spend time staying warm, and there are ways for bank fishermen to do this, other than just dressing warm.

Technologically speaking, hand-warmers have come a long ways in recent years, and for bank anglers, these are real time-savers. The key is activating the hand-warmers before you get cold. Place them in a glove or pocket and you're set. You can also put them in your socks to keep feet and lower legs warm.

But hand-warmers can be taken a step further. When living in Alaska, I'd often take two hand-warmers, activate them and use a sports wrap bandage to wrap around my body and hold the hand warmers in place against my kidneys. This goes a long way in keeping the body warm on those bone-chilling winter steelhead days. There are even large versions of these "hand" warmers now made for the body, and they can make the difference between spending a miserable day on the river or having fun and catching lots of fish.

If you haven't checked out the newest innovations on the hand-warmer market, it's time to do so. You'll find that in this day and age, there's no reason to spend a cold day on the river, or worse yet, be forced to call it quits just because you're cold. This is especially true when there are fish to be caught.

On cold days like this, pocket hand-warmers can help make things more comfortable. Bret Stuart nailed this early-morning steelhead on a cold, brisk morning.

W hen the commitment has been made to invest in a boat, be it a drift or sled, your fishing experiences will be forever changed. More than any facet of the sport, if you want to purchase something that will increase your chances of catching fish, a boat is it.

Once you get a boat, or boats as the case may be, everything else will fall into place. Boats open up opportunities for anglers to not only access waters they otherwise would not be able to, but to apply techniques that can't be presented any other way.

As with most elements within the fishing world, the exciting thing about boats is that they are always progressing. In this case, change is good, for designs are being made which help anglers more proficiently apply specific techniques. When I first started rowing a boat there was pretty much one to choose from, the ol' wooden McKenzie River drift boat. In fact, the first few boats we owned were ones we built ourselves, and having been born and raised on the McKenzie River, near where these boats were invented, there was a certain sense of pride that came with them.

Today, however, things have changed. Technology on the gear side of the fishing industry has allowed

Chapter 3 Boat Fishing

anglers to learn new techniques, and now, boats are being constructed to further help in meeting angler's needs. Want a drift boat for side-drifting? It's there. What about a sled for side-drifting? It's there, too. How about a 20-foot, extra-wide drift boat to accommodate more people, complete with a seat in the back? Got it. These are just basic examples of what's out there.

There seems to be no limit to the style, functionality and personal preferences that can be injected into boat designs. Want all the bells and whistles? As long as you have the cash, it can be done. The best part, every aspect of this state-of-the-art boat construction craze is done with one thing in mind: to help people catch more fish. True, many of the new design's are meant for comfort, but if you're comfortable you'll fish longer and in more harsh conditions, and the more you fish the more fish you'll catch.

In this section we'll take a look at the things boat owners can do to help further increase their fishing time, efficiency while on the water, and what can be done to catch more fish. Some of these pointers have to do with the boats themselves, while others look more at detailed tactical approaches that can be applied. What you'll find is, when it comes to boats and all that's associated with them, you get what you pay for. That also goes for gear that may need to be purchased in order to apply certain methods that can only be presented from a boat.

133. Fire-Up Motor

Prior to the start of the season, be sure to fire-up that motor and make certain all working parts are in order. Be it a kicker mounted on a driftboat, a jet on a sled or a backup motor on a big-water boat, it's a good idea to get that motor running before backing down to the ramp for the first time. I've seen a fair number of anglers over the years pull into a ramp, launch their boats and try starting the motor, only to discover that it doesn't run. Their day was cut short, in fact, they never left the dock.

The excuse, "It ran fine at the end of last season," may be true, but won't get you fishing that day, and few situations can be more frustrating, especially when your fishing time is limited and the bite is on. Before storing a motor at the end of the season, make sure all the gas is purged. I failed to do this one season and it cost me over $500 and two weeks of good fishing time while it was being fixed. Also, make sure new spark plugs are on-hand, as flooding can be a problem when a motor is slow to start.

When preparing for a trip, use high-octane fuel and quality oil to optimize motor performance. On jets, lube the unit properly; on prop' motors, make sure the oil is changed regularly, especially if running the motor hard.

To increase the life of your motor, once done fishing in salt or brackish water for the day, back into a freshwater setting and run it for a few minutes. This will ensure all the salt water is pumped out of the system and helps clean and preserve external parts as well. Keep on top if it and you won't lose any fishing time.

134. Comfortable Seats

No matter how big or fancy your boat may be; no matter how many bells and whistles may be attached, if the anglers aren't comfortable, it's going to make for a long day and will likely impact their overall performance. If you've ever been in a boat with uncomfortable seats, you know what I mean.

Many boats, no matter what brand, come with basic seat packages. Before purchasing a boat, ask about the upgraded seat options. The size boat you're getting and how you plan on fishing from it will have some bearing on the size and style of seats you will get. If you want thickly padded seats that hug the lower back, get 'em. If it's chairs with arm rests that interest you, get 'em.

There's no price tag that can be put on comfort, and when you're taking people down the river, you want them to enjoy the trip, stay focused, maintain a positive mental spirit, and most of all, do what's necessary to catch fish. Subpar seats can physically wear down a person, whereby rendering them less than efficient by the middle of the day. In the long run, this can equate to fewer fish being caught. If at all possible, try not to cut corners by pinching pennies at this stage in the game. I often ordered my seats from Three Rivers Marine (www.3riversmarine.com) in Washington. My wife and kids could not be more comfortable in them, meaning they passed the ultimate test.

135. Load Boat Properly

The day prior to taking the boat out fishing, take the time to properly load it. This applies more to drift boats than sleds, but can relate to both, depending on the situation. What's meant by this is that all the gear is safely stored, easily accessible and properly balanced.

Make sure tackle boxes are in a place that, when the boat moves, they won't be upended. Rods, nets and coolers should be out of the way of anchor ropes. Bow lines should not be covered by clothes or tackle. Lifejackets, by law, should be in easy reach. Everything should be easily accessible by both the boat operator and those who are fishing.

If you know specific techniques will be applied that day, set up the boat accordingly to make certain there is nothing in the way to inhibit anglers. The last thing you want is people stepping over the extra oar, tackle boxes, coolers and other bulky items, as sudden shifts in weight can turn a normal day on the river into potential disaster.

Once the boat is loaded with all the essential gear, hop in and make sure it's what you envision. Sit or stand at each person's spot and confirm that all is in order. Then, as soon as you hit the water, do the same. A boat balances much differently on water than on the trailer, and it may be necessary to make a few quick changes before everyone loads into the boat.

By taking the time to ensure balanced, safe loading of a boat before running it on the water, the chances of a mishap occurring are much less. Not only that, you'll spend less time jostling things around all day, less time looking for needed gear and more time fishing.

136. Rod Lockers

Maneuvering around rods that are tossed about in the boat can be frustrating, no matter how big of a boat you own. These days, rod lockers built into sleds are a common sight, and are a wise way to go. They can even be put in drift boats. On sleds, these top-loading, top-locking boxes are situated in the gunnels, and not only save valued space, but are safe places to store rods and other gear overnight. They are also great for storing rods while on the road. Just the time they save in hauling rods in and out of the boat make them worth it.

Being able to store rods in these lockers at the end of each day, where they are ready to fish the next, is a big plus. Not only can various rod set-ups be stored and ready to go, but rods and reels of many lengths and sizes can be stowed. When it comes to saving space, this rod-holding system is highly efficient and easy to work with.

An added bonus of this rod-storage system is that when fishing multiple rod set-ups throughout the day, they can be rotated in and out of the lockers. If done drift-fishing, for instance, simply put that rod away and grab your back-bouncing set-up. In addition, the space these lockers save let anglers move more freely around the boat, allowing terminal gear to be precisely maneuvered into the strike zone. At the same time, the added space is vital when fighting big fish that may lead you all over the river. Bottom line, rod lockers equate to efficiency, and the more efficient you are on the water, the more fish you'll catch.

137. Velcro Rod Straps

Carrying rods in a river boat is something that has spawned many inventions. On of the most efficient approaches I've seen came from John Gross, an Oregon guide whose meticulous demeanor affords him many great days on the river. Using a 22-inch-long Velcro strap, Gross holds a dozen or more rods in safe keeping in the boat, be it on the water or being trailered on the freeway.

Secure the top half of a standard rod holder—the plastic version lined with foam designed to mount to a wall—to the front edge of the box at the side of the oarsman's seat. Set the butt sections of the rods on the floor and slip the mid-section of the rods into the plastic rod holder. At this point, fully-extended rods bounce around so much, they often bang into one another, getting tangled or worse yet, breaking.

This is where the Velcro strap comes in. By sewing the tail end of the strap to the gunnel, behind the oarsman's seat, the rod tips can be placed between the Velcro and held in place. You can also have snaps put on the end of the strap, so it can be installed and removed at the beginning and end of the day. This allows the transport of fully equipped, totally extended rods to be held in place. The advantage is hauling rods that are strung and ready to fish at a moment's notice.

Rather than taking time to piece rods together, or re-rig with different terminal gear, the rods are ready to fish, allowing more time with the line in the water. If fishing rivers with a wide range in habitat, where you might be back-trolling plugs in one hole, dragging bait in another and casting hardware in yet another, this rod-hauling system offers a major advantage. Gross figures he has increased his actual fishing time by 30%, thanks to the Velcro straps, and has never damaged a rod over many years of using this system.

138. Rod Racks

Another way to store rods in a boat has to do with rack systems. The purpose of rod racks are to store multiple rods,

out of the way, yet within easy access so quick change-outs can be made if needed. Over the years I've seen numerous versions of rod racks, mostly home-made jobs, and they are impressive. The nice thing about making them yourself, they can be designed to meet your specific needs and fishing styles.

Rod racks that are installed in boats take many forms and can be as basic as screwing plastic rod holders—those intended to store rods in a garage—into place on a seat, the floor or off gunnels. Or, they can be as advanced as welding rod-butt holders on a plate, then mounting that inside the boat, along with another bracket that runs across the back of the boat to support the mid-sections of rods.

What you install comes down to personal preference, but the objectives are the same, and that's to save space, safely store rods and have them in an easy-to-get-to place. Personally, I prefer rod racks that spread out the rods, rather than having them stacked upon one another. Stacked rods lead to tangles and lost time.

If one slot can be devoted per rod, then that one rod can quickly be accessed. This is very important should you break a line or snap a rod and find yourself needing a quick replacement. In the event that you find yourself drifting downstream, side-drifting let's say, and want to toss a jig tight to shore, simply real in the drift rod, grab a jig rod and cast. The more accessible the rods, the more fishing time you'll get.

Be sure every rod in the rod holder is rigged and ready to go. Don't bait them, but have all else in place, so they can be quickly reached when necessary. When fishing from a boat, multiple methods can be applied which means lots of rods can be on board—we routinely have over a dozen, sometimes more than 20—and having them organized, ready to fish does make a difference.

139. In-Seat Tackle Boxes

When fishing three or four anglers in a drift boat, space is a valuable commodity. Good friend and guide, John Gross, has saved a great deal of space in his river boat by converting the storage area beneath his front seats into a tackle box. Drawer slots are cut into the backside of the seat, and the boxes made to easily slide. A locking panel system on the outside allows all the tackle to be stored safely when not on the water.

These custom boxes can be spendy, but once you see how efficient they are, I think you'll agree it's a good investment; the hard part is convincing your spouse of it. Properly constructed, you'll never have a problem with water leaking in. When anchored in a hole and fishing it, where people are moving around inside the boat, this set-up creates a great deal more space.

Not only can these boxes be accessed from the oarsman's position, but by lifting the seats as well. By accessing from the top, rain gear, extra boots and other loose gear can be stored between the drawers and the sides. Broken-down rods can even be laid on top of the boxes, making for safe and easy transport. This is a great way to organize a wide range of gear for anglers who fish a variety of water types, something that often requires a large gear selection.

140. Gunnel Tackle Boxes

There are many steps anglers can take to increase their level of performance on the river, and this is one of them. Noted guide and longtime friend, Bret Stuart, crafts his own tackle boxes that slip over the gunnels. Made of 1/8-inch or thinner metal, these work well on a drift boat or a sled. The idea is to have easy access to presorted gear and save floor space. They are also easy to remove, making for safe keeping in the garage should you be storing the boat outside.

The boxes can be made in a wide array of sizes to meet your needs. Deep, shallow, narrow or wide, or a combination of the above, customizing your hanging tackle boxes is easy. The boxes hang on either side of the boat, and can be positioned in easy reach of the oarsman or boat operator. If more people are in the boat, the boxes can be moved about to optimize desired space.

Organizing the tackle within these boxes is left to the individual using them and the fish species being targeted. If going after salmon and steelhead on the same trip, organize the boxes accordingly. The same goes if hitting only chinook, but where several tactical approaches are used to reach fish holding in and traveling through varied water types is where these boxes really pay off. Keep it simple, stay organized and fishing time will increase.

141. Bait Box/Leader Tree

There are a variety of bait-box contraptions and separate leader dispensers out there, but finding a set-up that includes both is a real time-saver. One of the best I've seen consists of a diamond-plated steel box that clips onto the gunnel (available at www.3riversmarine.com). The easy-to-access lid flips open and closed, to keep water and sunlight out. By pre-cutting a number of baits directly into the box, re-baiting is easy, saving valued time during the course of a day.

On the bottom of the tray, two flanges stick down from each side. With a hole drilled in the bottom of each flange, a steel bar can be slid in between them. Around this steel bar, a length of pipe insulation can be placed, which fits nicely beneath the box. Upwards of two dozen pre-tied hooks can be wrapped around the insulation; they can even be pre-rigged with desired drift bobber types and colors.

By having the leader pre-tied and ready to go, all you have to do when a leader is lost—or it becomes frayed and needs replacing—is spool off a leader, tie it on and re-bait. Because the bait is so close to the leader, the change-out is quick. No more digging through tackle boxes in search of leader boxes, then rummaging through coolers looking for egg containers. The bait, leader and drift bobber are all in one place, making for a speedy change-over. It's surprising the number of minutes this one element will add to your day of fishing, and in rivers where hangups are the norm, it's invaluable.

Versions of this box also contain a slot to place an ice pack in, directly beneath the baits, in order to keep them cool on hot days. And with the advent of quality hooks, worrying about rust formation over continued use is not a problem.

142. Bait Boxes

If you don't want to hook a bait box onto your gunnels, or if you don't like the open-style leader tree, having some type of bait box handy will help keep things clean and moving efficiently. If fishing more than one or two people in the boat, where baits are being passed around, a designated bait box is a good idea. Rather than storing baits in bulky coolers with the lunches or drinks, having them in their own container makes them easy to get to.

Bait boxes can be as basic as a small cooler or as advanced as a custom-made metal box with multiple features. What type of bait box you use depends on how you fish and how many people may fish with you. If fishing with eggs and shrimp, you'll want to keep both baits cool and dry. It may be that you have multiple egg cures, in which case they need to be stored, accordingly. If using baitfish, they may be in a wet brine. Fillets of baitfish may be in a salt or borax dry brine. Prawns or crawdads might also be used. Point is, there are lots of bait options, and storing them for proper preservation and easy access can greatly increase fishing time.

You may want your bait box to have a lift-out shelf, where shrimp, eggs or dyed prawns can be placed. Below that might be a place for several bags of bait, all of different cures, or ice, to keep baits cool on those hot days. Three Rivers Marine has a ready-made model that works well for this purpose (www.3riversmarine.com).

When strictly egg fishing for kings in Alaska, we'll often have a medium-sized cooler filled with one-gallon sealable baggies of different cures. We know we'll be rifling through the baits and want them ready to go. On the other hand, when fishing summer steelhead and springers on the same river back in the Northwest, we'll want to keep the sand shrimp alive and the eggs cool. Bait boxes are an organizational tool that help things move forward more smoothly, and that, in itself, goes a long way.

143. Scent Boxes

In recent years the number and variety of scent-based products that have been developed for salmon and steelhead anglers has never been greater. From gels to sprays, liquids to pastes, companies are now providing fishermen with what they need to catch more fish. Partially, the bass industry is to thank for this, where extensive studies have been conducted on how well fish smell. Thankfully, findings in these studies have carried over to the salmon and steelhead world.

Whether you choose to apply scents to eggs, shrimp or other baits, lures, plugs or drift-bobbers, there's no doubting the effectiveness of these items. Scents are particularly effective on salmon, and do work well on steelhead. While sight-fishing, I've caught several steelhead over the years that I know I wouldn't have gotten were it not for scents.

Scents can be applied to baits during the curing or brining process, or when fishing on the river. Some anglers prefer having baits soak in scents, so the odors become impregnated in the tissues. Another approach is to wait until you're on the river, then apply the scents because it's not certain which flavor the fish may prefer on any given day. Both approaches work. Scents can also be injected into baits.

As for lures, plugs an other artificial presentations, pastes can be applied to them, whereby adding a scent factor to the visual effect. Pastes adhere surprisingly well to these artificials, opening many opportunities for anglers.

As with baits, it's a good idea to bring several types of scents along. Placing them all in a single container, one that fits easily in the boat and can be readily accessed, will increase the likelihood of their being used and will ensure cleanliness. I have a small, plastic container that holds about a dozen types and flavors of scents that sits right next to me in the boat, where I can easily reach what I need.

Don't be afraid to try different scents, even if they are not indigenous to the waters being fished. Sometimes crawfish works better than shrimp, or herring over anise. The key is finding a smell the fish like, for once it's discovered the bite can turn on quickly.

144. Lead-Weight Storage Systems

Having a storage system whereby sinkers can be easily accessed, without making too much of a clutter in the boat, will increase your fishing time. Such a system can take on many forms, and what you desire comes down to what you like.

One of my favorite approaches is to take a few small, plastic containers and fill them with what weights I'll need for that day. If I'm salmon fishing, for instance, and know I'll be using 1 1/2- and

2-ounce sinkers, that's what I'll take. Each weight category gets its own container, so you don't have to waste time sifting through a mixed bin in search of the one you need. I'll position these in the gunnel trays, on the bow, in drink-holder slots or next to the oarsman's seat, wherever they need to be for easy access.

If room is not a concern, then you may opt out of the little, plastic containers for something larger. Shallow, slotted boxes or trays, even ones with dimples in them, are excellent for holding weights. These make for quick and easy access, as weights are in plain sight and simple to identify.

Another approach is to color-code your sinkers. If you have a range of cannonball sinkers you'll be using, for instance, you may want to color the numbers of the 1-ouncers red, the 2-ouncers blue, the 3-ouncers black, and so on. This means you can put them all in one compact container and simply look at the colors to quickly identify what you need.

Each one of these approaches works well, keeping in mind that what fits your needs may be different than what works for other anglers. Whatever sinker storage device you come up with, make sure it's out of the way and makes for easy access, because when going through lots of gear, this really can add time to your fishing day.

145. Hot-Water Basin

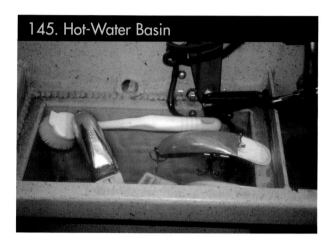

On sleds, the water that pumps through a motor can be rerouted into a holding bin in the back of the boat. There are many boats now featuring this option, and if you're a bait-fisherman, it's a luxury to have. If working with cured eggs or plugs wrapped with baits, keeping things clean can be a challenge. With this hot-water bath, keeping plugs and hands clean is quick and easy.

The water that runs through the motor becomes heated, and rather than kicking it out of the manifold and back into the river, a hose can be connected to route the water into a specially-made holding bin. The bin features a plug to control the flow of hot water into the bin throughout the day. Using warm water to rinse off plugs and other fishing gear not only keeps them in better fishing condition, but it allows anglers to keep their hands clean, something that can impact a salmon bite. Remember, salmon have a sense of smell measured in parts per billion, meaning we need all the advantages we can get, and this equates to clean hands with which to handle baits and gear.

Should rod handles or reels get gummed with borax, simply dip them in the hot-water basin and wipe clean with a rag. Rags, knives, pliers and other tools can also be kept clean of blood and potential bacteria-laden contaminants that are often transferred

to fishing baits. The hot water also feels relieving when thawing the hands on those cold winter days on the river. Keep the lemon-scented Joy soap, a scrub brush and some clean rags by the hot-water basin and you'll be amazed how much you use them, and what a difference it makes in keeping things clean and helping you catch more fish.

146. Double Anchor

When fishing rivers, especially smaller systems, boat positioning in any given hole can make the difference between a limit of fish or going home without a single bite. Oftentimes, if you're not in the slot, you're not going to catch fish, no matter how good the bait you're using. The thing is, if your positioning is off by only a matter of inches in some holes, you won't be able to access the sweet spot.

Take a swirl hole for instance, where salmon travel through a single, narrow seam to reach a specific holding zone at the upper end. Such holes can be a salmon angler's best friend, or worst nightmare if you can't hit the sweet-spot. Take the same hole in high, turbulent conditions and reaching those honey holes can be even tougher. Oftentimes boats with a single anchor get tossed or even moved around 360°, and believe me, it's nearly impossible to effectively fish a hole like this; I know, I've tried it.

I don't know how many times we've watched anglers fishing boiling holes without hooking a fish, only to move in after they left and hammer the salmon. The only noticeable difference: we dropped two anchors which allowed us to be in key position to more effectively fish the target water. In big boils and rough water like this, it's hard managing your line, and if you're not in control of it, you're wasting valuable fishing time.

A two-anchor set-up—one off the back and one off the bow—will keep that boat in precise position and allow accurate casts and drifts to be achieved. I've seen boats with duo-anchor set-ups absolutely nail fish while anglers in single-anchor boats, working the same hole, struggled. On my double-anchor set-up, I prefer having a 30-pound anchor on the back, a 10-pounder up front. Having both anchors run on a pulley system so the oarsman can control them, is most efficient, especially when fishing alone. This much weight will ensure the boat stays in one position, allowing you to thoroughly cover a hole.

147. Launch Early

Haugen with a hefty silver salmon caught at first light.

One of the greatest advantages boaters have is the ability to put themselves where the fish are. Often it comes down to how badly you want to catch fish. If you want fish badly enough, you'll be willing to do everything within your means to make something happen, and this includes launching the boat early.

One morning a buddy and I launched the boat at 2:00 a.m. to get into a hot-producing salmon hole. We were shocked to discover someone else had beat us to it. How? They spent the night on the water, in their drift boat. Fortunately, he caught his limit within a few casts, then we moved in and did the same. Since that time, we've spent many a night in boats, just to get the right spot.

Though spending the night in a boat can be a bit hard on the body, people do it all the time. If running unfamiliar rivers, you'll want to launch before dark, the previous day, so as not to risk navigating any dangerous waters. On those clear, moonlit nights, we've even run downstream in the middle of the night to get into prime position. Monitor the situation, how well you know the river and be honest with your boat-handling skills in these conditions. If in doubt, play it smart.

The primary reason to launch a boat early is to beat other anglers to the sweet-spot. In some salmon and steelhead holes, narrow slots, only large enough to accommodate one boat, may be where the fish are holding or traveling through at first light. Making the effort to be the one occupying this slot can make a big difference in your success. It's work, and makes for a long day, but if you want fish, spending the night on the water or launching in the middle of the night is an option worth considering.

148. Launch Late

If you're not an early morning person, or if work or other obligations keep you from launching a boat early enough to be the first one in a hole, don't worry. Casting off later in the morning does have its benefits, and does save some wear and tear on the body and the mind.

Rather than feeling you have to be first on the river, try following boat traffic. I know of several guides who have clients that simply do not want to get up at 3:00 in the morning to fish. Instead, they'll have a big breakfast and meet at the ramp around 7:00 or 8:00 in the morning. Though the guides would rather be fishing early, to have the chance of at least catching another fish or two before other anglers got to the holes, they still do pretty well. After a while, if fish have been caught or the bite is not happening, boaters often go in search of them. This leaves vacancies throughout the river, meaning there are opportunities for those coming down later.

If launching late, keep in mind you may not get the best spots in every hole, which means it's a good idea to learn to fish a hole from multiple positions. This may require mastering a variety of techniques, but that's something that should be done anyhow.

Once boats have passed over fish, they will often shift to different holding water than where you'd find them at first light. At the same time, once the sun hits the water, this can send fish into deeper or more broken waters, where they feel safe.

By launching late, knowing where to find fish and how to reach them, you can boost catch rates. This also holds true for the boater who shoves off in the dark and chooses to spend the entire day on the river. The fish are in the system, it's up to you to catch them.

149. Cover Water

One of the advantages boaters have is their ability to move around. This is especially true for boats with motors. There

Guide Jeff Boggs covered the water to get Gene Shands on this chrome king.

are some days on the river when bites are simply hard to come by, and on such days, it may pay off to cover water and find fish.

On a couple of the rivers I fish close to home, 99% of the boats are drifters. There are a couple guys who run sleds, and on most days, they outfish everyone. Their techniques are the same, but they aren't afraid to burn fuel to find fish. They may fish one hole four or five times a day, maybe more. Their mindset of being aggressive, covering water to find fish, is highly successful.

More and more drift boaters are discovering the value of motors, especially when side-drifting, for they allow you to fish holes, run back up and do it all over again. Once you do find fish, motors can be instrumental in keeping you in the zone. Pumping on the oars can sometimes achieve the same effect, but often you only get one shot at a hole when drifting without a motor.

No matter how you go about it, the theory behind covering water comes down to hitting a spot, fishing it hard for 15-20 minutes and if nothing bites, moving on. Depending on the hole, you may be able to fish it from several different angles, searching for fish. This is a good approach for oar-powered boats. Once that hole has been worked, move on and maybe come back later, if possible, to see if fish have filtered in.

If fishing from a drift boat, it may be necessary to relaunch the boat, repeating the same run. You can also make longer runs, stopping when you find fish. By being assertive and going on the search for fish by covering water, a lot can be learned about where fish hold at certain times of the day, even parts of the season. In this case, being aggressive can have its rewards.

150. Float Long Sections

For drift boaters without a motor, it may be necessary to cover long stretches of water in order to find fish. Rather than making a single run, say from one boat launch to another, it can be a huge benefit to make two or three runs in a day's time.

Typically, these extended drifts come when you have a full day to devote to it. One drift we commonly make takes about five hours. To extend it to the next take-out adds another three hours. The third take-out tacks on another four or five hours. Of course, once fish are located, progress slows in an effort to catch them, for there's never any telling what lies downstream.

When covering so much water, once you find fish, you want to stick with them. The drawback to this can come on these long runs, when you find fish late in the day and still need to cover lots of water to make it to the next ramp by nightfall. In this case, use your best judgment and don't push things. Often when you find where fish are stacked, you can devote time to catching your

limit there, then pushing downstream in a hurry; it's surprising how quickly you can cover water when not stopping to fish every spot.

One of the most challenging decisions when making long drifts lies in not knowing where you'll be taking out. A good rule here is, take the mountain bike with you, in case you tag out early and can ride back from the first ramp you reach. Leave a shuttle rig at the second spot, and should you find yourself going all the way to the furthest take-out, have the cell phone to call for a shuttle.

Making extended drifts is a good way to learn the water and where fish may be. On those slow days, it might be a good idea to devote some time to covering water and locating fish, you may just discover a new honey-hole.

151. Relaunch

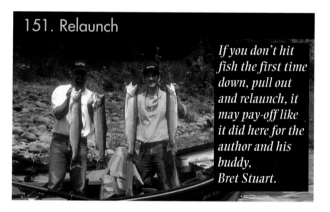

If you don't hit fish the first time down, pull out and relaunch, it may pay-off like it did here for the author and his buddy, Bret Stuart.

Drift boaters always face the dilemma of staying put or pushing downstream. They know that if they move, they'll not be able to come back to the hole. They also know that if the action is slow, and they don't move, someone else may beat them to the fish further downstream.

One of the answers to this predicament is making a quick run, early in the morning, then making the same run later in the day. Of course, if you hit fish early, stay with them. Moving downstream and finding fish ahead of other boat traffic is the goal, but it doesn't always work out this way.

If you're not tagged out by the time you reach the ramp, load the boat on the trailer and relaunch, making the same run. You can learn a great deal from your first run. Note where the bites—if any—came, where fish were rolling, where you saw fish as you passed overtop them in the boat, and so on. Knowing these things will help you to decide where efforts should be focused on the next run in order to best catch fish.

When covering so much water, be aware that multiple techniques may need to be applied. Have the appropriate rods rigged and ready, baits and scents in place, and be willing to do what's necessary to catch fish. Another point to consider is that the boat traffic that may now be ahead of you could have forced fish to move into different water or hold tighter in holes.

Nonetheless, you're still at the advantage here, for based on your early run, you know where the fish were, thus should be. It only takes a bit more effort to relaunch a boat, and the rewards can be great once you locate fish.

152. Stay Put

Depending on what kind of boat you're fishing from, time of day, river conditions and overall pressure on the river, you may want to find a good hole and fish it for several hours. This is contradictory to covering as much water as possible, but makes sense in certain situations.

In low-water conditions, fish, especially salmon, may tend to hang in a single hole for extended periods of time. They can remain in these areas for days or even weeks, and knowing the fish are there is half the battle. Warming water temperatures can also confine fish to a single hole. If the hole is deep enough, fish will often retreat to the bottom, where darkness and cooler temperatures protect them. In these conditions, fish may be found there at any time in the season.

In larger holes, you may be able to break it down into sections and spend several hours fishing the entire thing. In one of my favorite salmon holes, for example, the fish are at the upper end of a riffle early in the morning. Soon after daylight they drop back and stack against a ledge, in about 12 feet of water. About midday, as daylight hits the water, the fish will move to the deepest part of the hole, where it drops off to about 25 feet. Late in the afternoon, salmon start moving again, and new arrivals begin trickling over a tailout at the lower end, then holding in a big flat. During the course of the day, every single spot can be fished and fished again by simply relocating the boat. A variety of methods can be applied and spending the time often pays off.

There's a similar steelhead hole I like to fish. It can be plugged early on, high in the riffle, jig fished through a slick later in the morning, then drift fished in the fast water the rest of the day.

The key to spending time in one hole is knowing the fish and the anatomy of the hole. It's imperative to learn when the fish will move, what factors might force them to move and where they might go. Another key has to do with applying the best techniques that will get fish to respond at various times in the day, amid different types of water. Be persistent, observer and diversify, it can work when fishing one hole.

153. Dissect Hole

A large majority of salmon and steelhead holes can be fished from multiple angles, in a variety of ways. For a boater who is willing to move around, breaking down a hole—that is, dissecting it into specific parts—can lead to a greater number of fish being caught.

One of the most influential factors of where a fish holds within a given hole correlates to water levels. If fishing a river that experiences a great deal of fluctuation, be it through excessive rainfall, snow melt or dam regulations, it pays to monitor river levels and where fish are during certain times.

On rivers such as short coastal streams, where a winter storm can quickly swell waters, it's a good idea to monitor weather conditions to determine what level the river is at or will be at when you plan on fishing it. The same holds true for rivers whose levels are controlled by dams, where flow rates can be monitored, thus allowing river levels to be pinpointed. Once river levels are known, you can figure out how to best fish a hole, often in multiple areas.

Not always, but sometimes high waters can increase the amount of area that can be fished within a given hole. By taking the time to seek out fish during periods of various water levels, you can learn where they congregate. For example, one of the best winter steelhead and spring chinook areas within holes on some rivers can be found tight to a corner, where water flows over a normally exposed gravel bar. It may only be a foot or two deep here, but these fish like taking the shortcut over the now covered gravel bar. While other anglers stick to the main current, it might be worth plunking or plugging these corners.

The options for how to break down a hole and find fish are many. The important part lies in knowing that this option exists, then doing what's necessary to learn where the fish are hiding.

154. Anchor And Wait

Peer pressure. It's something we've dealt with since childhood, and even as adults we encounter it from time to time. Feeling pressured to do something we don't particularly want to do or something that may be uncomfortable is normal, and part of life, even in the world of fishing.

For many anglers it's their nature to want to be first to the next fishing hole, or to not allow others to beat them to the best spots. If you want to fish a particular place that's already occupied, without infringing on a fellow angler's territory, try sitting in wait. Simply move the boat near where you'd like to fish, without getting in the way, drop anchor and wait for them to move.

I don't know how many times over the years Dad and I have watched boats work a hole, in what we determined to be poor position. We knew fish were in there, but the anglers simply were not in the right place to make the proper presentation. Rather than push downstream, we'll pull off to the side, drop anchor and just sit there, waiting. Eventually the other boats move on. Oftentimes you can slip in and quickly catch fish.

It may only take a slight adjustment in boat position to get that terminal gear down to where the fish are, and if you know they are in there, it can be well worth the wait. This is particularly effective on days when the river is crowded, where you know moving downstream will likely result in your not getting to fish the spots you want to. Sometimes the wait may take only a matter of minutes, other times it may be a couple of hours. How long you should sit in wait, not fishing, depends on several factors which you will have to be the judge of based on your situation that particular day. Be courteous, allow plenty of room for fellow boaters to fish while you wait and you may be surprised at how opportunities open up.

155. Anchoring In Big Water

When fishing big rivers where dropping anchor alongside other boats is the rule, there are important things to know in order to be safe, access more water and catch more fish. Choosing the right anchor is a good starting point, and generally speaking, a bigger anchor is better. If unsure as to what size to get, dealers can help you gauge the weight to match your boat's length.

As for anchor styles, the Fluke anchor is ideal for sandy bottoms, a Rocking Chair anchor with two to four tines is best in rocks and a Kedge anchor good in fast, shallow waters with a gravel bottom. Having a breakaway anchor is almost a must, so you can pull it with the ball if hung up and quickly detach from it should you have to move downstream after fish. The anchor is attached to a 5/16" chain, with one foot of chain for every one foot of boat length being the rule of thumb on how long the chain should be. Some anglers believe this is overkill on longer boats, and will shorten it up a few feet.

The chain can be tied to a braided 3/8-inch nylon rope. This small-diameter rope creates less drag compared to larger sizes and is plenty strong. Rope length varies, usually between five and seven feet for every one foot of water depth being fished (the Army Corps of Engineers suggests seven feet of rope for every foot of water). In 40 feet or less of water, 125-150 feet of anchor rope is what many anglers opt to use. The bumper rope—connecting the nylon rope to the boat—is about 30 feet long, and can be polypropylene, as it floats, making it easy to handle around the bow.

A ball of size A3 or A4 is ideal. It's a good idea to mount two to three bow chocks on both sides of your anchor davit, off the bow. This will allow you to center the boat should it plane to one side or another once the anchor has been dropped, and saves from having to pull and reposition the anchor. Sea anchors—a windsock used under water—are also good investments which allow you to keep aligned in high winds. These are dropped off the back of the boat, and act like a chock, you can even use two, one off each side, if needed.

If you're serious about big-water anchor fishing, spend the time and money to do it right. Practice when no one is around, for this is a serious process. Once you get comfortable with it, you will reach more water and catch more fish, safely.

156. Mark Where Bite Occurs

When fishing a hole, it's natural to track your line. Sometimes, however, it's easy to get so tuned-in to where your line is going into the water, that you lose sight of where it's positioned in the hole—in relationship to the bank—when a bite occurs. This is particularly the case in big rivers, or when working deep, swirling holes where line movement is fast and random.

When a bite does occur, not only is it a good idea to mark where in the water the line was when it happened, but also mark it on the bank. Ideally, if you can take your boat's position and line it up with an identifiable object on the opposite shore, then you increase your chances of getting that terminal gear back to where the strike came. Even better is if you can pinpoint two landmarks, one on each shoreline, and then mark your line's position when the bite came, but this is not always possible, especially in big rivers.

The objective is to know exactly where your line was entering the water at the time of a bite, as multiple salmon and steelhead can be pulled from the same spot, not only on that day, but over years of fishing. Oftentimes the water's surface may appear uniform, with no identifying features, whereby making it tough to locate exactly where the bite came. Other times the surface features may change with the slightest hint of river fluctuation. By paying close attention to where the line is at the time of a bite, and keying in on landmarks, you'll be better able to position the boat, and your terminal gear, to where they need to be to catch more fish.

At the same time, if learning a new hole, identifying landmarks and positioning the boat where you want it from the outset, will save valued time. The more you learn a hole and the more fish you catch from it, you'll narrow down the options of where you want the boat to be positioned, exactly. The more precise your initial drop of the anchor, the better your ability to cover the best water, the more fish you will catch.

157. Spooking The Bite

When the bite is slow to come and you know fish are in the hole, you can often use the boat to your advantage to help make something happen. This is especially true in shallow-water fisheries, where fish can be seen. This technique can be applied from a drift boat or a sled, and is best done when you have the hole to yourself, so as not to risk upsetting other anglers.

Ideally, it's best to spot fish first, so you can observe their reaction to your boat's movement as you approach them. Oftentimes all it takes to trigger a stubborn fish or school of fish into biting is a slight nudge, something to get their attention and force them to tense-up, even change position. Not always will this trigger a bite, but when nothing else seems to be working, this aproach can be worth a try.

Initially, start moving slowly toward the fish. At the first sign of nervous movement, back off. You want to alert the fish to your presence, not run them out of the hole. Keep an eye on the fish and reposition the boat back away from them, so you can cast without further spooking them. It's a good idea to wait five to ten minutes, to allow the fish to settle down, whereby disassociating what startled them from the bait which now floats in front of them.

Another option is to be aggressive. It may be necessary to drift, row or idle downstream, directly over the fish in order to stir them up. This seems to be most effective when lots of fish are around. Once you've passed over the fish, gently row or motor back upstream—off to the side so as not to further spook them from where they just moved to—give them some time to settle down and start fishing.

158. Motor Disturbance To Trigger Bite

While fishing Alaska's famed Situk River for steelhead one spring, the bite was tough in coming. One of the sled boats that's grandfathered in to that river sped by where I was bank fishing. I'd been there for two hours and hooked only one fish, despite seeing several of them in the hole in front of me. Minutes after the boat passed, and the fish settled back down, a buddy and I landed and released 11 bright steelies. Coincidence? No. The boat triggered the bite, no question.

Later that morning I observed the same boat working a hole. They tried many approaches, and none drew results. Then the guide got on the motor and started cutting cookies in the water, directly over where the fish were holding. They then pulled over, ate a snack and resumed fishing 20 minutes later. Before it was all over, they pulled multiple steelhead from that hole. Again, the boat was used as a tool to trigger a bite.

Using your boat's motor to stir up the fish can be effective, though is often used as a last resort when the fish simply aren't biting. It's best applied in deeper holes, where fish are congregating and are reluctant to move out, no matter how much they may be irritated. It's also wise to do it when alone, so as not to upset fellow anglers who may not be advocates of this technique.

Agitating fish into biting with the use of a motor hinges on the issue of improper ethics amid some anglers. Some feel it stresses the fish too much, others argue it's something the fish see daily, whereby experiencing minimal stress and a quick recovery. Whether or not you choose to apply this technique is your call, but there's no disputing its effectiveness in the right situations.

159. Let Boats Pass To Trigger Bite

When boat traffic is high, letting them pass by might move fish around, as it did here for the author.

Often boaters get hung-up on being the first ones down the river, believing that such aggressiveness increases their chance of catching fish by staying ahead of the competition. While this may be true in some situations, staying ahead of the pack is not always the best option. It might be best to sit and wait, especially if you know fish are in the hole you're working but aren't biting.

If boat traffic is a concern, rather than pushing ahead, try lagging back, letting boats pass in front of you. Oftentimes, especially when the bite is slow to come, this aggravation can turn on a bite. I've found this to be especially true on summer and winter steelhead, as well as spring chinook that are in a holding phase; that is, not moving from one particular hole to another.

In fact, you can take it one step further and request that passing boats not hug tight to shore in an effort to be courteous and avoid disturbing your water. Instead, ask them to pass by directly over the fish, whereby increasing the hopes of disturbing them. If the fish get nervous enough to move, there's an increased chance that they may strike.

This is a trick some wise bank anglers have been relying on for years, requesting boats to pass over holding fish rather than close to shore. Sometimes it pays off, moving the fish tighter to shore and giving them an adrenaline boost, a combination that can result in a bite. If the fish are there—and you know it—but aren't biting, what is there to lose?

160. Back 'em Down To Trigger Bite

Seeing and not catching steelhead, both summer and winter runs, can be one of the most frustrating experiences anglers encounter. If in a boat, it's likely multiple techniques can be applied to find what the fish like, or don't like. But if drifting eggs, floating a jig or tossing hardware in front of them does not pay off, try backing the fish down.

This is best done by way of back-trolling or back-bouncing plugs or bait. Simply align yourself with the fish that have been seen, start well upstream of their position and begin backing down the presentation. If the bite doesn't come, and you no longer see the fish when passing by the point where they were last marked, keep working the presentation downstream. Often that fish, and sometimes multiple others, will back downstream to the lower end of the section of water being fished. If the fish spook and spurt upstream without a bite, nothing's lost as they weren't biting anyway.

Once you feel the fish are backing down, be sure and work it all the way to the end of the drift. More times than not these fish will recede to the very edge of a tailout and hold there. If you've made it this far, work the bait back and forth, along the face of the tailout, in an effort to find the fish. Often they grow so irritated, they will strike out of aggression.

This approach seems to be more effective with the more lines you have in the water, whereby decreasing the amount of escape water the fish can retreat to. If drifting the river with a fellow boater, try positioning your boats side-by-side and running a wall of plugs or baits downstream. Putting out, say, six lines, as opposed to one or two, will often do the trick. It may also be a good choice to use plugs with rattles or baits with good action and plenty of scent. In extremely low, clear conditions, downsizing the presentation may be necessary so as not to excessively spook the fish.

161. Drift The Middle And Cast To Sides

Other than following natural current lines, two other factors commonly push fish to shore: high-water conditions and pressure from fellow boaters. If you find yourself floating downstream, facing any of these conditions, evaluate what has to be done to get the terminal gear into the strike zone.

When it comes to some summer steelhead and spring chinook rivers, and in particular winter steelhead and fall chinook streams, working close to shore can yield big rewards. How many times have we been guilty of—and seen others doing it—working the middle of a river, or seams only on the outside edge of the main current? When conditions and/or situations warrant, these may in fact, be the least likely place to find fish. Instead, study the water close to shore and do what's necessary to position your presentation in the proper spot.

In working close to shore, search for current lines, seems coming off small points of land, bedrock channels, brushlines, submerged gravel bars and other conditions that appeal to fish. If boat traffic is high, fish may retreat to less traditional holding water in an effort to escape pressure. In this case, perhaps it would be wise to let several boats pass in front of you, whereby forcing more fish toward the bank, then focus on working the edges of the river.

Jigs, plugs and casting lures tight to shore will often elicit a strike in areas overlooked by fellow anglers. I once watched a boat work behind us in high-water conditions. We threw everything (or so we thought) toward the shoreline, without success. The trailing boat had the same idea, but they tossed plugs and quickly retrieved them. The fish like it, and responded to this near-shore, aggressive presentation.

In the right conditions, working the shoreline with the right gear combination can produce fish when nothing else will. Mind you, the water does not have to be deep for this to happen. Salmon can be pulled from four feet of water, steelhead even shallower than that.

162. Side-Drifting

Side-drifting is arguably the most effective technique there is when it comes to steelhead, even salmon, fishing in rivers. This is especially true with winter steelhead. Side-drifting is one of the best ways there is to cover large amounts of water, and the natural style of presentation entices fish to bite a high percentage of the time when compared to other techniques.

But there are some important factors to consider when side-drifting, and it starts with the proper rod. The best side-drifting rod I've found for steelhead is the G. Loomis STR 1141S. Couple this with appropriate line and leader to meet the conditions being fished, then focus on the terminal gear. I've fished a wide array of side-drifting presentations over the years, from double-hook bait set-ups topped with a drift-bobber to bare eggs on a hook so small you'd think a trout would have trouble finding it.

My favorite presentation in clear water conditions is a size-1 or -2 octopus-style hook with no more than four or five cured

Side-drifting proved fruitful for Buzz Ramsey and the author.

eggs placed in the loop. Run a short, two- to three-inch dropper and attach a weight that is light enough to occasionally tick the bottom during the drift. Avoid too much weight, which results in dragging, not allowing the bait to be channeled by natural currents into food funnels. In very low conditions, a larger bait with no weight can be effective.

Thread on a Puff Ball, barely exposing the tip of the hook. This will keep the hook's point riding upright, whereby decreasing the chance of it hanging up during a drift. Have multiple rods rigged and ready to go, along with precut baits and pre-tied leaders, should the terminal gear be lost.

Anglers should simultaneously cast slightly upstream of the boat, parallel to one another. The oarsman or motor operator takes over from there, positioning and timing the rate at which the boat moves downstream to that of the lines. Bites when side-drifting are often delayed, so avoid the tendency to immediately jerk every time you see or feel something.

163. Rod Holder Position

Rod holders keep rods in precise position while back-trolling, trolling or plunking, and alleviate the physical strain of the angler holding a rod for extended periods. But where these devices are placed in a boat is critical to how the rods in them fish, and how the captain runs a boat.

Positioning rods on the sides of boats is simple, but often the oarsman or motor operator won't fish due to the hassles of handling a rod. If fishing three people in a boat, and only two have rods out, that's 33% of the fishing time being lost. By mounting a rod holder between the two front seats or on the deck of a drift boat or on the handle of a motor at the back of a sled, fishing time can be increased.

It might even be necessary to mount multiple rod holders in the boat and use them as conditions require. Small streams, for instance, may find you wanting to run rods tight to the boat, whereas larger rivers may allow you to spread things out a bit more. Though rod holders can be pivoted about to change position, sometimes current flows are too great to allow you to cover the desired water.

Some anglers will mount multiple bases on both sides of the boat, then move the inserts to the ones that will best allow them to fish the target water. I have had great success with the innovative sliding rod holders created by Three Rivers Marine (www.3riversmarine.com), both on my drift boat and on sleds. Of course, flow rates, methods and size of gear being used along with angler preference are just some of the influences factoring in to where rod holders will be positioned.

By taking measures to strategically locate rod holders throughout your boat, the amount of time every angler spends with their line in the water will dramatically increase. The end result should be more fish in the boat.

164. Tune Plugs

No matter what type of plug you choose to use, always be sure to tune it prior to dropping it into position or casting it. Start by tying it on the line, then let out a few feet of line or drag it through the water to see that it does not pull to one side or another.

If the plug pulls to the right or left, take a pair of needlenose pliers and slightly twist the eyescrew, accordingly. It only takes a small microadjustment to get the plug up and running properly. Some plugs will be perfectly tuned right out of the box, others may never tune to your liking.

Once a plug has been tuned and fished, then stored at the end of the trip, make sure to check and see that it's still properly tuned the next time you choose to use it. Sometimes it gets knocked around in the tackle box or the eye shifts when cinching the knot, whereby causing it to not run true.

A plug that veers to one side or another will not reach the target water, thus decreases the chance of getting strikes. If there's a severe pull, the plug will pop out of the water, or result in serious line twist.

It only takes a few seconds, and sounds basic, but tuning a plug is something that should not be overlooked, especially if you're new to the sport. It's just another one of those little hints that will help increase your effective fishing time.

165. Bacon-Wrapped Plugs

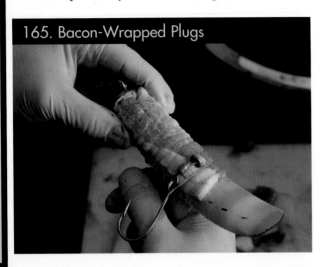

For years anglers have been experimenting with wrapping baits on plugs such as Kwikfish. This added scent provides another dimension by which anglers can target another of the fish's senses, specifically, smell.

While herring, sardines and anchovies rank among the top baits of choice for wrapping plugs, smelt and even trimmed shad will work. A bait wrap that was brought to my attention while fishing in Alaska, is bacon.

Bret Brown, co-owner of Alaska King Salmon Adventures Camp on the Nushagak River (www.alaskakingsalmon.com), told me of this trick, and we used it with surprising success, outfishing all sardine wraps in the boat over a two-day period. It was late in the season, and the bite was slow in Nushagak terms. Brown had used bacon with success in Pacific Northwest streams, as had some of his guides. We tried it, it worked, and since then I've had success on other rivers.

Think about it, and bacon wraps make sense. They are high in oil content, have a sweet smell and are designed for wrapping. Bacon strips are streamline, the perfect width and hold up to the most treacherous waters.

What's more, we've had them tied on plugs and left them there during the heat of day, while fishing other methods. Some six hours later, the bacon looked cooked on the plug, and oozed oils to the point it almost appeared that it needed to be replaced. But the released oils were a good thing, and that plug caught the first four fish that evening.

The bacon is wrapped on raw, and the more fat a piece has, the more effective it seems to be. On the other hand, as the meat gets wet, the grain opens up, whereby accepting artificial scents well. A wrap that's about 75% fat, 25% meat seems to be a good

choice. The use of bacon is one of those things that, once accepted, your confidence will grow, and more fish will be caught.

166. Back-bounce Plugs

Back-bouncing bait is a popular approach for salmon anglers, and to some extent, steelheaders. As far as I can dig up, the back-bouncing technique has been around since the 1950s, maybe earlier. But one approach that's often overlooked is back-bouncing plugs.

Rig the sinker on a slider set-up, then tie the plug onto two to four feet of leader. How far you drop the plug back depends on how deep you want the plug to run. The shorter the leader, the tighter to the bottom it will run; the longer the leader, the higher. If searching for fish that may be suspended, perhaps a longer leader may be best. On traveling fish that move tight to the bottom, a short leader will allow you to more precisely present the lure.

Back-bouncing plugs, no matter what the brand, style or size, can be done from an anchored or moving position. Which method you choose comes down to the water being fished and the fish being targeted. If you're not one to sit on the pick, waiting for fish to come to you, don't feel like you have to conform to doing it just because everyone else is. Pull anchor and work your way downstream, back-bouncing the plug in an effort to find fish on the move.

Back-bouncing plugs, especially wrapped Kwikfish or Flatfish, is a prime example of a method that works well on one river, but anglers may be reluctant to use on another. I've been fortunate to apply this technique very effectively on numerous streams, from California to Alaska. If you can back-bounce bait, you can back-bounce plugs, and most streams are conducive for both approaches. If the conditions are right, you'll be surprised with the results.

167. Back-troll Baits

Back-trolling baits can be done in many ways, be it with a diver, plug or flashing attractant. No matter how you go about back-trolling, the objective—when using bait, as opposed to straight plugs—is to present the bait in such a way so as to lay a scent line fish can follow. This scent-based delivery will allow fish to track the smell, following it to its point of origin (the bait). Of course, the better the bait, the greater the likelihood of fish finding it.

No matter what the bait, it can be back-trolled. We've had steady success on eggs, shrimp, a shrimp cocktail, tuna balls, herring strips, and more. The diver can either be attached to a swivel, or hooked on a slider. In most waters I prefer rigging it on a sliding system, so when a fish grabs the bait and takes off with it, there is little resistance against the diver. In shallow, rough water where the diver is hitting the bottom and the chances of hanging up are greater, a fixed position diver can be good, allowing you to better detect if you're hung up.

Leader length can vary from 18 inches to six feet. If targeting fish that are on the move, in shallow water, a shorter leader will allow you to better keep the bait in the target zone. In deeper holes, a longer leader will offer more movement, thus increasing the odds of finding fish that may be suspended off the bottom.

Back-trolling baits can work when back-trolling plain plugs will not. Baits can be topped with any of a number of drift-bobbers, or run alone. As with plugs, back down the presentation at about 1/3 the normal flow of the current. This is a great way to cover water and search for fish, then focusing on those fish once they are located. It's also a great way to appeal to a salmon or steelhead's sense of smell, in addition to sight and sound. It's a very controlled presentation that can be applied in a wide range of waters, one that's worth the effort of mastering.

168. Boondogging

Boondogging paid off for the author (left) and his dad, Jerry Haugen (right). Mike Perusse was the man on the motor who set the tempo of the presentation.

It has many names, but whatever you call it, boondogging, boomdoggin', free-drifting or dragging, there's no disputing the effectiveness of this presentation in certain situations. It works best in rivers with a smooth, gravel bottom, where hangups are minimized. Main currents, seams, side-waters and deep holes are some of the more popular boondogging habitats.

Unlike back-trolling bait, boondogging is a much faster presentation, one where the speed of the bait is moving at the natural flow of the river. Due to the quick nature of this presentation, it's an ideal way to seek out fish. Simply set the boat sideways and have all anglers cast upstream. Keep the boat parallel to the lines, whereby allowing all the presentations to "drag" downstream at equal rates.

Sinkers can be rigged on a sliding system, so resistance is minimal should the fish hit and immediately turn downstream, whereby decreasing the amount of resistance. A fixed sinker set-up on a six-inch dropper will suffice, since the majority of hits are aggressive moves made by fish heading upstream—they can, however, turn and chase it downstream.

A fresh bait, usually firm eggs or eggs tipped with a small herring strip, are good for this method, for they will withstand the punishment this approach can deliver. If the bait is dragging too much, and the hook is getting hung up, try attaching a drift-bobber or slipping a puff ball onto the hook. These will add buoyancy, whereby cutting down on the chance of the hook getting hung-up.

As for the dropper, make it out of lighter line, so when it does get hung, it will easily break off. In waters where hang-ups are many, it's a good idea to have multiple weights pre-rigged, so they can be easily replaced. The quicker you can retie, the quicker you can get that line in the water.

169. Hot Wings With Plugs

One sunny winter day, a buddy and I were back-trolling plugs. The water was still in a recovery stage, and a good bit off-color. We tried switching plug colors, styles and sizes, even adding scents and covering wider swaths of water, but nothing worked. Then we added a flasher.

Tying on a Mack's Lure Hot-Wings (www.mackslure.com), we soon started hitting fish. In this situation, there's no doubt the added flashing of color in the silty water helped draw the attention of fish. Since then, we've used it in similar situations in other rivers, and with good success. It's worked well on both steelhead and salmon, even trout.

Tying the Hot Wings directly to the mainline, then running a three-foot leader off that, the plug can be back-trolled as normal. If pulling small-size plugs in clear water, and feel that they are not pulling deep enough, add an inline sinker above the Hot Wings. If doing this, be sure to use a bead-chain swivel to prevent line twist.

The Hot Wings come in a variety of colors, and as with plugs, have their place in different waters. Which one to use when may come down to personal preference. The mylar wings are very forgiving, rotating under the slightest of pressure. The blades can also be shaped into position to provide a tighter or wider rotation.

The Hot Wings are a prime example of how important it is, and how effective it can be, to have a diversity of gear to enhance your presentation. They can be worked above both back-trolled plugs or bait. They also work on back-bouncing set-ups, be it plugs or bait, that are being delivered.

170. Jumbo Jet Divers

When it comes to back-trolling some plugs, and especially bait presentations, the tendency is to go with smaller divers the more shallow the conditions become. Though this may be applicable in some streams and some settings, many salmon and steelhead rivers are moving so fast, smaller divers can have a hard time digging in and carrying the bait all the way to the bottom. If they aren't digging in, they're not getting down to where the fish are.

Many western rivers are fast moving, yet fairly shallow—say four to ten feet in depth—in places where fish can be found. Salmon will often travel in such water, while steelhead may stage in them. When there, these fish tend to travel and hold tight to the bottom, and success can hinge on whether or not the presentation is placed on their nose. An inch or two can make a real difference here.

If facing situations such as this, where you feel your presentation might be moving overtop fish, try upsizing to a large diver. The one I've had the best success with over the years is the Luhr Jensen Jumbo Jet Diver. These large divers can be found at stores such as G.I. Joe's, as well as other sporting goods supply and tackle shop companies.

Black is my preferred color in clear or green waters, simply because I've experienced salmon coming up and striking the green, red and blue ones. I like the metallic-finished Jumbos in certain conditions, especially murky waters or in high, turbid conditions.

The benefit of these magnum divers is to dig down to the bottom, helping to put the terminal gear smack on the nose of a fish. This diver has worked for us in numerous rivers over the years, and I'm confident, has allowed us to catch fish when nothing else would have worked. Don't be afraid, however, to try other size divers of various colors, as they all work, it's just a matter of finding what works best on any given day.

171. Vary Leader Length Of Divers

Not only can the size, shape and style of diver you choose to use make a difference in reaching fish, but so, too, can the length of the leader. No matter what the size of the diver, leader length plays a major role in where you're actually fishing, depth wise.

For example, a longer leader will move around more behind a diver, while a shorter one will remain consistently behind the diver, and at a more constant depth. If running diver and bait into a hole where you're not sure of the depth, or not sure of the depth at which fish may be hanging, adapt. If, after the first pass you don't hit a fish yet feel confident they are down there, then rerun the drift, this time with a longer or shorter leader.

A longer leader gets tossed around more in the current than a shorter one, and if you want to see if fish are suspended, then top the bait of the longer leader with a drift-bobber. The larger the drift-bobber, the higher in the water column the bait will rise. It will also move side-to-side, but not as much as one might think; of course, just how much it gets tossed around depends on the turbulence of the water and size of the bottom structure being fished.

If wanting to hit specific slots, channels and seams, then a shorter leader will allow you to more precisely reach the desired target water. At the same time, a smaller drift-bobber will cut down on the buoyancy and drag of a bait, allowing an accurate presentation to be made. Assess the situation and don't be afraid to experiment with leader length, it can make a big difference.

172. Plugs As Divers

If looking to add some action to your bait, try substituting a plug as a diver. In doing this, be sure to remove the hooks, then

paint the plug black. I prefer flat black, as this will cut down on the number of strikes the plug receives. Some anglers prefer leaving them colored, using that as a visual attractor. Run a leader length just as you would behind a diver.

The benefits of running plugs as divers are that they offer a more erratic, side-to-side action, which transfers to the bait. At the same time, some plugs feature rattles inside, which helps capture the attention of fish by keying on their auditory senses. You can also put scented pastes on a these—or any divers, for that matter—to help establish a scent line. The only drawback here is that a fish may bite the diver rather than the bait.

Mud Bugs are a favorite of mine, due to their exaggerated movement. They come in 1/4-ounce models which are 3" long, and 5/8-ounce versions that are 3 1/2" long. The larger model dives deeper and with its loud rattle is ideal for salmon. The 1/4-ounce model works well for steelhead, especially in shallow, moderately moving waters. Heavy-water steelheading may require the larger version.

Other plugs such as the Fat Fish, Brad's Wigglers, Hot-n-Tots, Tad Pollys and more, can also be used with effectiveness. Let your imagination go to work and try to figure out which plug may best serve your specific needs. These devices can, and do, work.

173. Detecting Slack-Line Bites

Dave Eng had no trouble detecting the slack-line bite of this fall chinook.

This point is not so much a tip as it is a brief discussion in detecting a bite. But it's worth mentioning because once learned, or recognized, you will catch more fish.

A slack-line bite is most commonly associated with trolling spinners for fall chinook. It happens when a fish approaches the spinner from behind, takes it in its mouth, then continues swimming upstream, taking the weight and all with it. When this happens, rather than feeling the usual tug on the end of the line, it simply goes slack. Because the fish is traveling upstream with the bait in its mouth, the line will go limp, whereby creating slack in the line. When this happens, you have what's called a slack-line bite.

However, that's not to say a slack-line bite won't happen with other presentations. I've experienced slack-line bites while trolling plugs, herring, even drift fishing. Side-drifters experience such bites, too, as the aggressive fish often follows the presentation and continues moving upstream. Whenever a fish grabs the bait and moves toward the angler, whereby pulling the weight with it, there's a chance of experiencing a slack-line bite.

Once the line goes limp, the rod will often relax. At this point many anglers think they are hungup, and they may well be. Hungup or not, as soon as the line relaxes, yank on it. It's better to set the hook on a hangup than chance losing a fish.

Not always does a fish turn on the bait once its taken, whereby creating a viscous strike. Sometimes, though be it on rare occasions, the fish will pick up the bait and keep moving in the same direction. It can happen anywhere, at any time, but no matter how prepared you are, it often catches you by surprise. Once you get tuned-in to detecting these bites, you'll begin to realize how many slack-line bites you may have missed over the years.

174. Timing Casts

One of my biggest pet peeves is fishing with three or more people in a boat, and everyone's casting is out of synch. There's nothing more frustrating than having someone cast ahead of you, forcing you to wait to cast. Whether talking a single hole, or throughout the course of the day, this can cost valued time.

All it takes to get synchronized is communication. Everyone in the boat needs to understand where the casts must fall, where the drift will occur and when the retrieve will come. If there's a clear understanding of these points, the chances of tangling up, missing a strike and losing time while waiting on others, greatly diminishes.

Once rods get crossed—where you're fishing under, around or over fellow anglers—your ability to detect a bite can decline. Not only that, if you are in an awkward position, it can be tough setting the hook, even if you do detect a bite. I've seen rods broken in this way, where a strong hookset found two rods clashing, and busting, due to anglers being out of position.

If the boat is large enough that anglers can spread out, that's even better. If not, and anglers are forced to reach around or over one another, then communicate the plan before making that first cast so as to avoid this mess. In most scenarios, the person on the downriver side should cast first, followed by the next person upstream, then the next, and so on. This ensures that the person at the lowest end of the drift will have their line cleared first, and will result in fewer hangups and increased fishing time.

175. Salmon Bungee

In the trout world we call them snubbers, or rubber snubbers. In the world of salmon fishing, they are refered to as bungees. Salmon Bungees were introduced by Luhr Jensen, just after the turn of the century. They come in black, hot red and chartreuse and their primary function is to soften the bite. Their coloration can also impact fishing success.

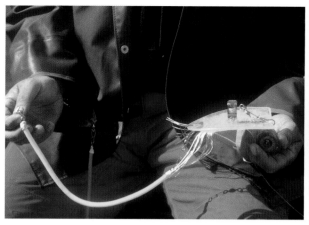

If running divers with a Salmon Bungee, try mixing and matching color schemes. On a past fall salmon trip, I wasn't having any luck on my chartreuse Double Deep Six diver and flame Salmon Bungee. As soon as I switched to a chartreuse bungee, I couldn't keep the salmon away. This has happened on multiple occasions, and it's amazing how changing one simple factor can make or break a day on the water.

The diver and bungee set-up is ideal in high, fast water, when back-trolling bait or hardware. Because the bite can be subtle, especially in high water, the Salmon Bungee is a good tool as it serves as a shock absorber, allowing fish to mouth the bait longer, without meeting immediate resistance. The result of using the Salmon Bungee is a higher hook-to-catch ratio.

If you're having trouble with short strikes while trolling or back-trolling, consider giving a bungee a try. They are rigged in-line, and come with complete, easy-to-follow instructions that will allow for simple assembly. They can be added to diver and bait set-ups, when flatlining plugs or when trolling bait with a sinker and/or flasher set-up. A basic change like this can have a big impact on your season.

176. Hook Placement In Baits

While trolling plug-cut herring one day, we were getting lots of hits, but a very low percentage of hookups. In an effort to boost our hookup rates, we tried changing things until we found something that worked. One of us rehooked the herring in a different way, to achieve a different spin, the other slid the top hook of the double-hook set-up an inch farther up the line and let the trailing hook dangle free. It was the second option that worked and we soon limited out on the fish that had been seemingly striking short all morning.

When it comes to trolling baits, in particular, hook placement can make a big difference. We've even used a trailing hook when fishing large egg clusters for big kings, and caught fish I'm confident we would have otherwise not hooked.

If hits seem to be coming—or not coming—but the hookups aren't happening, try repositioning the hook or hooks to achieve a different movement of the bait. Threading the leading hook of a herring, be it through a fillet or plug-cut, in a slightly different position can speed or slow the spin. In a prawn, hook placement also dictates the amount of spin that's achieved. If running a big shrimp cocktail (sand shrimp and egg combination), then maybe a double-hook set-up will better allow you to present the bait, thus attain more hookups.

The key is trying to make something happen, and this comes through experimentation and change. You won't know unless you try, and asking local anglers for advice can also pay off. Some folks firmly believe that specific deliveries work best on certain rivers; there may be some truth to it, so it's worth a try if your approach doesn't work.

177. Knife Rack

One of the biggest time-savers when on the water is having easy access to such things as knives, scissors, pliers and a file. If you have to dig through your tackle box every time you need one of these tools, or take time out from your fishing to pass an item to a buddy, you're losing valuable time during the course of the day. Instead, make an effort to have them handy and within reach at a moment's notice.

The best set-up I've seen was one crafted for Alumaweld sleds, by Three Rivers Marine (www.3riversmarine.com). They now make them for a wide-range of makes and models of boats. It's a rack that bolts on to the transom, but they can be placed anywhere you wish. The rack is made from white UHMW, a thick plastic material. Carved into the four-inch-wide, ten-inch-long (or whatever size you like) piece are six to eight slots. Each slot is sized to specifically fit the aforementioned tools.

These racks can be screwed on to virtually anywhere you desire, be it in a sled or drift boat, and their size can vary to meet your personal needs. To figure out where one will best meet your needs, assess where you spend the most time in your boat, especially when it comes to fighting and landing fish, and retying riggings. These are the times you most likely need such tools, and having them within easy reach is important. I'm and advocate of having two racks mounted in the boat, one for you, one for the passenger or passengers.

I've found that by having a pair of scissors handy, I'm less likely to bite line with my teeth. At the same time, a file within easy reach will find me sharpening hooks much more frequently. As for pliers, they're always in need and should be easy to access.

178. Cleaning Table

Some sled boats have a built-in cleaning table which goes a long way in saving time at the end of the day. In places where you're able to clean your fish on the water, these tables are slick and save you from having to do the job once home. They allow you to clean fish before getting home, ensuring the quality of the meat. Simply pop them into place and start cleaning. This can be done by one person while another cleans and puts away all the gear. If alone, it beats cleaning them at home, when you feel like doing other things.

These tables typically break down and are stored under a seat, in the fish box or in another storage compartment (it depends on the size and style of your boat). They snap into the gunnel and offer a clean, easy place to process your catch. For drift boaters, a simple cutting board may be all that's needed.

It should be noted that some states and/or rivers prevent the disposal of fish remains back into the water. This was brought on by people cleaning fish at boat ramps, and leaving the guts on the bank, whereby creating foul odors as it rotted. The ugly scene soured attitudes toward anglers. If this rule applies, be sure to take a garbage bag along and dispose of the waste accordingly. You can use the remains for fertilizer or crabbing bait.

In sleds, a washdown pump helps keep things clean. If no washdown pump exists, simply remove and wash with river water. While this tip doesn't necessarily increase your fishing time, it does prevent you from having to take the time to clean fish once you get home, or back to camp. If you're looking to save time after a long day on the water, a portable cleaning table may be worth the investment.

179. Washdown Pumps

Knowing a salmon's sense of smell, every step an angler can take to keep his gear clean will pay off. As soon as a fish hits the deck, the slime they carry and the blood they lose can get everywhere. As bacteria builds up, foul odors can be transferred to terminal gear such as a plug or bait that's laid in the bottom of the boat. By keeping the boat clean, unwanted scents are prevented from spreading.

For every fish that comes into the boat, it's worth washing down the floorboards. When eggs and sardine remains botch the deck, take a minute to wash it clean. On blistering hot days, it's a good idea to wet the deck prior to bringing a slimy fish on board, for once it hits the floor, the slime seems to almost cook in, and can be very difficult to remove.

A washdown pump installed in the back of a sled boat is perfect for keeping the boat clean. In big sleds, installing a second washdown pump toward the front end also helps. Before slime, blood and mud from boots sets-up in the bottom of a boat, these pumps are great for cleaning the surface. Having a bottle of Joy soap and a long-handled scrub brush on-hand is even better. At the end of each day, be sure to thoroughly clean the boat to prevent decaying matter from contaminating gear and the boat on future trips.

180. Rubber Floor Mat

For sled-boat owners who devote a great deal of time to trolling for salmon in shallow water, placing a rubber mat on the floor boards can greatly minimize noise and vibration. Does it allow you to really catch more fish? It's hard to say, as this is one of those impossible-to-measure elements. Who is to say it was a quiet floor versus lure color or trolling speed that elicited the strike? In the mind of the angler, it's one of those aspects that gives a boost of confidence, which really can make a difference in your ability to catch fish.

Fact is, the rubber mat does dampen the sound by way of absorbing vibration, and if you've ever been under the water when a metal boat moves by, the amount of sound it gives off is surprising, especially in shallow, rocky rivers. Noted Northwest and Alaskan guide, Jeremy Toman, has his sled floor covered in 3/4" rubber matting. You can also go with 3/8" material.

The drawback is the amount of weight the rubber adds to the boat, but if you're not running far during a day of fishing, or you have plenty of horsepower, it's really not that bad. When passing over salmon holding in six to eight feet of water, where spinners or baits are being pulled just off the propwash, stealth can be the key to hooking up. Rubber mats are one of those small parts of the overall picture anglers are in control of, so if you fish these types of waters, it can be worth the investment.

181. Zinc Anodes

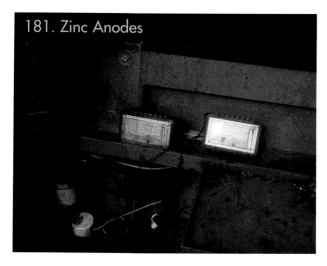

If you spend any time in an aluminum boat fishing bays or estuaries, where salinity levels run high, then zinc anodes are a must. This is another tool that was brought to my attention by Jeremy Toman and his dad, Bob Toman.

Zinc anodes perform multiple functions which will help catch more fish. They also help protect your boat against rust and corrosion. Electrolysis, a chemical change caused by the passage of an electrical current through an electrolyte, can eat away at an aluminum boat as it cruises through salty water. Zinc anodes will ensure the right kind of charge to protect the boat from destructive electrolysis.

At the same time, zinc anodes placed in the metal hull of a boat will help create a low-level positive charge, something that's been scientifically proven to attract fish. The anodes can be welded or bolted to the hull of a boat. Some anglers attach one anode to the underside of the hull and simply set another in the bottom of the boat, where water may pool. Make sure the anodes are kept clean, and this is best done with a stainless-steel or brass-bristled brush. Avoid cleaning the anodes with a steel-bristled brush, as this will cut down on their overall performance levels. The cleaner the anodes, the greater their likelihood of producing an electrical charge that appeals to salmon and simultaneously helps protect your boat.

182. Wash Oar Handles

Oar handles are a bacterial trap. Sweat and oil from your hands are easily transferred to oar handles. Residue from baits, grease, gas cans, clothes, food, fish slime, blood and everything else we touch will build-up on oar handles, no matter what material they are made of. Even when wearing rubber gloves, unwanted residues can be transferred to the oar handles, then likely relayed to baits, something the fish will detect.

Over time the build-up of these obtrusive smells will accrue, and no doubt be transferred to baits, lures and plugs when fishing. Taking a moment to clean the handles several times a day can make a difference. Keeping a bottle of lemon-scented Joy dishwashing soap in the boat makes it easy for frequent washing of the grips. At the end of the trip, make sure to wash them thoroughly to avoid bacterial build-up.

To help ensure oar handles are kept clean, it's a good idea to have plenty of dry, clean rags to start the day. This will encourage you to keep things clean the whole day long, but be sure to wash the rags at day's end, so they'll be clean and ready for the next trip.

Once the handles become dried and encrusted, it can be very difficult to get them clean. Stay on top of things and keep the handles clean—especially on hot days—along with the rest of the boat. The result will be a cleaner boat that does not harbor offending smells, and a less likely chance of contaminating baits.

183. Secure Oarlocks

Standing along the banks of Oregon's famed Rogue River, I watched as a drift boat picked its way through the head end of some whitewater. Pivoting the boat into position, the oarsman struck a rock with one oar. Instantly the oarlock shot out; the boater didn't have a chance. The boat, fishing tackle and all their gear was lost, as was a prized dog. It could have been worse, yet the whole thing could have been prevented if the oarlock would have been securely fastened.

No matter what type of river you run a drift boat in, make sure the oarlock is secured at the bottom. This is easily done by

running a pin or bolt through the eye at the bottom of the post of the oarlock. It won't keep the oarlock from pivoting, but from popping out through the top. The goal is to keep the oar and the oarlock in place at all times, so pinpoint maneuvering can be done.

Not only is clipping the oarlocks in place a major safety precaution, but it can lead to a better day of fishing, especially when pumping on the oars in fast water, say for plugging or back-trolling diver and bait. If an oar does pop out, it's usually in rough water, often when trying to jockey the boat into position to work a prime fishing hole. Secure your oarlocks and maybe even take it the extra step to carry a backup should one snap.

184. Extra Oar

One of the biggest safety precautions a drift-boater can take is having an extra oar on-board at all times. This can save your life, and if an oar is lost early on a trip, it can make or break the fishing experience. Ever since I was a kid, Dad always taught

me to have an extra oar in the boat, and I have, just like he has. I've seen what not having an extra oar on-hand can be like, and it's not pretty.

If cost is a factor, it's not necessary to go with top-of-the-line oars that may serve as your primary pair. Some brands of oars detach at the middle, making stowing them easier, but if you get one of these, make certain it's assembled prior to launching the boat.

If fishing or running through rough water, you never know what circumstances may unfold, leaving you reliant upon that extra oar. I've seen boats flip over, helplessly drift downstream in heavy water and get smashed into rootwads and rocks because the oarsman neglected to have an extra oar on hand. Many of the accidents I've seen could have been prevented had an extra oar been handy.

Hopefully you'll never need it. If you've ever had the experience of popping an oar or splitting one, it's not fun, and it takes no convincing for you to carry an extra. If you haven't, good, I hope it stays that way, but please, have that extra on-hand, just in case.

185. Rasp Oar Ropes

It was a calm, sunny day, and we were some 500 yards ahead of the next boat. Pumping the oars to get through a long stretch of frog-water, it was quiet and peaceful. Stopping to admire a pair of Canadian geese, a loud, screeching sound caught our ear. It took several seconds to figure out what it was. It emanated from the boat above us, and echoed every time he pulled on the oars.

The high-pitched, loud, screeching sound easily carried through the river valley. If it carried that far above water, there's no doubting some of the sound was transferred through the water. The conditions were tough; extremely low and clear water, which made it very challenging to find cooperative fish.

We ended up with four bright steelies, but worked hard for them. The boat behind us didn't have so much as a bite. They were using the same method we were, and I couldn't help but wonder if their squeaky oars were the cause.

Sounds travel from the oars, down the side of the boat and into the water, and this is something I believe fish can sense. It could possibly have been that the cause of their misfortune was due, to the loud oars. I've heard of other boaters having this problem, not hooking fish, then fixing their oars only to find immediate success.

When you've worn your oar ropes to the point they are flat, hard and screechy, take a rasp and rough them up. Run the large-toothed rasp over every bit of hard, compressed rope. Not only will this eliminate the annoying sound, but it will give you better oar control. It only takes a few minutes, and is worth the effort.

186. No Knot In End Of Anchor Rope

It was a high-water year. The fish were in but the river conditions were tough, both for fishing and navigating. Above us, a boat ran the rapids we'd just gone through. As they zigged and zagged through rough water, dodging boulders and boils, their anchor popped out of the davit. The boat was in too tight of

quarters to do anything about it, and the oarsman had no choice but to focus his attention on navigating while the anchor line freely fed out...until it reached the end.

At the end of the anchor rope there was a knot, and as soon as it caught in the last pulley, it sucked the back end of the boat down. It immediately filled with water. It's scary how fast it can happen, and fortunately all this guy lost was his boat and some gear. Other boaters haven't been so fortunate.

It may seem like a trivial thing, but if you've ever had it happen to you, or seen it happen, getting an anchor hung in fast water—where you can literally do nothing about it—can be more than humbling. To avoid the dangers of catching an anchor and risking capsizing the boat, do not tie a knot in the end of your anchor rope. Anchor rope and an anchor is cheap compared to the price of a boat, your gear, and the lives of the boaters involved.

The only benefit of having a knot in the end of the anchor rope is if the line accidentally gets let out, whereby a knot can save your anchor. But if you're paying attention, this rarely, if ever, happens. The alternative is to keep the end of the anchor rope knot-free, in case it gets hung and you can't get it loose in a sticky situation. It's a basic precaution, and can save more than just fishing time, it can save lives.

187. Extra Anchor/Anchor Net

If you have ever lost an anchor early in the trip, you know it can ruin a day's fishing. It's not the end of the world, but the loss of an anchor can keep you from fishing specific waters and various techniques that could very likely cost you fish. The alternative is to take an extra anchor along, or an anchor net.

I'll often have a bow anchor, only weighing about 10 pounds, that serves as a fair backup should the need arise. It's lighter than what I'd prefer, but in a pinch it can be made to work. An alternative can be to carry another, full-size anchor, but that much added weight in the boat is hard to justify for the few

anchors you may actually lose in a lifetime of fishing. Some folks never lose an anchor, while I know of other's who have lost two in as many days. It's all a matter of chance.

If you don't want the hassle of carrying a second anchor, there's a nifty device which works well in a pinch. It's a mesh bag that holds a wide range of various-sized river rocks. The bag easily attaches on to the end of your anchor rope and takes up virtually no space in the boat. And, of course, it weighs next to nothing.

With the anchor net, all you have to do is fill it with rocks, or a rock, of the size you desire, attach it to the anchor rope and get back to fishing. At the end of the day, empty the bag. It's simple, economical and can, no doubt, turn a gloomy day of fishing into a productive one. This uniquely designed bag is available at www.jonescalls.com, and is one of the many outdoor-related items this company continues to offer.

188. Freeing A Hung Anchor

Position is important when trying to free a hung anchor.

If you do have an anchor that gets hung-up, there are efforts you can make to help free it. However, the key is knowing when to give up. You do not want to risk losing a boat, or human lives, for a chunk of lead.

That said, how you go about freeing an anchor depends on what type of water it's hung in, and how much room you have to work with. If it's as simple as rowing or running upstream to lift from a different angle, dislodging an anchor can be quick and easy. If, however, it's in fast, turbulent water, the remedy may not be so direct.

In fast-water situations, be sure that whatever you do, the boat remains balanced. This means avoid short-lining the anchor rope, which causes sudden shifts of the boat, especially as you move toward the back end to lift and maneuver the rope.

If you can't row above the hung anchor and work from there, the next best bet may be to add additional rope. Simply run the existing anchor rope through the last eye, pulley or davit, and tie on another section of rope. I carry an extra 100' section for such emergencies. The added length of rope should allow you to row toward the bank, out of the main current, then back upstream, above the hung anchor. In smaller rivers, the additional rope may allow you to reach the bank, and try working the hung anchor free from a safe position off the shore. Working from the upstream side of the hung anchor is usually the best, and safest, position from which to free it.

As a final resort, you may need to cut the anchor rope. I've seen several folks get their anchor hung and not be able to get it free, whereby they simply tossed all their anchor rope overboard. This creates potential hangups for fellow anglers, so try to avoid littering the river with heavy anchor rope. Instead, cut it as close to the water as possible. Don't risk leaning over the back of the boat in rough water, simply cut at the safest point which will allow you to retain the most rope.

189. Boat Heaters

Thank goodness, those good old days of winter fishing are gone. Hands, toes and face turned so numb you could hardly articulate any of them. Back then, a bucket of briquettes served as the sole source of heat, and it was barely enough to get the job done. Today, with the advent of high-tech boat designs, fancy heating systems and even portable heaters, a cold day on the water can be much more comfortable.

When you pick out a boat, consider all the potential conditions under which you might fish. If cold days will be spent in pursuit of winter steelhead or fall chinook, then it's worth investing a few extra dollars to be more comfortable, whereby increasing your fishing time. Heating systems can be installed in many boats. They can range from running multiple heaters off one propane tank, to dedicating each heater to a specific tank. They can be run from the oarsman's chair to both passenger seats in a drift boat, to wherever you desire in a sled boat.

If having permanent heaters installed in your boat concerns you, or you don't think you'll be using them enough, then perhaps the portable heaters are for you. Coleman makes a line of portable heaters that are very fuel efficient, light weight, easy to use and get the job done. They run off small propane cans that are easy to replace. These heaters work well in any boat as well as off the bank, if building a fire is not an option.

At the very least, equip yourself with multiple hand-warmers, to help take off that cold edge. On bone-chilling days, the warmer your body, the more fishing you'll get done.

190. Depth Finders

An increasing number of salmon and steelhead anglers are discovering the value of a depth finder. Trout anglers have been using them for years, but these devices have a place in river fishing as well.

One key feature of this valued piece of equipment is not only its ability to find fish, but also to help learn the anatomy of the bottom, so you can determine where fish will travel and hold. Determining an accurate depth-reading of holes being fished allows you to better prepare for the presentations you plan on delivering. It may require a different sinker set-up to best cover the water, or an alteration of terminal gear.

In holes, this tool can help you find the fish. In big, deep salmon holes, finding where the fish are laying can be an invaluable lesson. You may discover the fish actually suspend there, rather than hugging the bottom, so you will have to adjust your approaches accordingly. Fish finders are also effective for tracking the movement of fish in such holes. This tells you not only where fish are moving to and from, but in which direction the current may be flowing, thus what the best angle will be to present your bait.

Some anglers have a depth finder running in their boat at all times. This allows them to track the movement of fish throughout the day and try to put some reasoning as to where they are moving and why. Correlate these movements with such factors as water temperature, weather conditions, barometric pressure and more, and you can see that these devices do serve a need in helping catch more fish.

Other anglers may use a depth finder but once a year on any given river. The approach here is to chart (or memorize) the anatomy of specific holes and keep that in mind throughout the season. Some anglers like taking a test run, prior to the start of the season, to focus efforts on operating the depth finder in order to learn if the bottom structure has changed in any form over the course of the year. However you choose to apply them, there's no question depth finders can help increase your knowledge of a river, and your ability to catch more fish.

191. Prearrange Shuttles

If fishing alone, or taking only one vehicle to the river, finding a shuttle rig to take you back to the launch site is a necessity, unless walking or biking is an option. Having a prearranged shuttle not only keeps your mind at ease, but it can increase your fishing time. Knowing that your rig will be at the take-out when you arrive means you can spend more time fishing, which is the ultimate goal.

Often-times anglers figure they'll just catch a ride back to the launch once they reach the take-out. Usually this works fine, but on the times it doesn't it can be very frustrating. On those slow days when you want to keep fishing in order to take meat home, you may find yourself wanting to fish right up until dark. Such extended fishing can make for a potentially dangerous hitchhiking or biking situation, and it takes the pressure off if your rig is already waiting for you.

Many area fisheries, even rural ones, offer a form of shuttle service. Check with local tackle shops, gas stations, markets and even diners to see what they have to offer, or if they can point you in the direction of someone who does operate a nearby shuttle service.

The prices for a shuttle are usually fairly reasonable, considering how much time it can potentially save you on the river. But whether or not you choose to utilize a shuttle service comes down to personal preference and your fishing situation. The question you have to ask yourself is, "Will getting a shuttle increase my fishing time?" If the answer is yes, you know what the next step is.

192. Drop Bike For Shuttle

A shuttle option that offers independence is dropping a bike at your designated place of take-out. This means that when you arrive at the ramp, you can bike your way back to the launch site. Such is a great option if wanting to work on your own timeline and not worry about whether or not someone was able to shuttle your vehicle. It can also help save costs where shuttle fees are exorbitant.

I've been in situations where, within minutes of fishing, I was tagged out, called it a morning and pushed to the take-out. There I had the mountain bike waiting for me, and I could peddle back to the launch at my leisure. Had I been forced to wait for a shuttle rig, there's no telling how long I could have been there.

On your way upriver, simply drop a bike at your designated take-out. Be sure to securely lock the bike so no one steals it, passing the chain through the frame and both tires. Even better, lock the bike frame and remove the front wheel (perhaps the back one, too) and toss in the boat with you. This ensures no one will cut the chain and ride off with the bike.

Another option is to simply toss the bike into the back of the boat. This allows you to take out at whichever ramp you choose. You may tag out early and want to pull out at the first ramp. Then

again, you may want to keep fishing if there's nothing in the box by the time you reach the first take-out. If fishing with a buddy and you tag-out early, you can stop right there; one of you riding the bike back up to the launch, the other rowing the boat to the take-out. It's a great time-saver.

Of course, biking back to the launch may not be for everyone. The country may be too steep, or maybe it's a long haul. Perhaps the path back leads along a dangerous highway. Whatever the situation, and your personal circumstances, evaluate it all and see if there's a benefit to using your own shuttle bike.

193. Team-Up First Time Down

The first time you make a run down a river, it's a good idea to team-up with someone who has already done it. This is especially true for novice boaters who are learning how to operate a boat, as well as read water.

When it comes to boating, there's no substitute for experience, and the more time you spend on the water, the more proficient of a boater and angler you'll become. But the first time down a river or stretch of river cannot only find you questioning the best routes to take, but also scratching your head as to where the prime fishing spots may be.

I know of guys who've been fishing the same river for five years, even longer, who have never caught a salmon or steelhead from it. This may not be due to their lack of fishing knowledge, rather their inability to read water and recognize where fish will be moving or holding on any given day.

One of the greatest aspects of fishing is that there is always so much to learn, and the more knowledge seasoned anglers can share with newcomers, the better chance we have of preserving our sport and carrying it on to future generations. If new to boating, it's worth the time and effort to seek out assistance to help guide you down the river.

Speaking of guides, some guides will hire out, teaching you how to run a river, read water and even educate you on proven fishing techniques. If contacting a guide to inquire about such an option, be sure to be up-front with them; tell them you're a boat owner and are looking to learn how to run a river and read water. They may require a minimum number of trips to fit in all the lessons, even tack on some added costs due to the extra level of involvement on their end, so be precise in what you're looking for. Note, not all guides offer such services, so it may take some searching to find what you desire.

194. Good Nets

It may not seem like it's that big of a deal, but having a good net is a luxury worth investing in. Look for a net that has a big hoop, is weighted to allow the mesh to sink as it's plunged beneath the surface, and has a sturdy handle to withstand the weight and tenacity of big fish.

Some people prefer nylon mesh, others like polypropylene. The kind of basket material you choose comes down to personal preference, so take time in researching what's out there and find the one that best suits your needs.

If you do a lot of angling, it may be worth investing in two nets, keeping both in the boat when the action is hot. There are

times when big fall chinook come into a system, and hooking up doubles are common. These are big, strong fish, and when you have an opportunity to get them to the boat, you want to take it. I've seen several fish, and heard of numerous others being lost, where two fish were hooked, they both came to the boat at the same time but only one could be netted at a time. By the time they got the fish untangled and out of the net, the other fish got off. It's a low percentage deal, but can happen, and I know guys who will carry two nets during peak seasons for this reason.

It should be noted here that when you net a salmon or steelhead, close the mouth of the net so the fish cannot escape, then *pull* the fish into the boat. Avoid lifting straight up on an open net, for fear of breaking the hoop from the handle and losing the fish; I've seen it done many times. Buy the best net you can afford, treat it right and have fun catching fish.

195. Seal Boat Bottom

Applying a protective coating to the bottom of your boat not only guards it from deterioration, but it allows the craft to more easily slide over rocks and can even make it more efficient to handle in the water. If you've ever been in an unsealed boat, and stuck on rocks or a partially exposed gravel bar, it can be frustrating, especially because valuable fishing time is lost.

For years, Gluvit was used, and still is by many boaters, to seal and protect the bottom of their boats. More recently, however, Coat-It, a specialty waterproof epoxy sealer that is impressively abrasion resistant thanks to reinforced Kevlar fibers, has been proving very effective for boat owners. Coat-It is cost efficient, lasts and performs well under rugged punishment.

Another sealing alternative I've heard good reports of, though have not personally used, is spray-on bed liners. Simply sand down the bottom of your boat, then take it in to any of the companies that spray bed liners into trucks (call ahead of time to confirm specific directions they may have). They can spray a thin layer over the bottom of your boat, and people I know of who've had it done say they would never go back to anything else. They even had their oar tips sprayed for further protection. According to the people I know who have used the spray-on sealer, their boat moves easily over rocks, glides smoothly in the

water and withstands all the punishment they care to put their boat through.

Whatever protective coating you choose to use, make sure your boat is coated prior to its maiden voyage. The protection these coatings offers will prolong the life of your boat, guaranteed, as well as improve your overall operating efficiency.

196. Kicker Or Trolling Motor

If fishing from a drift boat, one of the best ways to cover water, especially dead water, is with a motor. Once you've drifted through a stretch of water, and want to return to where the drift started, it can be painstaking to row your way back up. Firing-up the motor and heading back upstream can be a huge time-saver.

At the same time, if you're done fishing a stretch of water and needing to head through a long stretch of dead, unfishable water, a motor can make that happen much quicker. The idea is to cut down on your travel time, whereby increasing your fishing time.

You can either use a small kicker motor or go the electric route. Note that if going with the gas kicker, you will need a certified license in some states. That's why many anglers are switching to the high-power electrics, like Minkota's Maxim Pro80. For this big-thrust beast, you'll need two 12-volt batteries mounted on the transom. You can easily install a small onboard charger, which makes it easy to plug and recharge at day's end.

Not only are these small motors great for covering water, but they are very effective for applying certain fishing techniques, namely side-drifting and free-drifting. Being able to use a small motor, rather than pumping on the oars all day, definitely saves wear and tear on the body, and likely increases your fishing time. There's no question in how much time these pieces of luxury save when moving through dead water, making them what could be the most efficient time-saver in this book, depending on where you fish and how.

197. Propeller Guard

If you are running boats up and down the river, or using the motors to fish with as in side-drifting, it's a good idea to invest in a propeller guard. For the added protection of a propeller, it's worth investing the extra money in a stainless-steel version that lasts forever, not the plastic ones that can bend, flex and break. One day these prop' guards may become mandatory in the U.S., more geared toward recreational water-sports enthusiasts to protect people from becoming entangled in the blades.

But anglers will want the prop' guard for the protection it offers the blade and the overall stress on the motor. Running over gravel and rocks can wear blades down, even sheer a pin, which can result in the prop falling off the drive shaft.

Prop' guards come in a variety of shapes and sizes, so find what best fits your needs. It could be a simple plate, a series of plates or a round guard that surrounds the outside of the propeller blades. There's even a cage that attaches to the unit and protects the whole prop' system.

The more the propeller blades wear down, the less force they have. The less force they have the longer it takes to get where you're going. If you fish amid any rocky areas, a prop' guard is worth the investment simply for the time, and money, it will save you over years of extended use.

198. Be Quiet

Buzz Ramsey and Nick Amato doing what they do best.

Sound carries and can scare fish. It's as simple as that. I recall when aluminum boats first came out and many anglers were reluctant to use them, claiming they would be too noisy—remember, I was raised on the Mckenzie River, home of the original wooden McKenzie River drift boat, where change can come slow.

Over time this theory has faded, and now you're hard-pressed to see many wood boats on the water, even on the McKenzie. The upkeep of aluminum boats and their overall strength have made them a dominant force in the fishing industry, no question. But that doesn't mean we can get careless.

When in an aluminum boat, or any boat for that matter, make a conscious effort to keep noise to a minimum. Sound carries a long way, especially under water. In fact, sound travels faster through water than through air, due to its more dense substrate. This means that the quieter you are, the less likelihood you have of spooking fish.

Keeping quiet is especially important when fishing conditions are tough, where the water is low and clear. If sight-fishing, keeping quiet is even more vital, where stealth is the rule. From footsteps to moving gear around to squeaking and clanging parts and toning down loud vibrations, make sure all sounds are kept to a minimum if trying to put the move on fish without alerting them to your presence. It takes some effort, but can make the difference in the number of fish you catch come day's end.

199. Bilge Pump

We were in a small boat off Kodiak Island one day. It started out clear, but by noon a major rainstorm hit. Of course, we had taken out the bilge pump, which was a harebrained thing to do in Alaska. The craft filled so quickly with water, it took two of us scooping as quickly as possible to keep from sinking. It was touch-and-go for a while. We made it back to the mothership, with several gallons of water in the bottom of our boat. What I would have given for that bilge pump.

When fishing in situations where rain is possible, it's a good idea to have a hand-bilge pump on board. It's even a good idea to have one along on hot sunny days, should you take on water and need to get rid of it. Running heavy rapids, accidentally taking on water over the side or getting a crack in the boat are possibilities, and having a bilge pump on-hand to help remove the water is a big time-saver.

Jet sleds with a built-in bilge are perfect, for the flick of a switch does the work for you. Whatever boat you have, be sure there's some form of bilge, for there's nothing more frustrating than using empty pop cans, water bottles or small containers to empty excess water from a boat. Not only does it take a great amount of time, it takes away from your fishing.

200. Spare Tire On Trailer

Heading to launch the boat in the wee hours of the morning, we happened upon a fellow angler, stranded along the side of the rural road. He was alone, and miles from the nearest little town. He towed a drift boat, the trailer of which had a flat tire. He had no spare.

His dilemma was whether or not to leave the boat, take the tire and get it fixed, or just wait for someone to take it and get it fixed for him. His little truck, without a canopy, was too small to store his gear, lifejackets and oars, and he didn't want to leave his boat and gear for fear of having it stolen. It wouldn't have been an issue had he carried a spare.

Many boats don't come with a spare tire. Make sure to get one immediately upon purchase of the boat. Don't wait, you may forget, and by that time it could be too late, costing you a day's fishing at the very least.

You can get a spare tire with brackets that mount directly to the trailer, or simply pick up a spare and toss it in the back of the truck. Either way, be sure to have a spare on hand. I've seen too many instances over the years where anglers have neglected to get a spare trailer tire and it resulted in the loss of a fishing day, or at least missing the prime hours of the day. It's a small investment in preventative maintenance, one that's worth it.

201. Lock Boat Trailer

One of the most helpless feelings there is on the river is pulling up to the boat ramp only to discover your boat trailer has been stolen. Though I've not personally had it happen to me—knock on wood—I've seen it happen to fellow anglers. It puts a sick feeling in your stomach, and I hope it's not the result of "fellow anglers" committing the crime, rather lowlifes in need

of money. I can't imagine an angler ever stealing anything from another person, but it happens with tackle all the time, so why not a trailer?

To help prevent a trailer from being stolen, get a lock for it. A lock usually slips through the tongue latch, though depending on the hole size there, you may need to get a cable and lock it to the tow frame on the truck.

Obviously, this is more a time-saver tip for getting home, then again, if you happened to push through a run quickly, in hopes of making another run, it can cost you a half-day's fishing or more if the trailer disappears. It's worth investing a few extra dollars in a quality lock, to help prevent your property from being stolen.

Even with a trailer lock in place, make every effort to park near a road, under a street light or somewhere where people can easily see your rig. Be sure to have the trailer's serial number recorded so you can immediately report it should the unfortunate situation arise where it does get stolen.

202. Pontoon Boats

Many streams and low-water situations are simply too small to work a drift boat through. Add the fact that bank fishing is not an option due to being surrounded by private property, and access instantly becomes limited. But things can be saved with a pontoon boat.

Pontoon boats have opened up many great opportunities for anglers to access and explore streams and stretches of rivers they otherwise would not be able to. The fact these crafts are so lightweight, portable and easy to maneuver in low-water conditions make them ideal for increasing your fishing time.

When investing in a pontoon boat, ask yourself where you'll be using it, how often and for which species? There are many makes and models now on the market, and you can definitely find one that will meet most of your needs. Once purchased, be sure to organize your gear so as to get the utmost from your fishing experience.

Due to some of the dangers involved in drifting many small West Coast streams, it's advisable to team-up with a buddy when fishing from pontoon boats. In the event that a mishap should occur, it's always comforting to have help nearby, especially since much pontoon boat fishing takes place in waters that are set off the beaten path.

Open your eyes and mind to what's out there and you'll be surprised at the number of ways there are to increase your fishing opportunities, thus maximize your time on the water. Use these tools enough and in no time they'll pay for themselves in the form of fish. Besides, who wants to spend money on buying fish at the market when you can invest it in toys to help catch them?

Whether fishing from a boat or off the bank, there are certain measures that can be taken to help not only increase your fishing time, but the chance of catching more fish. Some of these are simple changes, others require forethought prior to heading to the river.

In any case, it comes down to having an open mind and the discipline to make the necessary changes to make something happen. One of the hardest things for anglers to do, especially ones who have been fishing for years, is try something new. This is understandable, for why fix it if it isn't broken?

Chapter 4   On the River

On the other hand, how will you ever learn better, more effective techniques if you don't experiment? With so many new inventions in the world of fishing, doors are continually being opened to trying new things; new approaches that may catch fish better than anything ever tried before.

Trying something new takes time, and having confidence in what you choose to apply definitely plays a factor in your ability to catch fish. But with an open mind and a willingness to try new approaches, you can catch more fish.

203. Scent Use

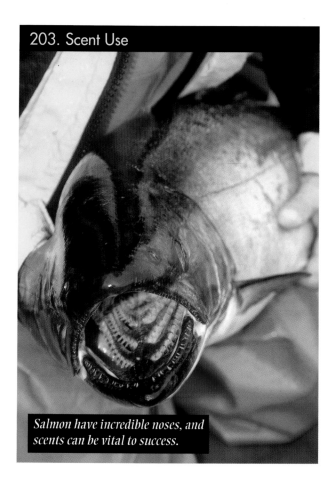

Salmon have incredible noses, and scents can be vital to success.

Since the 1990s, scent products have taken the salmon fishing industry to another level. I literally cannot count the number of fish that I've caught over the years that I believe were taken due to the scent being used. Even in the egg cure I grew up using as a kid, anise oil, the primary scent in the recipe, was always present and I feel, played a major role in the bait's ability to catch fish—it still does today.

But scents have progressed so much, and continue to improve and expand every year, that there's no question they are a key component in catching more fish, especially salmon. Salmon have a sense of smell measured in parts-per-billion, so their noses are, or should be, key targets for anglers. The more, and perhaps more variety, of scents we can offer fish, the greater our odds of catching them.

Scents can be applied to any terminal gear you fish. They can be mixed in to egg cures during the curing process, or added later. They can be injected into shrimp, herring, crawdads and more. The sticky pastes can be applied to lures and plugs, without washing away. They can even be spread onto drift-bobbers and rubbed into yarn to help carry scent to fish.

No matter what flavor scent you use or what you use it on, remember, you are delivering smell to a fish and want to do it in a way so they can find it. This means laying a scent trail that travels downstream in a consistent path so fish can detect it, follow it and snatch the bait. This is why plunking, back-bouncing and back-trolling plugs are so effective when using scents, because they are either in one position or moving downstream in a constant, steady path where fish can track them.

If you've yet to jump on the scent craze, do it. Our sport is growing ever more competitive and these scents can give you the upper hand needed to catch more fish.

204. Larson Lures

About the time this book was being written, Larson Lures was starting to make their way into the fishing market. I hope they stay around, or at least their concept, because they have many cutting-edge innovations, something that's not easy to come by in this day and age.

One of the most impressive lures they developed is the scent body spinner. The hollow body consists of two threaded parts, with strategically placed holes angled to perfection. The great thing about these lures, besides their state-of-the-art-design and striking paint jobs, is the fact that scents can be placed inside the body chamber (you can also add lead shot too for more weight). Simply take a small piece of foam, coat it with your scent of choice, place it inside the body and screw the two-part body together.

As the lure is fished, water passes through the holes, dispersing the scent. The first time I used this for coho salmon in Alaska, I was hooked. I was fishing with three other buddies, and all used different lures. Using a scent-bodied spinner packed with sardine Smelly Jelly, I hooked four fish before any of them got so much as a bite. I became a fast believer in these lures and see them making an indelible mark in this industry.

The scent-body lure also comes designed with a spinner blade in the middle, to add more action, color and to help disperse scent. Larson Lures also has an impressive line of vibrating-type spinners that are among the most effective I've ever used. To learn more about these lures and keep up with their latest innovations, visit www.larsonlures.com.

205. Fool-A-Fish

Another new product that was making a mark in the fishing world just prior to this book being penned was Fool-A-Fish. Fall chinook anglers, in particular, have found Fool-A-Fish to be effective, but I've also had good success on springers, as well as summer-run kings in Alaska.

Though Fool-A-Fish has proven particularly successful on an array of presentations, reports I've heard from fall chinook anglers is that it really paid-off when applied to herring, or other forms of baitfish being used. In a spray form, Fool-A-Fish creates a polymer film on the bait, a film which reflects a high percentage of the ultraviolet light, something fish are reportedly capable of seeing and are attracted to.

It's one of those products like scents, that can be tough to use for the first time simply because you question its effectiveness, being a new product and all. However, you never know unless you try. The first time I used it on cured salmon eggs for kings, I didn't see much difference when compared to fellow anglers in the boat. But I stuck with it, and by the middle of the day was outfishing my buddies three-to-one. They all started applying the spray to both eggs and sardine chunks, and catching fish. In this instance I'm a firm believer it resulted in our catching more salmon, for it seemed to turn on the bite when other things wouldn't. To learn more, visit www.foolafish.com.

206. Toothpaste To Polish Spinners

When pulling spinners, the blades can pick up scum from the water or algae, whereby degrading their sheen and overall reflection value. In salt water, the salt can be hard on the spinner, tarnishing the blades and inhibiting their overall effectiveness.

To help keep the blades shiny and working to their full potential, many anglers wash them with a scrub brush and soap. However, they can be hard to get clean with soap and water. This is where toothpaste can make a big difference, for the little grains of grit do a great job in breaking down scum and salt-water residue.

Simply squirt a dab of toothpaste on each side of the spinner blade and work it around with your thumb and forefinger. The more aggressive your rubbing, the better the toothpaste works at polishing the blade. The more you work it in, the more dull the blade becomes, due to the makeup of the toothpaste. But once you've thoroughly scrubbed the entire blade, wash the toothpaste away with water and you'll see its effectiveness.

Using toothpaste to polish lures is a concept that's been around for years. The reassuring thing, it works, and is still used by many of old-timers who believe in it, and catch lots of fish because of it. As for which flavor or which brand of toothpaste to use, I've not heard any conclusions drawn on that. The simple form of toothpaste seems to get the job done just fine.

207. Vary Bait Size

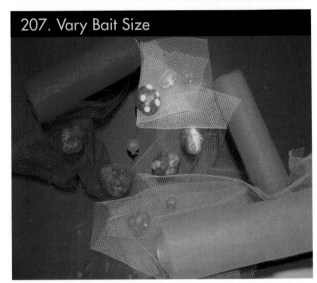

If you find yourself on the river and are confident fish are around, but they aren't biting, it's time to change things around until you find what they like. One of the simplest changes that often goes overlooked is varying your bait size. Whether it's eggs, shrimp, sardines, drift-bobbers, even hooks: changing the size of your delivery can make a difference.

Whatever size you're fishing, if the strikes aren't coming, try using either larger or smaller baits. If focusing on big kings, I tend to progress toward larger baits. Kings have big mouths and incredible noses which means those senses need to be targeted. A larger bait is not only easier for fish to see, it also holds more scent and dyes, something that can appeal to big fish.

If fishing shy steelhead in shallow water, downsizing the bait may be the ticket. Rather than fishing a whole sand shrimp, try using only the tail. If you've been using a quarter-sized egg cluster on a 2/0 hook, try only a few eggs on a size-1 or size-2 hook.

When up or downsizing baits, be sure to match the drift-bobber to the hook size being used. Too large of drift-bobbers cover the point of the hook, and too small of ones may not provide enough lift to keep the bait off the bottom.

Once you find what size bait the fish like, keep with it. You may wish to continue up or downsizing in the direction you were going, to see if what you have to offer can be made even more appealing. It sounds like a simple concept, and it is, but it's one that's underutilized by many anglers. The great part is, it does work.

208. Bait Changes

Not only is altering the *size* of your bait important, but changing the *kind* of bait you're using can be just as, if not more, critical. In those times when fish are around, but not biting, try offering them a different bait.

The change may come in the form of a simple egg cure, say offering fish a red borax-based cure rather than hot-orange sodium sulfite-based cure. Then again, a bait change can be more complex. Two of the most effective bait changes I've seen while fishing for salmon involved starting with eggs, and moving to shrimp and sardines. In both cases, the eggs were kept on, just downsized to make room for the full sand shrimp to be threaded on the hook. The same was true for the sardine, which was cut in a small chunk and slid over the tip of the hook and let to hang in the bend of the hook.

Both of these changeups have proven very effective for me over the years, in a variety of waters. In fact, they've been so successful that there's no question in my mind it was the bait change which resulted in fish being caught.

Other times you may want to switch out baits, all together. Maybe eggs or shrimp, alone, aren't getting the job done, so you go to a prawn. Perhaps a plug-cut herring isn't working like you'd planned, so you go to trolling a strip or fillet. Changing bait is one of the elements we, as anglers, have control over, so why not resort to it when the bite's slow, and do what you can to help turn things on?

209. Drift-bobber Changes

Sometimes changing the bait isn't good enough. Often a change may need to take place in parts. If a bait change didn't work try something else, maybe a longer or shorter leader, more weight, fluorocarbon leader; the list goes on. But one of the most basic changes that really can make a difference is that of the drift-bobber. It's critical, however, to first understand what drift-bobbers do, before experimenting with them.

Drift-bobbers come in many designs, sizes and colors. They add color, movement and shape to baits. Some also add buoyancy.

Some have wings, some are round. Some are painted, others metallic. The variations are many, and they work when fished with bait as well as fished alone.

Once you know what you wish to accomplish by changing drift-bobbers, then you can experiment away. Perhaps the water is off-color. In this case, maybe going to a winged drift-bobber, like a Flashing and Spinning Cheater or Spin-N-Glo will get the job done. Maybe upsizing a Corky or going to a different colored presentation is what it takes. It could be you want more lift on your bait, to target semi-suspended fish, thus go to a larger drift-bobber to elevate that bait higher off the bottom.

The point is, change can be a good thing, and you never know what will work unless you try. Invest in a wide-range of drift-bobbers, in color, size and shape. But don't be afraid to use them. You will likely find that some colors and styles work better on one particular river than another. It's an interesting facet of the sport, and one worth delving into, for changing drift-bobbers can make a difference in the number of fish you actually catch.

210. Stacking Drift-bobbers

In addition to experimenting with drift-bobber color and design change, there's another option that can work really well. I've had good success with this approach on both salmon and steelhead, and it has to do with using multiple drift-bobbers rather than just one.

Stacking drift-bobbers on top of one another not only adds buoyancy, causing the bait to ride a bit higher off the bottom, it also creates more visibility and movement, so the presentation can be more easily seen by fish. The manner in which drift-bobbers can be stacked is only limited by the imagination.

You can stack a pair of the same-size drift-bobbers, say small sizes for steelhead, larger ones for salmon. You can also stack a degree of sizes, say from smaller versions close to the hook, to larger ones on top. Maybe you want a basic drift-bobber on the bottom, a winged version on top. Perhaps a pink one situated beneath an orange one is the color combination you're after.

Whatever the choice, there's no questioning that stacking drift-bobbers will work. I've found this approach to be particularly effective on summer steelhead and spring chinook.

It's worth noting that with the added buoyancy that's gained from using stacked drift-bobbers, there can be a tendency for the top one to ride up the line. In this case, it's a good idea to have some toothpicks in your pocket so you can peg the top drift-bobber so it doesn't ride up the line, leading the fish to strike away from the hook.

There are no limits when stacking drift-bobbers, and the change can produce impressive results. I've spent days on the river where the only thing we could catch both salmon and steelhead on were stacked drift-bobbers. Try it some time, hopefully you'll be just as impressed as I've been.

211. Remove Spinning Drift-bobber Wing

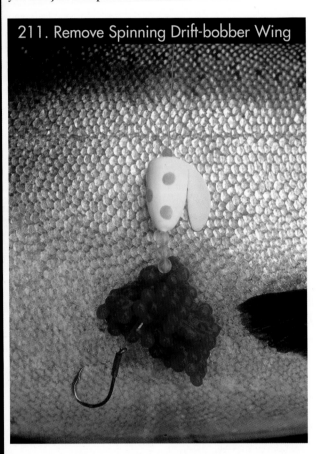

I'd seen and heard of this trick before, but the first time I tried it was while fishing with friend and noted guide, Brett Gesh, on Alaska's Kenai River. We were after big kings, and the morning bite was rather slow. Bringing in our lines, Gesh proceeded to remove the wings of our magnum-size Spin-N-Glos and Flashing & Spinning Cheaters. Over the course of the next three days, three of us would land 15 kings, keeping only three fish total, one being a 70-pound giant which graces the wall of my den that I can look up and see as I write these words. The interesting part of that memorable fishing trip, all but a couple of those fish were caught on one-winged drift-bobbers.

Since that time I've used the single-wing approach with good results on everything ranging from tiny drift-bobbers for summer steelhead to mid-sized versions for spring and fall chinook, and back up to huge ones for Alaskan kings. Removing the wing from one side of the drift-bobber creates a crippled movement that fish often react to. The uneven spinning is more sporadic

than when both wings are intact, and the range of movement is a bit wider.

I have found that when using one-winged drift-bobbers, it's a good idea to stack two to four beads beneath it, so the more intermittent rotation doesn't tangle with yarn or bait tissues. They can also be stacked on top of a smaller, round drift-bobber, like a Corky or Cheater. The combination of more color, exaggerated movement and enhanced motion may draw a bite when conventional presentations won't.

212. Lure Changes

It was a slow day on the river. The water was high and a bit off-color, though not too bad. The various size Hot Shots we pulled weren't working as planned, nor did any of the other style plugs we tried. Then we each tied on a K12 Kwikfish and worked slower water. Instantly a bite came, then another. Changing the plugs until we found something that worked meant going from a skunked day to having an exceptional one.

No matter how much confidence you have in a lure, be it a plug or spinner, if it's not working, consider changing it out. You never know what will work—or won't work—unless you try, and if you're not catching fish anyway, then you have nothing to lose.

Lure changes can come in the form of not only color, but size, shape and weight. Some lures make noise, while others glow, carry scent or cast illuminated light. Some move in tight confines, while others slowly flutter about, covering lots of water. Some are designed for fast water, some for slow, some for shallow, some for deep.

There are a multitude of lure designs out there, and they are put together that way for a specific reason. Find lures that fit the elements in which you're fishing, then be willing to use them. Talk with fellow angler, guides an tackle shop owners to see what's been effective on the river you plan on fishing, then gear-up accordingly.

By closely evaluating the water you plan on fishing, and determining where the fish you're after may be holding, then you can begin breaking down what you'll need to help catch fish. The more you do it, the more easily the skill develops of deciphering what lure will work best in any given situation. The great thing, not always is the answer what you may hypothesize it to be, there's always the possibility of discovering something unique to the situation you're fishing in. Either way, experiment, try new things and do all in your power to catch more fish.

213. Limit Bait Handling

Human odors are one of the most repulsive smells to fish, in theory. The oils found on human hands appear to have a repelling effect on fish, and the more effort taken to prevent the spread of these odors, the more fish will be caught, in theory.

When on the river, keep bait handling to a minimum. The best way to do this is by curing baits at home, with gloved hands. Make an effort to wear rubber gloves when curing eggs, so as to not contaminate them with human scent. To further reduce handling of baits, I like cutting them to fishing size at the time of curing, not when I'm on the river. Not only does this save time, it prevents excessive handling of the baits, often by bare hands.

At the same time, wrapping plugs with fillets can be done the night prior to hitting the water, again, with gloved hands. This maximizes fishing time, and will allow you to dedicate more attention to the task at hand, resulting in more efficient bait-handling and also eliminating the transfer of unwanted odors.

By having baits precut to proper size by the time you hit the water, all you have to do is grab a bait and slap it on. For plugs, having them pre-wrapped means handling only the plug, not the bait, when on the river. Doing these things in a controlled, spacious environment with gloved hands is more effective than when on the water, where you might find yourself handling baits with bare hands and spreading unwanted odors.

214. Suspend Bait Prior To Cast

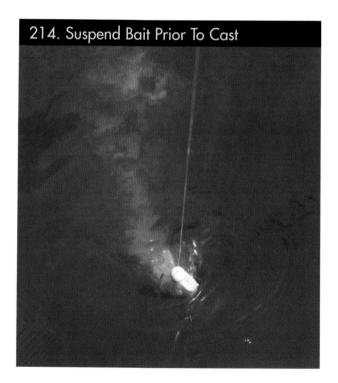

Once rods are baited, make sure the bait is suspended; that is, kept in the air. Applying gooey baits can be messy, so when cleaning your hands in a boat, avoid laying the bait on the floor, against the sides, on a seat or in the water. Laying them anywhere in the boat will result in the transfer of foul odors, and dropping them in the water causes them to lose their most potent smells. Instead, suspend them in the air, or lay the baited hook in the bait container while cleaning your hands.

For bank anglers, avoid laying baited riggings in the dirt or sand while taking the time to clean your hands. Instead, lay them on rock, or better yet, suspend them in the air. This can be done by leaning the rod against a bush or tree, cradling it in your arms, or placing it in a Rod Holster.

The first few casts with a fresh bait are the most effective. This is when they hold the most scent, color and have the most appealing texture. If a bait is flipped into the water while you clean your hands, it can milk out for several seconds. Each precious second the bait spends in the water, prior to the first cast being made, greatly reduces its overall effectiveness. To maximize a bait's potency, keep it suspended in the air while cleansing hands; it's a small point, but a valid one that can make a difference in filling that tag or not.

215. Sharpen Hooks

One of the most basic, yet overlooked, lessons to help catch more fish is keeping a sharp hook. Nowadays, many quality hooks exist, ones that are needle-sharp straight from the package. But no matter how sharp they are off the shelf, they can become easily dulled once you start fishing with them.

One thing you'll always find plenty of on an experienced angler is files. In their boat it's not unusual to have two or more files always within arm's reach. If bank fishing, always keep a file on your person, in a place that's easy to access.

No matter how good your bait or overall presentation, if you get a fish to bite and it doesn't stay hooked, all the efforts are for not if the hook isn't sharp. They key, however, does not lie in how many files you may own, but in using them on a regular basis. Keep the file in a place where it can be easily reached and used as needed.

If you find yourself having to dig through your tackle box or reach across the boat every time you need to sharpen a hook, the chances of you actually taking the time to do it drop, considerably. The result, missed fish. One buddy I fish with always has multiple files on hand. Every angler in his boat can easily reach a file or two. But the most important part is using them. Every time you get hung up, check the point of the hook. After every dozen or so casts, even if you're not getting hungup, check the hook. If it's dulled, pass the file over it. Regaining a sharp point takes only a few swipes of the file, and can be the key factor in whether or not you hook fish.

216. Vary Leader And Dropper Length

The tendency of getting caught in a rut is one of the greatest pitfalls of anglers. Doing the same thing, time after time, is not good if you're not catching fish. A rut that's easy to get caught in, especially when drift fishing, is using the same length leader with the same sinker presentation. This is one of the most basic things to change, and can make a difference in the number of fish you catch.

Say you've been fishing with a two-foot leader and six-inch dropper, both tied to a three-way swivel. This is a great set-up for targeting fish on the bottom, but if working where fish are shifting about in the water column, then you're limiting the amount of actual water being covered.

The author found the right depth to take this nice-sized hatchery summer steelhead on a jig.

In order to cover more water, consider going to a three-foot leader and putting the sinker on a slider. If you're not a fan of the sliding sinker (their biggest benefits are that they reduce resistance when a fish does pick up a bait, and they allow baits to work at a range of depths), then maybe a long dropper is worth a try.

When fishing a three-foot leader, a good way to cover more water is by making the dropper five to six feet in length. When using droppers of this length, I prefer going to a spider system on the sinker. Here, because the presentation is left to sit on the bottom for longer periods of time in order to allow the bait to swing and cover more water, the spider acts as cage of protection around the sinker, reducing the likelihood of it getting hung up. Combine this set-up with a larger drift-bobber or two, and you're now targeting slightly suspended fish. It works!

217. Hover Baits

When targeting suspended fish, one of the ways of doing it is with a bobber presentation. This is highly effective in many situations, especially from shore, but this approach can tie-up a lot of water. There's another alternative for targeting suspended fish, one commonly referred to as hover fishing.

Hover fishing is just that, where the angler presents the bait well off the bottom. This approach is primarily used on salmon, which tend to suspend in deep holes. For boaters, start at the head of a deep hole, letting out line until you hit the bottom. Then reel up the line so it's anywhere from two to five feet off the bottom. The boat, with the aide of the oars or a trolling motor, will slowly drift downstream, with the bait remaining near the boat, so the line doesn't get away from you. It may require a significant amount of lead (up to seven or eight ounces) to keep the line where you want it, but it's worth it.

Bank anglers, in the right situation, can also carry out a variation of hover fishing. It's best done from elevated bank positions, where fish gather along ledges. Often the fish will stack tight to these ledges, not along the bottom. If bank anglers can

maneuver into the right position, they can often walk a hovered bait through where these fish are holding. Then again, they may have to shift to bobber fishing.

The key to the hovering presentation is going slow, so as not to quickly pass through fish that may be suspended and moving about. Work as much of the hole as possible, preferably from top to bottom, and do it at a slow pace. Drop the weight to hit the bottom every few minutes, then reel it back up to the desired depth, just to ensure you're fishing at the target depth. If having trouble with the line getting away from you, add more weight. Be in control of the presentation at all times and it will work in the right situations.

218. Jig Depth

In the world of jig fishing, the general rule-of-thumb is to have that jig riding about 12 inches off the bottom. Some anglers like it closer, say within six inches of the bottom, others like it about 18 inches above the rocks. How deep you fish jigs comes down to personal preference, which is largely based on personal experience and success, or lack thereof.

However, when jig fishing, especially for steelhead, don't get caught in the rut of fishing the jig at the same depth or distance from the bottom, all the time. I've caught steelhead and silver salmon in two feet of water, with the jig no more than five inches below the surface. I've also caught steelhead in 14 feet of water, with the jig running seven feet off the bottom.

It's amazing how far a fish will travel for a jig it wants. Then again, I've floated jigs a foot over the heads of fish, and not until I dropped it to within a few inches of their nose—only five or six-inches off the bottom—did they attack it. Fish can be finicky, and their desires can change from day to day.

The key to finding what works is varying the depth of your jig. Fortunately, this is easily done by adjusting the position of your bobber-stop. In addition to varying jig depth, don't forget to experiment with color changes, even adding scents to the head or body. These changes, in whole or in part, can make a big difference in how effective jig fishing can be for you. Once you've found something that works, make note of the conditions and refer back to it. The more you fish jigs and experiment around with them, the more you'll discover what works.

219. Vary Speed Of Delivery

Once fish are located, it may be necessary to vary the speed of your delivery in order to catch more of them. Case in point: One day Dad and I were covering lots of water in search of fish. Three-quarters of the way through the run, we had out first strike, but missed it. We re-ran the drift and missed another strike. Then we added another ounce of weight, rowed back up and back-bounced our way along a narrow, rock ledge that plunged into a deep, swirling hole. The next six passes we hooked six springers, landing our limit of four.

Had we not slowed down our presentation, we could have kept missing the fish that were obviously stacked in the hole. On this particular day, the fish wanted something slow, and thankfully, we figured that out. At other times, the fish may react to a more aggressive, speedier presentation.

Finding what fish want, and at what speed they want it, can be tricky.

and times of the day they'll be there, then they'll work at it until they find success. Not always do you have to be on the go, worrying about beating fellow anglers to the next sweet-spot. Thoroughly fishing a hole at a leisurely pace, then moving on to do the same in another hole, often rewards anglers. Move slow, try a range of presentations and enjoy your time on the water.

221. Move Quickly

Sometimes covering water is the approach to take.

There are several factors that can play into how fast, or slow, a bait should be presented. Excessively cold or warm water temperatures tend to cause fish to move more slowly, where as mid-range temperatures can find them being highly active. Angler pressure, barometric pressure, cloud cover and more can all influence how a fish moves and reacts. The key is recognizing that behavioral changes can, and do, occur, then figuring out a way to catch more fish because of these changes.

It may be that a slow presentation parked on the bottom is what fish want. Or maybe they want a flashy, fast-moving offering swung in front of them. What fish want, and how we know what they want, is one of the great mysteries of this grand pastime, and what makes our sport so addicting...and frustrating at times.

220. Move Slowly

One of the greatest rewards of fishing is the level of tranquility it offers. For many anglers, simply being on the water is good enough, catching fish is just a bonus. With that mindset, one approach to finding more fish is taking a slow approach. That is, rather than being in a rush to cover as much water as possible, take your time and move slowly.

The slower you move, the more thoroughly you can fish a specific area. It takes time to experiment with various baits, bait sizes, drift-bobber combinations, even a range of presentations, be it jigs, plugs, lures or bait. Oftentimes, the more thorough and persistent you are at finding what works, the more fish you'll catch. The bonus with this approach is that it doesn't require being in a rush. Simply relax, know you're going to dedicate a certain period of time to fishing that hole, then do just that.

Even once you've fished a hole, you may elect to start all over at the top end, and cover it again. Maybe fish have moved in that weren't there when you began fishing. Maybe they are in there, but you just haven't found the right combination yet. It can take time and effort to get dialed-in.

There are some prized holes anglers make an effort to get into in the middle of the night, then they'll spend all day fishing it until they find what they're after. These anglers often know every inch of that hole, where fish will be in certain situations

If your schedule is tight, you may not have the luxury of taking your time to find fish. Maybe you have to be to work at a certain hour, or maybe you need to be at your kid's ball game in the afternoon. Whatever the reason, sometimes covering as much water as possible in a short amount of time is the route you choose to go.

Now, you could elect to spend your time in one hole, but if those fish aren't in there, no matter how hard you fish it, they aren't going to bite. This is where going on the move in an effort to quickly cover more water, can pay huge rewards.

If in a boat or off the bank, when searching for fish, have all the rods rigged and ready to go; this will help save time. Once entering a hole, hit the spots you know will, or should, hold fish. Once you've covered the target water, move on to the next spot. However, if you find fish, then it's worth spending time in that one place to try and pull more out of there.

Covering lots of water can require a lot of gear, especially when working from a boat. You may be drifting, running plugs, throwing spinners or dragging bait. Bank anglers won't have quite so many options. If you know you're going to be moving quickly, then make sure to have all gear ready to go the night prior, so you can save time on the water and more efficiently cover all the water you want to. Taking along six or eight rods in the boat, two or three on the bank, is not overkill if that's the number of approaches you plan on presenting.

Being aggressive and covering water can be productive. Do what best fits your schedule. The important part is that you're simply out there, fishing.

222. Move Quietly

When moving along the river, it's a good idea to do so quietly, so you don't risk spooking fish. This is especially true in low, clear conditions, where fish may be on edge. If wade-fishing, getting from point A to point B, may be best done by getting out of the water and walking the banks. If working from a boat, perhaps quietly slipping into the side of a new hole, rather than over the top of it, is appropriate.

The idea is to present baits without fish knowing of your presence. The more quietly this can be done, the less likely the fish are to spook. Generally speaking, a more relaxed fish is one that's more willing to strike, and once you've spooked them, there's no going back.

If bank fishing with a buddy, try and keep your voices down, especially when you know fish are near. Also, keep an eye on long shadows. I don't know how many times I've spooked, and seen fish spooked, by the shadow of approaching anglers. If focusing on sight-fishing, you might also want to wear earth-tone colors, so as to avoid alerting fish to your presence.

If in a boat, keep movement and noises to a minimum. At times, taking such precautions can make a difference. Then again, if I thought boats spooked fish, I wouldn't own one. Point is, use logical judgment and try to avoid alerting fish to your presence prior to making the initial casts in a hole.

As time passes, fish may become aware that you're around, and this may actually make them nervous, whereby triggering a bite. I like applying stealth first, then dropping my guard a little more as time rolls on.

223. Work Close To Your Feet

Working a jig by a cut-bank, right at his feet, the author struck silvers.

Have you ever been on the river and found yourself casting as far across stream as possible, while observing other anglers doing the same from the opposite side? Usually this is done to properly position your terminal gear to be fishing a specific spot as it's carried downstream, or to hit a slot near the other shore which anglers from that side can't access. But often, in a focused effort to work the opposite side, anglers neglect to first fish close to their feet.

One of the biggest mistakes anglers make is overlooking prime water right where they are standing or anchoring the boat. I'll never forget the time I waded too far into a summer steelheading hole, only to spook a school of fish that had stacked up behind a big rock I usually stood on. It was the first time I'd seen fish holding in this spot, but I learned from the mistake and caught several fish from there before the season came to a close.

If fishing from the bank, take the time to read the water you're about to fish, before wading into it. If working from a boat, look ahead and evaluate where you should position yourself in order to best fish the upcoming shorelines. It comes down to reading the water and knowing where fish hold and travel, then putting yourself into key position without spooking fish.

If new to a stream, take your time, so as not to spook fish. If you do spook fish, mark the spot, for chances are others will hold there as they move upstream. When banking it, try walking on land, rather than making noise by kicking up water and rocks. It may be that you are able to fish a slot close to shore from upstream, then position yourself in that spot you just fished in order to reach target water across the stream. Think before you move, and fish close if you feel there's any chance of fish holding there.

224. Cast To Opposite Bank

Casting to the opposite shore can be effective, given it's done in the right place, at the proper time. If there's a definite travel route or holding spot fish may occupy on the opposite bank, then by all means, it's a place worth spending time on. But avoid casting across the river just to see if you can do it. Each cast made should be well thought out, based on where you think the fish will be, given the circumstances.

One factor that can push fish to the opposite shoreline is pressure from other anglers. Bank anglers tend to spook fish into the middle of the river. Their presence may also keep fish from seeking less taxing waters, which is often along the shore from which they are fishing. Throw in some boats passing over-top, especially in low water, and the fish can be even more pressed to seek protective habitat.

Direct sunlight is another factor that can force fish to move about in a river, as are rising and dropping flows. Often, fish retreat to less powerful water, a place where they can relax without being threatened. Such places often exist along the opposite bank, and when the situation is right, fish can be pulled from there.

On a midday summer steelheading trip back in the early 1980s, the bank was lined with anglers. Several boats passed by, but one boat dropped anchor, almost in the middle of the river. He had no idea that he parked on the best water, and after a while of not catching fish, he moved on. As he started pulling anchor, I casted upstream and behind him, tight to the opposite bank. When my line came tight I set the hook and the fish launched himself out of the water between the boat and the far bank. I landed that fish, made another cast into the same place and landed a second chrome steely.

It was simple to figure out, really; all the fishing pressure had pushed the fish to the opposite shore, where they were holding in about two feet of water. There is a time and place for casting across to the opposite bank.

225. Repeated Casting To Trigger Bite

I don't know how many times over the years I've awaken way too early in the morning in order to get a spot on the river, only to get no strikes until mid-day. In numerous situations I could see the fish, be they steelhead holding or salmon jumping, so I knew they were there. The thing is, they simply were not biting.

Despite efforts that range from varying bait selection to more weight, longer leaders and even different approaches, there are times when a bite simply won't happen. In this case, when there's no reason to go in search of other fish, then the only thing left is persistence. Often, incessant casting can trigger a reactionary bite.

Repeated casting will, much of the time, result in getting a bite. The question is, how long are you willing to wait, and how many fish do you care to catch? But once the bite does turn on, land that fish and get the line back in the water as quickly as possible. It seems that a high percentage of the time, once one fish bites, others in the school start biting.

If you've ever spent several hours fishing a hole amid other anglers, then have someone finally hook a fish, it's like a chain-reaction, where more and more people immediately get strikes. Who really knows what triggered the bite, but there's no doubting the fact persistence played a factor, for without continued casting, nothing would have happened.

Keep casting, don't give up and maintain a positive attitude. The thing about fishing a place like this, it doesn't hurt to take a break once in a while. These fish aren't going anywhere, and you have the spot tied-up. Take a breather from time to time, give that arm a rest, then get back at it with a fresh mental spirit. It may take hours, several hours, but repeated casting can yield results.

226. Super Glue And Duct Tape

When on the water, numerous things can happen where you find yourself in need of some quick fixing. Some of the damages incurred will require more serious attention when you get home, but if you're looking to just get through the rest of the day, super glue and duct tape can make a big difference.

Super glue has a wide range of applications, and it's a good idea to have a bottle on-hand wherever you go, be it from the bank or out of a boat. Super glue can remedy everything from broken eyes on the rod to cuts. If you get small injuries, such as a line cut, a minor slice with a knife, or a hook puncture, clean the wound, dry it and place super glue on it. It's a great way to stop bleeding, prevent infection from setting in and start the healing process, quickly.

Super glue is also handy for sticking tape to plugs or spinners, should it start to come off. Should jig or fly heads, even wraps on the eye of your fishing pole start coming unraveled, super glue will stop it. Have a plug that's cracked, mylar or plastic that's ripped? Try super glue.

As for duct tape, it's likely one of the most universally owned products by sportsmen, and has more uses than can be listed. From sealing a boot leak to fixing seats in a boat, making handles to carry a load, and more, there's simply no shortage of ways this nifty invention can help save the day, at least until you get home. For bank anglers or folks looking to stow duct tape in their tackle box, you don't have to carry a big, heavy roll around. Forms of duct tape come in small, flat, plastic bags which are ideal for sticking in a vest, a pant pocket or tackle box. Between these two pieces of must-have gear, you'll be amazed at what can be fixed, and how it really can increase your fishing time.

227. Vary Angle Of Presentation

When fishing a hole or section of water, physical position has a major impact on where the terminal gear travels. From the time the cast hits the water, through the entire drift and all the way through the swing, where that bait ends up going is determined by where you're at when the cast is made. Granted, the amount of weight being used, float size, length of rod, how much line is on the water, even which reel you're using can all impact the pathway a drift takes, but largely, it comes down to where you are when the cast is made that has the greatest impact as to where the terminal gear will end up.

Once the target water has been identified, and you have a strong hunch where fish will be holding, closely observe the movement of surface water to see what it's doing. Determine how the water is acting the closer it gets to your target zone. Is it boiling, kicking left, shifting right or turning slick? Whatever it's doing, there's a reason for it, and it has to do with bottom structure, stream gradient and the amount of water moving downstream.

Casting position sounds simple, but believe it or not, all of these aspects factor in to where your cast will end up, thus, where it should begin. If having trouble finding bottom at the end of the drift, try freespooling out line to allow the weight to sink faster. Perhaps adding weight caused you to get hungup early in the drift, and not enough weight resulted in the gear being lifted out of the strike zone at the end of the drift. The best remedy may be to simply change positions.

If in a boat, a change may equate to moving a mere boat length. On the bank, the move may only amount to a few steps. Point is, a slight change in the angle of presentation can make a big difference in the rate at which the terminal gear is delivered. Remember, often times there are multiple angles from which a delivery can be made, the key is finding those angles in order to get that hook to where the fish are.

228. Go Back Over Pressured Water

If your favorite fishing spot is occupied, go back later.

Whether you're fishing from a boat or off the bank, retracing your steps can be a successful approach. Think about most river situations, where anglers continue coming and going throughout the course of the day. Fish in these waters receive constant pressure, and if you're confident fish are there, or that new arrivals could be showing up any moment, then it may be worth the time and effort to go over that pressured water, again.

Some folks will work-over one hole for several hours on end. They may start at the head end and fish it down, then repeat the approach. They may begin low, from the bank, and fish it up to the head, then fish it back down. No matter how you go about it, covering the same water is a good ploy.

Each time you start over you may want to consider changing offerings. By presenting different baits or lures to the fish upon each pass you make, you're increasing your odds of finding something they like. Think about why a newly arriving angler often gets a bite within the first few casts of showing up. Typically, it's

not because he was doing anything different, rather the fact he gave the fish something different to look at.

Be creative, don't give up and repeatedly cover that same water. If in a boat with a motor, you have the luxury of running back upstream as often as you like, and bank anglers can rework water until their legs give out. Whether you're refishing a hole, a short riffle or a mile-long stretch of prime staging water, dedicate yourself to doing it right. Don't get caught simply going through the motions. Think about where the fish will be and make each cast with as much precision as possible. It just might work.

229. Don't Leave Fish To Find Fish

Once you find fish, don't give up, the bite can quickly turn on.

One of the most challenging aspects of catching fish can be finding them first. Sometimes it happens fast, but often it takes a great deal of time to physically locate fish; that is, seeing them jump or swimming around. Variables such as lighting conditions, off-colored water or tannic-stained streams can make it tough to see fish from above the surface, and not always do fish jump. Oftentimes it's strikes or hitting fish with the line that alerts anglers to their presence below. Once fish are located, don't give up if the bite is slow in coming.

Unless you're fairly certain there are more fish elsewhere in the river, there's no reason to go searching if you've already found some. At the same time, if you are familiar with the hole and are confident fresh fish will move into the spot you're concentrating on, be patient. Anglers, myself included, often grow frustrated when surrounded by fish that aren't biting. In such a case, start changing things around to try and entice a bite.

Many times all it takes is a change in terminal gear, be it different bait, different colors or different sizes of the presentation, to trigger a bite. The speed at which the terminal gear is being offered may also be a factor; it may need to be slowed down or increased. Perhaps direct sunlight, foot or boat traffic has the fish nervous, which may require adjusting accordingly, based on how the fish are reacting. Once fish are located, it can mean spending serious time until they finally strike, but when it happens it often triggers a bite from numerous other fish in the school, meaning the action can light-up quickly. When this happens, you'll see why staying put pays-off.

230. Overnight Benefits

For most of us, when we think of spending a day on the river, that's it, a day. But the longer you can spend on the water, the more you'll learn about it and the fish you pursue. If traveling

any distance, it's a shame to have to return home after a day on the water, especially if the action is rockin'.

One winter day, Bret Stuart and I drove three hours to a river. We hooked 15 winter steelhead that day, then drove home. Bret owns 24-7 Guide Service, is a close personal friend, and is also my camera man for the shows we shoot for Wolf Creek Productions. So when we got home late at night, and Bret suggested we do it again in the morning, I didn't hesitate. Bret had a couple cancelations, we were done filming for the season and the fish were in. Three hours of sleep went fast, but we caught fish the following day. If we'd have been thinking ahead, we obviously should have just gotten a hotel room.

Staying in hotels is one option of keeping you in the vicinity you're fishing, camping along the river is another. Depending on the time of year you're fishing, and the amount of public camping available, it may be best to get a hotel room. Then again, if you can pull over on a gravel bar and crawl into the sleeping bag, great. Or maybe there's a campground nearby where you can pitch a tent or park a camper. Another option is sleeping in your boat, which I've done, and makes for a long day come sunup.

Do some checking prior to embarking on a trip that requires a drive, for it may be better to dedicate two or more days to the outing. If, on the first day that river does not produce, then drive to another river in search of fish. There's a lot that can be learned from overnighting on or near the river, not the least of which is figuring out how to catch more fish.

231. Eat On The Move

This is a tough one, but a rule I was born and raised knowing and still live by today, and that's eating on the move. When spending a day on the river, it's tempting to take time out for a nice lunch, kick back and enjoy the scenery. There's nothing wrong with that, as long as you are willing to sacrifice fishing time for eating. But over the years I've spent on the river, I can count on one hand the number of times I've actually stopped fishing to eat something. The payoff here comes in the number of fishing hours gained.

The only exceptions for eating while on the river might be if you're waiting for someone to move out of a hole you wish to fish, or if you're certain no fish are in a hole, but feel they'll move in soon. In these cases, it's obviously worth staying put in order to get your fishing time in later, and okay to eat lunch without worrying about wasting fishing time.

If bank fishing, consider snacking away while on the move. If working from a boat, eat when you have one hand free. I carry portable, high-energy snacks like jerky, trail mix and granola bars. Growing up, I remember Mom always giving Dad and I a hard time about coming home with the lunches she made, and not a bite missing. My wife was doing the same thing, so I wised up, and now eat it on the drive home. She hasn't caught on as to why I don't eat much at dinner on those nights.

Figure it takes 30 minutes to eat a relaxing lunch on the river. Tally that over the course of the year and calculate how many hours of fishing you've lost. It can be an eye-opener. If serious about doing something different to catch more fish, this is one place to consider, for the more that line is in the water, the greater the chance of getting that bite.

232. Respect The Space Of Others

When on the river, it's every angler's goal (or at least it should be) to have a good, safe, enjoyable experience. There's no questioning the fact we'd rather have a river to ourselves, but in our populated world, that's hard to come by these days unless you're in the Alaskan or Canadian wilderness.

When fishing amongst other anglers, keep in mind the need to respect their space. It's not the law, rather a common courtesy, something that will make the day more enjoyable for everyone. When pulling into a spot already occupied by anglers, ask if they mind if you join them; I feel this is especially important if where you plan to fish intersects the water they are covering. I can't recall a time I've ever been turned down by simply taking the time ask a fellow angler if they minded that I share the water with them.

But do more than just ask. Observe how others are fishing in the area. It's likely you'll need to use the same approach in order to prevent hanging up, tying up the hole, or getting large sinkers thrown at you. If people are drift fishing, it's probably not a good idea to start loose-lining a bobber and jig through the hole. Every season, almost on a weekly basis anymore, I encounter novice anglers infringing on waters I'm fishing, only to unknowingly (at least I hope it's unknowingly) tie-up my target water or keep me from fishing it all together.

Be aware of what's going on around you. If someone infringes on you, politely point out what they've just done. Use the same strategies others employ—or one that allows you to manage your line without interfering with them—and you're on the way to a fun and hopefully productive day of catching fish.

233. Anticipate Strikes

My high school football coach, Reanous Cochran, once said, "If you want to be winners, the biggest mistake you can make is getting used to losing." We were on the cusp of losing our second straight game, and that phrase hit me hard as we sat in the locker room at halftime. Ironically, those words have applied to more facets of my life than I ever would have imagined. Following a pep talk, we went out and won the game, and advanced to the state playoffs.

I've found the same to be true in fishing: If you really want to learn how to catch fish, the biggest mistake you can make is

Having confidence that strike will come is one of the biggest keys to maintaining a positive mental attitude, and catching fish.

getting used to not catching them. I know of anglers who have gone years without catching a salmon or steelhead, despite all the time, money and effort they put into it.

One of the biggest pitfalls anglers can face is finding themselves being content with going through the motions of casting. If you're randomly tossing a line in the water, hoping for a "lucky" crack at a fish, it's not going to happen. When you finally do catch a fish, evaluate all the elements involved when the bite occurred. You did something right to make it happen, and you should feel that every cast you make has the capability of catching fish. If you don't believe in each cast you make, why make it?

At the end of a day's fishing, I'm often mentally beat, especially on slow days. Why? Because my mind is constantly working to figure out what I can do to catch more fish. Successful anglers are continually evaluating the conditions, factoring in human pressure, time of day, fish behavior, the presentations they're using and more. Simply put, they expect to catch fish and do all in their power to make it happen. Anticipate the strike. Have confidence that it will happen, and it will.

234. Don't Overthink

Fishing can be a tough mental game, and remaining positive while on the river is crucial to success. However, there's a fine line between evaluating your approach and that of overthinking it. If you start inflicting doubt into your fishing strategy, you begin questioning what got you there in the first place. As this happens, your level of confidence wanes.

We've all been on the river and been outfished. If you haven't, be prepared, it will happen one day. It can be frustrating and cause grown men to act like kids. It's not pretty. I was with a buddy one time, fishing fall chinook. We hammered the fish, and all right in front of a top guide in the area. He had a boatload of

clients, and finally got fed up with seeing us catch fish. He fished the same way we did, and he's a very successful angler, usually. But he couldn't stand it. By mid-morning he called it quits and got off the river. The next day my buddy and I could not buy a fish, and everyone around us was slaying them. It's fishing, and when this happens, you have to roll with it.

Have confidence in how you're fishing and feel that what you're doing is right. Once you start inflicting doubt, you start doing things out of the norm. You might start moving around the river too much, rather than focusing on fishing where you know fish are at. You may try unconventional techniques you're not familiar with. When facing failure, we often resort to unorthodoxed behaviors, and it can cost us fish. When this starts to happen, don't overanalyze things; keep your head up and do what you feel will work. If it doesn't come together on that particular day, there's always tomorrow.

235. Keep Cork Handles Clean

Cork is a soft, opened-grain wood product, and as such, is susceptible to becoming imbedded with various things. There's nothing quite like the feel of a new, smooth, cork handle in your hands. But these rod handles can get dirty, and potentially impact your fishing.

If you're a bait fisherman, keeping your hands clean after handling baits, and prior to handling the rod, is important in the prevention of spreading potentially foul smells to the fish. The same is true after handling a fish you've just caught. The transfer of any blood, slime or egg residue to the fishing rod handle can permeate the cork. As these things sit there, they age, or rot. The more you handle the rod, the more these foul odors are transferred back to your hands.

From there, the odors can be carried to the baits or lures being fished, and this can impact the bite. The odors may be too miniscule for week human noses to detect, but fish can pick them out, and it's widely accepted that such rank odors can turn fish away.

In an effort to keep the cork rod handles from passing foul odors to the fish, keep them clean. This can be done by simply submerging them in the water if they've become messy. Perhaps giving them a rubdown with a scent-eliminating wipe or clean, wet rag will do the job. Maybe it takes a little more elbow grease to remove unwanted odors, meaning soap and water must enter the picture. If you have old cork grips that are so encrusted with residue that you can't get them clean, consider wrapping them with Rod Wraps. Rod Wraps (www.rodwraps.com) are easy to clean, plus they feel good in one's hands.

Keeping a clean rod handle is one of the little pieces to the all-important fish-catching puzzle. You may not believe that something so trivial can actually make a difference, but based on personal experience, I do. It takes minimal time to keep rod handles clean, and is worth the effort.

236. Keep Pliers Handy For Hook Removal

If you've ever had a big fish in the net, flopping in the bottom of the boat, then gotten a hook imbedded in your hand, you know it's not a pretty picture. It gets worse when the net gets hung on a seat or rod holder and you can't move to reach the pliers that lay where you last left them. For this reason alone, it's a good idea to have multiple pairs of long-nosed pliers handy, either laying in various places in the boat, in a pants pocket, or both.

Not only are pliers handy for performing crude hook-removal surgery, but they are also good preventatives from allowing getting a hook in the hand in the first place. When removing a hook from a fish's mouth, use pliers, not your hands. A quick move of a fish can send that hook flying, and if you're holding onto or reaching for the line, chances are it will end up in your hand.

My boys and I were on a pond one evening, catching trout. When trying to remove a treble hook from the jaw of rainbow, the fish slipped and the hook buried in my finger. I tried subduing the fish with my free hand, hoping Braxton, then age four, would not freak out. About that time, Kazden, then two years old, picked up the rod and starting running with it, yanking the fish and me along with him. It wasn't fun, especially since I was leaving on a wilderness elk hunt early the next morning; and it all could have been prevented had I used pliers to remove the hook.

There are endless uses for pliers in the salmon and steelhead fishing world, and I'd advocate always having a pair within easy reach. Doing so will allow you to carry out quick tasks that will result in increased fishing time.

237. Cut Tangles

Line tangles. They're inevitable, and no matter how you look at it, they are time-consuming. So, what's the best way to take care of tangles in order to maximize your fishing time? The answer comes down to how severe the tangle is.

If I tangle with another angler—someone across the river or in another boat—I make it a point to cut my line, and get theirs back to them as quickly as possible. If it's a simple tangle, I'll take a few seconds to try and get it undone. But if there's any question, I'll cut my line. It's a courtesy thing, one that goes a long way in establishing friendships on the river.

On line tangles that involve only your line or yours and your fishing partner's, assess how much time it will take to untangle the mess, without having to cut and retie anything. If in doubt, or if the tangle looks unmanageable, cut it and retie. However, if the line or leader have been wrapped around a swivel, lure body, hook or plug, check for abrasions or severe twists. If these are present, they can weaken the line, in which case you'll want to clip the line and start over with fresh line. Should there be abrasions or twists in the mainline, follow it up as far as necessary, cut it and retie.

I've seen many times—and have been guilty of it more than I care to admit—where valuable time has been wasted trying to untangle messes. At first it doesn't look so bad, then the more you get into it, you discover you should have just started over long ago. If your knot-tying skills aren't quite quick enough, consider tying droppers, leaders and other pieces of terminal gear onto snap-swivels. Oftentimes the tangles are such that all you have to do is unsnap the swivels, close them, untangle and reattach. In the long run, cutting through tangles, or attaching them to snap-swivels can save valued time.

238. GPS Coordinates

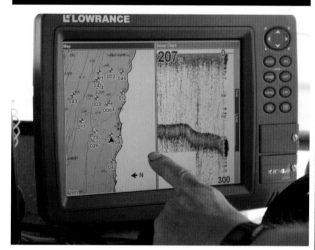

For years, ocean-going anglers have used global positioning systems (GPS) to mark waypoints where they catch fish. For big-river salmon and steelhead anglers, a GPS can be a piece of equipment that can make a difference in your catch rates. The biggest value of having a GPS on the water is that it allows you to quickly find key points where fish may hold, especially when it comes to deep salmon holes.

Combine a GPS with a depth finder, and the two tools can dramatically increase your efficiency. Some boats come with the option of having both GPS and depth finders built in, which, if you spend any time in bays or large rivers, can be a good investment.

Finding a good place to fish can take days, even years, and once you locate it, you don't want to lose it. Once such a hole is located, log the waypoint in your GPS. You'll also want to study the bottom structure with a depth finder, so you know precisely where to fish each time you return. You can take it one step further and identify landmarks on either side of the river, for this can help you quickly pick up and identify the place the next time around. However, in large systems, plotting your target hole by way of landmarks can be difficult, if not impossible.

Fog is just one factor that can keep you from finding your honey-hole in big rivers. Stormy weather and changing terrain due to flooding or severe winter storms are other reasons. The immense size of a body of water can be enough to make finding your mark a challenge, without the aide of technology. However you go about it, marking your key fishing holes with GPS can have time-saving results come future trips.

239. Cell Phones

Cell phones have many benefits when on the water.

Though I did manage to avoid it for years, I was eventually dragged into the world of cell phones. Once I figured out how they could help catch more fish, I was kicking myself for not having picked up on it earlier.

Cell phones are great tools of communication, and what really got me thinking about buying one was the time my buddy called from the river. "You better get away from your computer and get out here," urged Bret Stuart. "We've just landed our fourteenth fish of the morning!" Bret was calling from his cell phone. Within two hours I was on the water, and we ended up hooking more than a dozen salmon and steelhead, less than 15 minutes from my doorstep. Were it not for a cell phone, I would not have gotten the report until it was too late.

Cell phones also have their place while on the river. Not only are they good tools to communicate with shuttle changers or the family, but they are ideal when it comes to exchanging information with friends who are on the river.

If a buddy and I are teaming up with our boats, one of us will often hole-hop, quickly moving downstream until we find fish. The other will lag behind, trying a variety of techniques to try and get fish to bite. Whoever finds good numbers of fish calls the other person so we can work together in figuring out a way for both of us to benefit.

Cell phones are also valuable for communicating with fellow angler to help indicate what the fish they are picking up are biting on. You can also keep one another informed of boat traffic and other pieces of valuable information that can aide you in catching fish. Bottom line, cell phones are an ideal tool of communication that can help you attain immediate information which can, in turn, help you catch more fish.

240. Pick Up Trash

It's one of the most disheartening sights in nature; going to a tranquil river only to find it littered with trash. How and why "anglers" could hold such disrespect for the land and the rights of other anglers, is beyond the comprehension of many. What these people (and I know not all of them are fishermen) fail to realize is that their law-breaking, arrant, selfish and lazy habits are costing the rest of us valued fishing time, even sacrificing opportunities.

As I write these words, I just discovered that one of my favorite bank-fishing holes, a private piece of land I've been fishing since the 1960s, was recently closed. For years the landowner had let anyone cross his property and access the fishing hole which was on his land, without so much as even asking permission. But this spring he had all he could take. He got tired of seeing trash out his living room window, and having to pick it up himself. If people could not respect the land, he reasoned, then they are not deserving of fishing on it. He had a point.

Since boyhood, I remember my dad always picking up trash when we were on the river, and this was back in the day of few anglers, and more caring ones. "If you pack it in, pack it out," was Dad's motto, and if someone else fails to pack out their trash, pack it out for them if you want to keep fishing. From fishing line to glass pop bottles to beer cans, Dad always packed it out—he still does it today, and thanks to him, so do I.

In an effort to combat the ever-growing concern of river litter, many fishing clubs and organizations assemble volunteers to float and walk rivers picking up all the trash they can. Other individuals take it upon themselves to focus on picking up trash on a regular basis. I know of one man who leaves the rods at home and floats the river every two weeks in the summer, just to pick up trash on his home river. Talk about sacrificing your fishing time for others. It's this kind of dedication and discipline all sportsmen need to practice, but until that happens, it's up to you and I to carry the rest.

241. Fill In Punch Cards

In states where it's the law that you tag a fish immediately upon catching it, do it. There's no reason to taint a day that's going in the right direction and lose valuable fishing time. When a bite's happening, the last thing you want to do is waste time getting back into the action; worse yet is having a citation

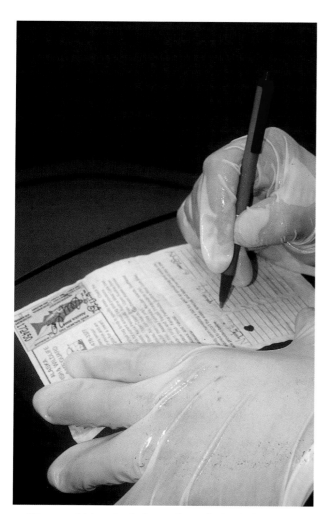

written up which not only hurts the pocketbook, but cuts into fishing.

Sometimes folks catch fish and then honestly forget to tag them before getting back to fishing. Other times, they figure they'll punch their tag later, and simply forget. There are routine instances where police officers hide in the brush and closely watch for anglers failing to tag fish. There are even cases where officials may follow anglers throughout the day, meeting them at the boat ramp after having observed them not tagging a single fish all day. The excuse that you were going to wait and tag the fish at the take-out is not valid, and could end up costing you more than a simple fine.

Also, avoid the urge to record a catch on someone else's tag. This act is not legal in many waters, so check state and area regulations, as well as special regulations that may be in effect, to make certain where things stand.

When I hear loathesome stories of folks who have conveniently "lost" punch cards, just so they don't have to purchase another one in order to catch more fish, it makes me sad and frustrated. Their deceitful ploy is to report the card as "lost," whereby getting another replacement card for a nominal fee. What anglers like this fail to realize is that fish-and-game offices rely on the feedback of punch cards—which they like seeing turned in at the end of the license-holding season—to establish fish harvest counts which in turn helps them more efficiently manage fisheries and set future seasons.

Laws are in place for a reason. Honor them, if not for your sake then for the sake of fellow anglers who may suffer repercussions of dishonest actions.

Many of the techniques discussed thus far deal with general themes or position-based approaches, like fishing off the bank or from a boat. And some of the techniques do touch on condition-related situations like habitat, hole anatomy and how to deal with pressure from fellow anglers.

In this section, we're going to take a closer look at approaches that can be used in high, turbid water. During the course of the year, both salmon and steelhead anglers encounter unfavorable fishing conditions, where they must contest high, off-colored water. Some anglers may choose to pass on fishing such water, opting instead for more favorable conditions.

Truth is, if you wait for the perfect conditions, you may not get much fishing in. What's more, fish can be caught in what many people consider to be way less than ideal conditions. This is especially true in high, dirty water, proving how these anadromous fish really do depend on their sense of smell for navigation, gathering food and overall survival.

Over the years I've caught salmon and steelhead in water carrying less than two feet of visibility. In fact, one spring, the water was so chocolate-colored, I figured visibility to be about 13 to 14 inches, and we still caught springers. The same is true for winter steelhead, where one time we estimated visibility to be 15 inches, and still caught what we were looking for. Though these figures are on the extreme end, the point is, fish were caught.

When fishing in such unfavorable conditions, there are certain measures anglers can take to help increase their success. Mind you, many of the points detailed here have been previously touched on, but not with the focus of fishing high-water conditions. The following points have been tailored to meet the demands of high-water fishing, and specifically focus on how to increase the ability of anglers to catch fish. In whole,

Chapter 5   High, Turbid Water

Knowing what to look for, and how to fish, in high water can greatly increase your time spent on the water.

all of these techniques increase your time on the water, for they allow you to get out and apply them under unfavorable conditions, when you likely would not be fishing in the first place.

Don't be intimidated by high-water situations. As long as the river is in a recovery stage, it's worth considering hitting the river. It's common knowledge that catching fish on a rising river is tough, and though it can be done, the regularity with which fish are caught on a rising river is highly sporadic, at best. Catching fish on a rising, muddy river is tough and not regularly productive, and the effort required is not usually worth the time. But once the barometric pressure changes and the river begins to drop back into shape, it's time to evaluate what can be done in order to catch more fish.

A few words of caution: When fishing high water, apply common sense and do not fish a river that's dangerously high to navigate. Strong currents, logs being swept downstream and other dangers commonly associated with high water are obstacles you do not want to deal with; they can be life-threatening. If the water you intend on fishing seems dangerously high, don't go. When a river is just starting to recover from flood stage, it may take a week or more before it becomes fishable, so be patient, continue to monitor its level and don't force it. Remember, the goal is to simply catch more fish, not put yourself into unnecessarily dangerous situations.

That said, the strategies discussed in this chapter are designed to increase your fishing time, whereby catching more fish, be it from the bank or out of a boat. They are intended to get you on the water days ahead of other anglers, the folks who are sitting at home waiting for the conditions to be just right. They are also designed to help you apply techniques you may not have thought of, techniques that have worked for me in high-water situations over the years.

242. Larger Baits

Salmon and steelhead have big mouths, and can devour big baits.

With high, colored water comes a need for anglers to do what they can to catch more fish, and one of the most effective tricks is increasing your bait size. A larger bait does two things: First, it presents a bigger package for the fish to see. With increased size comes more color, which equates to fish being able to more readily find the bait. Second, and I feel most important, a larger bait is a way to deliver more scent.

The larger the bait, the more scent it will carry. These may be scents that were applied to eggs during the curing process, or placed on baits just prior to fishing them. Upsizing your herring, shrimp, eggs or other baits being used, can make a difference.

With a larger bait, be sure to fish them in a setting where they will work for you. The objective of a bait is to carry a scent trail to the fish. And given the fact fish are commonly on the move in high water, it only makes sense to get the bait on the bottom, in the pathway through which fish are traveling. This is one reason why plunking is so effective in high water, because plunkers put their gear in the line of travel of the fish. They are also often on the water three or four days ahead of anglers who are using other techniques,

If targeting fish that may be holding in high water, say salmon in a swirl hole, a large bait will increase the odds of their finding it. If fish can smell a bait, they can track it down, it's just a matter of whether or not they want to bite it. But if they can't find the bait, they can't eat it. Think big and you will see a difference in your high-water catch rates.

243. Larger Plugs

As with baits, increasing the size of your plugs can make a difference. In high-water situations, many anglers prefer focusing their efforts near banks, where the majority of fish travel at this time. It's a good move. At the same time, many anglers opt to use plugs in high conditions, rather than bait, for the simple reason the plugs don't take the pounding baits do, thus their ability to fish for longer periods is greater.

But as with baits, the larger the plug, the better the odds of a fish finding it. Some people are apprehensive about using large plugs for fear of scaring fish away. Remember, the fish you're targeting are alive due to their success as predators in the ocean. They attack and devour baitfish on a regular basis, and some of the herring in the ocean are much larger than what you'll ever see in a river system. In other words, don't worry about plugs being too large and scaring fish.

Most anglers have stories of going after big kings, only to have a one-pound jack salmon nail their K16 Kwikfish. I don't know how many undersized fish I've caught on big plugs over the years, but it's mind-boggling. Even catching pink salmon and chums on magnum plugs is a common occurrence for king fishermen, a testimony to just how aggressive these fish can be.

The same holds true for steelhead. When Luhr Jensen came out with their SE series Hot Shot, I couldn't wait to try it in high-water conditions. It worked as planned, and still is a favorite high-water steelheading plug. Both winter and summer steelhead can also be taken on Kwikfish and Flatfish, on sizes that surprise many anglers—a K13 Kwikfish is not overkill. When fishing high water, don't be afraid to increase your plug size, and experiment with different colors, it just might be the ticket to more fish.

244. Plugs With Rattles

Bob Cobb relied on a wrapped K16 Kwikfish with rattles to take this nice Oregon springer.

While fishing with salmon and steelhead guru, Buzz Ramsey, he shared with me some interesting information one day. Buzz worked with Luhr Jensen for most of his career, and was instrumental in designing some of the most effective plugs in the industry.

"When rattles are inserted into a plug," Buzz shared, "that same model or color that didn't have a rattle pretty much becomes obsolete." In other words, every plug that comes out with a rattle inside runs the other ones of the same color and design off the shelf. Why? Because more anglers buy them. And why do they buy the plugs with rattles? Because they catch more fish.

Rattles in plugs send out sound vibrations, and fish do have a keen sense of sound and vibration-sensing ability. This is something not every salmon and steelhead angler thinks about, but the best time to consider using plugs with rattles is in high, turbid conditions. Being able to target a salmon or steelhead's sense of sound, in addition to sight and smell (if you're adding scents to plugs), provides one more advantage, an advantage that can result in more fish being landed.

Often, when on the water, we'll offer fish a range of items to look at. Maybe one rod runs a silver Hot Shot with a red head. Maybe another runs a blue Pirate with scent. Maybe a third rod carries a silver plug with a rattle. No matter what the range of offerings, over the years there's no question that the top-producing plug in most situations has been the one containing rattles. In fact, there have been many days when plugs with rattles were the only thing catching fish.

In other words, it's worth the time, money and effort to use plugs with rattles. In fact, about the only time I don't use a plug with a rattle is when the color combination or design I want to use is not offered in a rattle version. If you like the color and design, and it has rattles, use it.

245. Spinners

Jeremy Toman with proof of how knowing your spinners can yield rewards.

Just because the water rises and turns color, does not mean spinner-fishing techniques have to take a back seat to other methods. Spinner fishing in unfavorable conditions has proven effective for years, from Alaska to the temperamental streams of Northern California. The key is knowing which spinners work best in which situations.

Long-time spinner fisherman, Jeremy Toman (503-522-4327), spends many months a year in pursuit of fish, be it in Alaska or the Pacific Northwest. His dad, Bob Toman, is one of the top salmon fishermen on the planet, period, and his knowledge of spinner fishing is unparalleled. Growing up, Jeremy acquired much of his dad's knowledge, and has made quite a name for himself in the world of spinner-fishing for big kings. He knows far more about this topic than I, which is why I called on him for advice.

"When the water conditions turn bad, I go to a bigger spinner," shares Jeremy. "I will go to the bigger BT Thumpers, but increase the size of blade I'm using, say from a size 7 up to a size 13. As for which color blades work best in murky water, I like the chartreuse with a green dot, red/white, white/red and in the

evening, chartreuse/red. If the sun is high, I'll go to solid brass or brass with a red/white tip.

As for trolling speed, that roughly remains the same for Toman in ugly water. Both Jeremy and Bob like trolling their spinners at about the rate of 144 revolutions per minute. The thing about the BT Thumper, is the spinner blade is so active, each time it rotates it twitches the end of the rod, so you can actually see the blade "turn." By counting the number of rod ticks over a minute's time, the Toman's have found that 144 revolutions per minute is the ideal trolling speed for spinner fishing. Jeremy may vary his speed, dropping to 120 turns per minute, when things aren't happening like he envisions. Between the color, size and speed, Toman is dialed-in to this technique and catches more fish because of it. You can, too.

246. Smile Blades

The first time I saw a Mack's Lure Smile Blade work, I knew it would have a place in the salmon and steelheading world, going beyond the trout, bass and walleye it was geared toward. And the first time I tried it on early season summer steelhead, it worked. I'd passed bait and jigs through the stretch of choppy water first. Without so much as a strike, I threaded on a few 3mm beads to my leader, then slipped a Smile Blade over those. The water was high and light brown, brown enough that I wanted something bigger, brighter and with more action than the drift-bobber and jigs I'd been throwing at the fish.

That change came in the form of a Smile Blade, and after only a few casts through the same water I'd been covering for over an hour, a strike came. My buddy quickly tied on a Smile Blade, and within a couple casts he landed a steelhead, too. Since then I've taken both steelhead and salmon on this spinning, mylar-wing attractant, and am a strong advocate of its performance.

The thing that really impresses me about the Smile Blade is its ability to rotate in slow-moving water. In high-river situations, where fish often seek out less taxing water closer to shore, Smile Blades work well. They can be plunked, back-bounced or drift-fished with ease, and the array of color combinations allow anglers to pick what they believe will be most effective.

The Smile Blade also comes in various sizes, further opening doors to when and where they can be used (www.macks lure.com). These are one of those tools that salmon and steelhead anglers may require some time to warm-up to, but if you give them a chance, especially in high-water conditions, I think you'll find they do have a place in your arsenal.

247. Diver And Bait

Running a diver-and-bait combination is one of my favorite ways to get on salmon and steelhead in river systems. One reason is because it has a wide range of applicability, meaning it can be practiced in a variety of conditions, for just about any salmon and steelhead you wish to pursue. Another reason this approach is so effective comes down to the fact that anglers have such control over the presentation.

In high water, being able to control where you want the bait can be a challenge, and this is where back-trolling a diver and bait really proves its worth. Being able to control where you want your terminal gear to be means, in the case of diver and bait, establishing a scent trail fish can detect. In high, turbid water, churning, switching currents can make it very tough to lay a scent line, especially when dragging, boondogging or drift fishing. However, establishing a scent trail in colored water is a big plus, especially since the visual aspect of the presentation greatly declines due to poor visibility.

A diver and bait allows you to reach the target depth, and keep the bait in that zone. You can either anchor in wait, whereby letting the diver do the work for you, or back-troll the presentation. What you choose to do depends on the conditions, the size of the channel you're fishing and the amount of fishing pressure the hole is receiving.

If boaters are back-trolling through a section of water, you can slip in and do the same. In this case, avoid dropping anchor and tying up the hole; this may sound obvious, but I see it done every year, and it does nothing but upset fellow anglers by eliminating the possibility for them to fish.

When working diver-and-bait in high, tinted water, sway efforts toward the large divers, like Luhr Jensen's Jumbo Jet Diver. Using plugs with rattles in them as a diver is also effective in high conditions. Consider using larger-sized baits than normal, as well as larger drift-bobbers and more scent. Combining all these strategies will increase your chances of catching fish.

248. More Scent

When the fishing conditions grow tough, anglers need all the elements that they can muster up. The use of scent is something many people stick to, no matter what the conditions.

But when rivers run high and chocolate, or in the case of some coastal streams that are tannic in color, applying more scent to your presentation can make a big difference.

Whether you're fishing bait or plugs, spinners or jigs, the application of scent is something anglers have control over. Not only can applying more scent to these terminal-gear set-ups help the fish to better find them, but reapplying the scents more often can have a direct impact on their ability to attract fish.

When fishing rough water commonly associated with high conditions, some of the paste scents are good choices. These scent forms stay on the lure and bait surface surprisingly well, keeping the presentation fishing stronger and longer.

You can also impregnate some baits with scent, be it in the form of injecting liquids directly into the bait, or soaking the baits with scent during the curing process. There are artificial lures that will also take scent injections or insertions, widening their ability to be more than just a visual attractant; these can be ideal in high-water situations.

Having a range of scent flavors, even brands, can mean the difference between going home with fish or not. Fish are finicky, especially in unstable conditions associated with high, murky water. Being able to offer them a variety of scent flavors can make a difference. Keep in mind not all scent factories use the same formulas, meaning the anise or shrimp smell of one may not be the same as the anise or shrimp smell of another. Experiment, diversify and adapt and your efforts will be rewarded.

249. Heavier Lines

Fish have an innate ability to use water current to the best of their advantage, and nowhere is this more evident than once they are hooked. The knack these fish have, especially the big fish, to find currents and fast water to assist in their fleeing danger is remarkable, and if you've ever fought a big king for 20 minutes or more, you know what I mean.

To help control these fish and decrease the chance of losing them—either by breaking off or the hook pulling out—consider going to a heavier mainline and leader. Another consideration to take into account, especially for salmon, is their sharp teeth. Fall chinook, in particular, have well-developed, very sharp teeth, going to a stronger line—high water or not—is almost a necessity.

For high-water salmon, stepping up to a 40-pound mainline and 20-pound leader is common. Many anglers will opt for 60 pound mainline and 40- or even 60-pound leader. Salmon are not leader-shy, and the heavier the line, the better the chance of landing them. If heavy lines raise doubt, consider commercial fishermen who troll plugs with 80-pound line or heavier, even wire leaders. They make their living catching these fish, and can't afford losing them.

For steelhead, upsizing the line can also be effective. I once hooked and lost three big winter steelhead in a row, all of which took me into the brushline. I switched out the 12-pound mainline and 10-pound leader for 20-pound mainline and 15-pound leader and didn't lose a fish in the brush the rest of the trip. Over the years we've also caught I don't know how many summer steelhead while back-trolling or back-bouncing 20-pound mainline and 17-pound leader for chinook—these fish obviously were not leader-shy given the conditions. The use of heavier line in high water will allow for better control of the fish, and increase your catch.

250. Heavier Rods

While heavy line is one approach to landing more fish in high-water scenarios, increasing the size of your fishing rod can also make a big difference. Depending on the technique being applied, some rods simply fish certain techniques with specific line weights better than others. Follow the line ratings on the rod you're fishing, for these figures are in place based on the rod's spine specifications, how the rod loads-up and overall design.

If increasing the size of the line you use, and especially the amount of weight being used in high water, be sure to match the rod ratings. This is important in not only being able to accurately and precisely fish the way you want to, but once a fish is hooked you can more easily manage it in the more challenging conditions.

A common switch when looking to utilize a more stout rod is to go to a shorter, stiffer selection. These often come in one-piece designs that allow for a considerable increase in line and sinker weight usage. Given the modern technology of today's rod designs, even though these rods are shorter, thicker and very strong, they are light weight enough to allow for easy handling all day long.

If dropping to a shorter, stiffer rod is not to your liking, consider going with a longer rod. Longer rods, such as noodle rods and float rods, disperse the pressure of the fight over a longer distance, whereby allowing you to handle fish in challenging situations. The only drawback with this choice can be the lack of control these longer, more limber rods typically display. When trying to manage big, hot-fighting fish in high water, it's often required that you have to lay the pressure to them to control where they are going, or where you want them to go; this can be hard to accomplish with a long, limber rod, which is why I prefer a shorter, stout rod that I can bear down on.

251. Bigger Hooks

The cliché we've heard since childhood, usually when wetting a worm for bluegill is, "Bigger baits catch bigger fish." But I believe the saying has relevancy, in fact much relevancy, in the salmon and steelhead world. And nowhere do I believe it to be more true than when targeting high-water fish.

The bigger the bait, the easier it is to see and smell, especially in less than ideal conditions. But with the use of bigger baits should come the use of bigger hooks. Keep in mind, however, that some streams and states have hook-size restrictions, so check current regulations before hitting the water with magnum-sized hooks.

That said, big hooks are necessary when using larger baits in order to have more of the point of the hook exposed, so as not to miss a strike. If the hook is completely obscured by the bait there's a chance that when the fish hits, it may not get barbed, even on the best of hook-sets.

In high-water situations for steelhead, both summer and winter runs, a 3/0 hook is one I've been using for years, and with good success. In no way do I feel the oversized hook has cost me fish, in fact, just the contrary. I feel the big hook has allowed me to hook, fight and land more fish than if using a smaller hook under the same conditions. Having more hook buried into a fish's jaw provides more leverage, which correlates to increased landing rates.

As for chinook, a 5/0 is not overkill when fishing bait. When targeting kings that go 40 pounds and higher, a 7/0 hook is not overkill. I've even used 9/0 hooks when working waters with the potential to kick out 70-pound fish or larger.

The interesting thing about using big hooks is the number of smaller fish that are still caught on them. From jack salmon to small steelhead to rainbows and Dollys barely weighing more than the bait itself, it goes to show these anadromous fish are not afraid of gobbling big packages. Of course, these larger hooks also accommodate the use of heavier line, with more shank surface on which to tie leaders. The result is a stronger set-up that can make a difference in fast, high water.

252. Vary Depths

In high-water situations, fish, especially salmon, have the tendency to hold at various depths. This is particularly true in holding water. It's important to understand that as a river rises, current seems, eddies, boils and riffles can undergo change. Often these changes are apparent on the surface, while subsurface changes are not as evident. Sometimes subsurface currents even change direction, or experience more upwelling.

Due to these factors, and the simple fact an increased volume of water can lead to more challenging currents for fish to hold in, it's important to vary the depth of your terminal gear, to seek out fish that may be suspended. This can be done by simply lengthening your leader and/or dropper. If fishing a six-inch dropper and 24-inch leader, change one or both of them. Maybe go to a 48-inch leader and a three- to five-foot dropper. Perhaps changing the amount of weight you use will help vary the depth at which you fish.

Another good idea is to suspend baits below a float, with a sinker tied inline between the two. With the simple adjustment of a bobber stop, you can alter your depth, accordingly. If running plugs, try downsizing the diver, or going without one in waters that may hold suspended fish. Being flexible is the key here, and once you find fish, make note of where and the exact conditions; it can pay off in the future.

253. Work Less Taxing Water

High-water conditions can be physically demanding on fish, and to save energy, they will often seek out less taxing waters. In high-water conditions, we've targeted springers in less than two feet of water, tight to shore, and consistently nailed the fish. The same is true for summer and winter steelhead. These fish will, in the right conditions, move tight to shore.

One winter steelhead year, many anglers dismissed the poor fishing results to the fact that the water was so high, fish were shooting upstream at accelerated rates, moving by anglers. We fished hard, and in two days a buddy and I landed over 20 fish. They were holding in two places: In boils where you'd most likely target salmon, and so tight to shore it was tough getting to them under the overhanging brush. But our search paid-off and, not only were we rewarded with fish, but what we learned greatly expanded our fishing knowledge which has since proven effective on various other rivers in the same conditions over the years.

For winter steelhead and spring chinook, plunking close to shore, both from a boat and the bank, is a good approach. The fish will often migrate up the shallow, inside corners, and waiting for them can work well. For summer steelhead I've found they hold, more than travel, in the waters close to shore. Here, back-trolling plugs, diver and bait and working jigs can be quite productive.

Once you find where the fish are traveling or holding, you can adapt your presentations, accordingly. Make the approach you choose to use fit the conditions. It may be that multiple approaches can be presented. If so, find what works best in that given situation and be persistent.

254. Hit Tailouts

In high-water settings, the increased volume of flow often pushes fish downstream, where they hold in more relaxed water commonly associated with tailouts. For this reason, don't overlook these areas, be it for salmon or steelhead. Oftentimes, as these fish move through heavy rapids, they will hold and recuperate in the nearest, most comfortable water. This often comes in the form of a tailout.

How hard the water pushes into the rising bottom of a typical tailout will determine where the fish lay. It may be a different holding zone for every tailout you come across. A good, general rule here is to note where fish may be holding in normal conditions, then try those spots in high-water situations. If there are no fish to be found, then progressively work tighter to shore, until you find where they may be.

It's important to realize, however, that high-water tailouts can be hit and miss. While the fish will stage in such zones, it's typically not for extended periods of time. My favorite time to hit these waters is in the morning, early in the evening and after a big freshet, when fish are more inclined to move. At the same time, mid-day can be productive in these areas when the fishing pressure is intense on the upper end of the hole, forcing the fish to stay low.

The important thing when fishing these waters is to not get hung-up on pounding them to death. Grid the water, run a quick series of casts through there, all the while making sure to keep the bait on the bottom. Before moving on, put out the plugs and make a pass, or cast jigs through the area on the way downstream. This is often overlooked habitat, habitat that can hold fish.

255. Fish The Eyes Of Swirls

For springers, in particular, swirl holes can be very good areas in which to concentrate fishing efforts. The thing about fishing high-water swirls, they can be tough keeping the terminal gear in the sweet-spot. What swirl holes have to offer salmon is less demanding water due to the high degree of upwelling. This means salmon may be found at various depths within the swirl hole, which makes it even more challenging to find them.

Generally speaking, try to start fishing a swirl hole from the bottom, up. To do this effectively will require the use of more weight, a lot more weight. In areas where you would normally use two ounces of lead, it may require five or six ounces to effectively get down into a swirl hole. Not only is the increased weight necessary in getting your bait down, but keeping control of it once it's down there.

Managing your line at the bottom of a swirl hole is one of the most challenging forms of salmon fishing, and is a main reason these habitats get passed by. Once you get that terminal gear into the eye—or along the edges of the eye—it's important to keep it there. Keep a tight line, maintain constant contact with the bottom and don't allow your gear to be kicked out of the bullseye.

It's also a good idea to go with a short leader, say 18 inches or so, in order to keep the bait low to the bottom, where fish often hold in these settings. If the swirl being fished is near a vertical rock ledge, then consider starting on the bottom, then working up. Oftentimes salmon, and even steelhead, will hold higher in the water column, nosing in to the rock ledge. To effectively fish these zones, find the bottom, bring up the rigging a couple feet and let it work. Usually you'll feel the line bouncing into the rock ledge, which is good, for it shows that the current is moving the terminal gear, hopefully within the same seams in which the fish are holding. The great thing about swirls, if the fish are in, they can be present in big numbers.

256. Get A Motor

Not only can high waters be taxing on fish, but on fishermen as well. This is especially true for drift boaters, where pumping on the oars all day can wear you down. In fact, it can be so tiring that it causes you to pass-up prime fishing spots you would not otherwise surrender if you had a motor. This is particularly true when side-drifting and back-trolling.

When fishing from a drift boat, it's very frustrating to make one pass through a section of water, hook fish, and not be able to run back upstream and repeat the drift. Often in high conditions, the water near shore is actually less powerful, and allows boaters to row back upstream and repeat a drift. But such is not always the case. This is where a motor comes in handy.

The same can be said for back-trolling baits and plugs. In high, fast water you may only get one pass, or not even be able to complete an entire drift due to too hard of conditions. This is where a motor takes the pressure off.

Investing in a small kicker motor, or one of the new megastyle electrics, can pay huge dividends. Not only will these motors allow you to cover an increased amount of water, but they will allow for better, more efficient control of your presentations. And once a fish is hooked, these motors can be counted on to keep you in the hole, or close to it, whereby not passing by prime water that would otherwise go unfished.

In states that require it, make sure you have the proper licensing needed to run a gas motor. For the electric motors, investing in two batteries, then rigging a simple recharging system that plugs in to the boat (rather than having to remove each motor for charging) is time-saving.

257. Boondogging

In high conditions, it's often necessary to cover a great deal of water in order to find fish. And what better way to search for fish than to actually fish while you're doing it. One of the best ways to cover water quickly while fishing is boondogging. Whatever you call it, boondogging, free-drifting or dragging, the fact you're moving at the same rate of the river, versus holding against the current, means you can effectively cover more water.

The important part here is making sure the terminal gear is in the right place because you only get one, quick pass—you don't want to miss it. This is where it's best to have three anglers in the boat, even more in a roomy sled. The more lines you have in the water, the more water can be covered, the greater the odds of catching fish, period.

When boondogging through high water, I like increasing the size of baits, usually eggs, as well as the drift-bobber. I'll also go with a bit longer leader than normal, to allow for increased movement of the bait. Sinkers are usually run on either a short dropper, or on a slider, to keep things close to the bottom, where fish are holding in these settings.

Once fish are located, move back up and make the run again. But be sure to start further upstream, as these fish are usually on the move, meaning by the time you hook and land a fish, the pod could have moved a considerable distance before you get back on them. This is where the value of a motor comes in, too. When dragging, try to hit the center of seams, as well as the sides of them, where they begin to get shallow. In high-water conditions, fish can be in a wide range of depths, which is why this method can be a good one when it comes to locating them.

258. Back-bounce Edges of Seams

Because fish may hold on the edges of seams, taking your time through such water may be the key to success. If you're not finding fish in the main currents or close to shore, try dissecting the edges of seams, more specifically, the outside edges of seams.

Perhaps the best way to do this is by back-bouncing. Drift-fishing does not allow the terminal gear to remain in the sweat-spot long enough, and often the water is too boiling to effectively back-troll or run jigs. Back-bouncing bait is usually the most efficient approach here, for it allows you to control the position of the terminal gear, keeping it in the strike zone.

The only things that might vary here—compared to back-bouncing in normal water conditions—are the increased amount of lead and larger baits. Bigger baits allow for more scent to be dispersed, and are easier for fish to see. The use of scents can also be of great value, where keeping the bait on the bottom lays a good scent trail fish can follow. Increased sinker sizes allow for better control, not only when backing the presentation downstream, but also when keeping the terminal gear from being kicked out of the target water, something which routinely happens with lighter weight sinkers.

Due to the swirling nature of these waters, it's best to anchor at the upper end, then back-bounce downstream. However, it's not always possible to hold the boat straight in such roiling water, which means slowly moving the boat downstream while back-bouncing is the only option. Doing this with a motor is best, for it allows the captain to fish rather than row. Back-bouncing seams is a great approach, and you'll find that not only can it be very productive in high water, but under a range of conditions. Just match the terminal gear set-up to the conditions and you're set.

259. Rock Gardens

It was early in the spring. The water was high, which meant the fish were moving into the system faster than normal. A buddy and I worked several of our favorite salmon holes, but only caught a single fish after half a day of effort. Opting to give up on springers, we decided to see if any steelhead had moved in.

We baited up the back-trolling rods and moved down to a favorite rock garden, a place steelhead normally like to hang. The rock garden stretched for about 75 yards, and on this day, offered the perfect setting for both salmon and steelhead to hold in. Before leaving that hole, we landed eight springers and three steelhead, keeping our limits, releasing the rest. The water was about two feet higher than normal, and a bit discolored, proving to be the perfect hideout.

Since discovering that place, we've pulled more salmon from it, as well as others like it. Some of these rock gardens, however, are too boulder-strewn to back-troll through. In such cases, pull off to the side, drop anchor and drift fish it. Due to the increased amount of rocks, this is where a slinky sinker, caterpillar or even a spider sinker can make a big difference. Whichever sinker set-up you choose to use, the key is one that minimizes hangups. It's no secret lead has a propensity to stick to rocks, so if you can cover that lead, the chances of attaining more complete drifts will result, which will increase fishing time and number of fish you catch.

260. Spider Sinker Value

Whether drift fishing, back-bouncing, working main seams, ledges, the edges of seams or boils, arguably the biggest time-saver I've personally encountered in high-water situations is that of the spider sinker. I've documented cases, whereby comparing the number of sinkers lost by a fellow angler not using a spider to one using a spider; the results are mind-boggling.

In one day that stands out in my mind, the person using the spider set-up lost three sinkers, the other angler lost 27. That's a difference of 24 sinkers being lost. Now, take into account that

many of these lost sinkers were more than that, they were the loss of every bit of terminal gear. To retie all the terminal gear, figure the time it takes you, roughly a two-minute average, let's say. That equates to more than 45 minutes of lost fishing time, which can be huge, especially if your time is limited.

The examples go on and on. I've been using spider sinkers since the late 1970s, and have gained an immense amount of fishing time over the years because of them. The little protective cages do take time to create, and I do this at home, not on the river when I should be fishing. But once done and ready to go, these little devices will increase your fishing time, by eliminating hangups, like nothing else I know. See Tip 51 for building instructions.

261. Scent On Plugs

Whether fishing a Kwikfish or flatfish, many people believe that they should be wrapped any time it's possible. Their reasoning makes sense, especially in high water, and that is, "Why fish a bare lure when you can introduce scents at the same time?"

Wrapping plugs with herring, sardines, anchovies or crawdads are good bets. When low on baitfish, I've had good results wrapping shad fillets. Simply trim the cut to shape, remove the oversized scales and wrap as you would any other baitfish. As with other baitfish, the high oil content of the shad fillet is what you're after, and they do work.

If out of bait, Sponge Wraps can also be wrapped onto the plugs. Patches of absorbent cotton (sometimes mixed with other materials) can be wrapped onto your plug, then saturated with your favorite scent. Sponge Wraps are available through tackle shops and sporting goods stores, and are wrapped onto the plug just as you would a fillet. They are soft, meaning they won't hinder the bite of a fish, and if they do harden from setting in the sun, simply soak in water to regain their shape and pliability.

If baitfish and sponges are not an option, apply scent directly to the plug. The extra sticky scents produced today will stick to the plug, and last. Placing some scent in the bill and amid the O-rings of the hooks are good places to ensure the scent remains on the plug. When applying scents here, check to make sure the application of the scents does not effect the tuning of the plug.

There are many options when it comes to introducing scents on plugs. And in high-water scenarios, it's one approach that's well worth the effort.

262. Bell Beads

Along with high-water conditions comes an increased amount of debris. Dealing with moss, lichen, grass, weeds and other foreign objects drifting downstream due to high water flows cannot only be frustrating, but it can decrease your fishing time and overall effectiveness.

As sediments are carried downstream, they can come into contact with your line. As they contact your line, they can be carried all the way down it, to the terminal gear. The more sediment that stacks up on the lure, plug or bait, the less effective it is. This is where bell beads come in handy.

Bell beads are just that, plastic beads that are shaped like a bell. The bell bead slides on to your line so the narrow end points upstream. In this way, sediments that contact the line and are carried down to the bead are shed once contact is made with the bead. The result is less, or no, unwanted sediments gathering on your line.

If flatlining plugs, for instance, once the smallest piece of grass hangs on the bill or swivel that attaches to the eye-ring, the action changes, often to the point it will not catch fish. The same is true for a diver and bait; once grass accumulates at the head end of the diver, the action and performance of that diver is shot.

To remedy the plug problem, simply tie a barrel swivel three to five feet above the plug. Above the swivel, on the mainline end, first thread on the bell bead, then tie the line to the swivel. Not only will the swivel help prevent line twists, but the bell bead will shed sediments, keeping the plug functioning the way it was intended. When back-trolling baits, position the bell bead in the same place, above the top swivel, or if the diver is being run on a slider, above that point. The better your gear works, the more fish you'll catch.

263. Frequent Bait Check

When fishing high water, it's a good idea to frequently check your bait. This should be done more often than when fishing under normal conditions, for two reasons: First of all, the propensity for sediments to accumulate on the line are greater. Second, high water often means heavier, more turbulent situations, which can expedite the deterioration of baits.

Not only can sediments hinder the operation of lures, plugs and drift-bobbers, but it can prevent a fish from biting. Spinning drift-bobbers are a prime example of how sediments can have a negative impact on your gear. Once tiny pieces of grass make their way down the line, into the hole of the drift-bobber, they are spun into the hole, around the line. This prevents the drift-bobber from rotating the way it's intended. The same can happen to plugs, spinners and other hardware.

Finding which bait fish want can be a challenge.

Likewise, baits that become laden with sediment can turn off approaching fish. If you've ever observed underwater footage of how often a salmon approaches a bait, and doesn't bite it, it's quite humbling. Why they don't bite baits more often may forever remain a mystery, but it goes to show that anglers need to have everything running as clean and efficiently as possible in order to entice a bite; this includes keeping baits clean.

Finally, heavy water can pound baits, quickly breaking down egg skeins and tearing the flesh of baitfish. For this reason alone, it's worth taking a few seconds to check your bait to make sure it's intact. The better the quality of the overall presentation, the more fish will like it.

264. Creek Mouths

One winter the little coastal stream we fished was just coming into shape following days of torrential rain. We were on the water a day earlier than we probably should have been, so the fact we had the river to ourselves wasn't much of a consolation. But we fished, and fished hard...with no success.

Drifting downstream, enthusiasm waning, I tossed a jig toward the mouth of a small creek that flowed into the river. Fish on. We backed up and my buddy landed another dime-bright steelhead. Over the years, that spot has come to be one of my favorite high-water holes on the river. We've found similar high-water success at creek mouths for summer steelhead and spring chinook.

Such feeder creeks are smaller than the river, too small for fish to migrate up, yet large enough to offer food and the allure of fresh water, something anadromous fish thrive on. Because these creeks are smaller, they have a quicker recovery time when compared to rivers, thus the influx of fresh, clean water. In the right situation, such creeks can be very productive during times of high water.

The most fertile creeks I've found to catch fish in front of are where the size of the alluvial fan is small. The stacking up of small sediments into a pile at the mouth of a creek (the alluvial fan) can actually drive fish away, especially steelhead who do not like holding on or near sand. Rather than spend time fishing directly over these fans, move out and downstream, into a position where you can still profit from the surge of fresh water. If the water is deep enough, fish will often be there.

Fishing in low water can be one of the most challenging, and frustrating, experiences a salmon and steelhead angler can face. As if it's not bad enough when you're not hooking fish, but seeing them laying right there in front of you, and still not getting them to bite, is even more frustrating. What makes it worse, sometimes, the harder you try, the more frustrating the experience becomes.

Low-stream conditions bring with it more than just clear water. Low river levels often result in a rise in water temperature, something that, alone, can turn off a bite. Low water also forces the fish to hold in confined areas, which can put them on edge, also curtailing the bite. Where fish congregate, so too, do anglers, and this increased pressure can really cause fish to be close-mouthed.

Chapter 6   Low, Clear Water

The list of why it's so hard to really catch fish in clear, low rivers, goes on and on. And because fishing in these conditions grows so challenging, many anglers choose not to face them. But there are measures that can be taken to increase the odds of catching fish in these tough situations.

The adage, "10% of the fishermen catch 90% of the fish," really proves itself when the going gets tough. It's your choice, you can either hang it up and wait for conditions to return to perfect—which may take weeks, even months, or worse yet, never happen until the following season—or do what has to be done to catch fish. Following are approaches that have worked well for me over the years when fishing less than ideal low-water conditions. Do they work all of the time? Of course not, nothing does. But they have worked some of the time, and the confidence they lend, along with a positive attitude, goes a long way in catching fish in adverse situations.

265. Smaller Baits

In low-water settings, one of the first things to consider is down-sizing the baits. This is done for two reasons: First, the fish have a clear window of visibility, meaning they can see the bait coming toward them—or see it as they approach, as the case may be—from a greater distance, thus there's no need for larger presentations. Second, shallow-water fish can be edgy, and big, gaudy baits often spook them. I think this is more applicable to steelhead, who will react to small baits, be it shying away from them at first sight, or traveling great distances to devour them.

I don't know how many steelhead we've seen move from beyond 10 feet in the distance to strike a small bait. Sometimes, if they see a bait and they want it there's no stopping them, and I find the smaller baits often trigger this response. Perhaps this is due to the more natural flow associated with smaller baits.

Smaller baits are also less intrusive than larger ones. When fishing among boulders, sometimes the bait pops up in front of the fish, and boom, it's smack on their snout. Larger baits seem to have a tendency to spook more fish in these conditions.

On steelhead, going from a full sand shrimp to a shrimp tail, or from a quarter-sized piece of egg cluster to a dime-sized one, can make a big difference. When going this small, either affix the smallest drift-bobber you can find, like a size-14 Corky, or go without.

For salmon, decreasing the size of egg cluster, prawn, or whatever bait is being used, can also make a difference. Here, it's important to also remember to downsize the drift-bobber as well as the hook, to present a less-offensive offering and one that will float more naturally in the current. If you're seeing fish, or know they are down there, but they're not biting, try introducing smaller baits.

266. Smaller Plugs

24/7 Guidervice

Back-trolling plugs, or casting them off the bank, can be done in low water, it just seems to be more effective when smaller sizes are used. If you've ever stood on a high bank and watched someone run plugs down in front of you, it's incredible to see how quickly the fish will sometimes react to the presentation. It's stunning to see a fish move 15 feet or more to nail a plug. Then again, if they don't want it, the plug can bounce off their nose and they may not even open their mouth. It's called fishing, not catching.

But when conditions do drop and become challenging, consider decreasing the size of your plugs. Rather than pulling a 35 series Hot Shot, perhaps a 50, or even 70 series will be what it takes. I've seen these mini plugs work magic on summer steelhead, too many times to count, over the years. The same holds true for salmon. If that K16 Kwikfish feels too big, drop down a few sizes.

We've made passes through sections of water with large plugs, not having so much as a bite. Then we downsized the plugs, reran the same water and caught fish. This doesn't always happen, especially in low water, for the fish usually spook and clamp their mouths closed. But sometimes it does.

A stealthy approach is crucial when plugging low water. Move slowly, quietly, let out more line than normal and run the plugs flatlined, without the aid of a diver. I'll often let out 20 feet more line than when plugging water at normal levels; as long as the plug keeps digging into the water, you're fine. But if the plug rises to the surface, bring it in a little closer, so the bill meets more resistance. Also note that running the plugs out greater distances may cause a delayed reaction to the boat's movement, so gauge it accordingly. Be persistent, creative and patient, and downsizing plugs can be just the trick.

267. Micro Jigs

I once fished a small, clear Alaskan stream. The steelhead were stacked in a hole, but would not so much as move toward the 1/4-ounce jig I ran over them. They didn't appear spooked, for I used my polarized glasses and presented the jig from well upstream. They simply didn't want it.

So, I gave them time. I pulled out a snack and munched on it, letting the fish relax and hopefully forget about the jig that had been pestering them. I tied on a 1/32-ounce Stuart Steelhead Bullet Jig and, on the first pass, nailed a bright steelhead, still dripping with sea lice. Two casts later, another fish, then another.

That wasn't the first time I'd seen how effective micro jigs can be, nor the last.

Shallow-water steelhead can be finicky, and when talking about pursuing these great fish in two to three feet of water, you don't want to upset them. Start well upstream of where you see fish holding, or anticipate them to be holding, and start feeding line downstream. Let the current naturally carry the jig and float—or indicator if using a fly set-up—downstream toward the fish. I've pegged the float to the swivel, and gone with only six inches of leader and had fish move up and take these micro jigs, and that goes for spring and fall steelhead, coho and pink salmon. There's no question, even in big rivers, that micro jigs do have a place in clear, low-water situations.

268. Fluorocarbon Leader

With clear-water conditions comes the ability for fish to see better. I don't much worry about line when it comes to salmon seeing it, but I do when it comes to steelhead. Having sight-fished steelhead for many years, there's no question in my mind that I have spooked numerous fish due to line. Then I started using fluorocarbon.

Fluorocarbon has a refraction index nearly identical to water, meaning it's virtually invisible under water. When targeting edgy steelhead in clear conditions, using a good fluorocarbon leader could be the best kept secret there is. The key here having a good line.

Since their inception, fluorocarbons have come a long way. I've used several brands, but the one you'll always find me with, well, almost always, is PLine's fluorocarbon. Once on the river, the conditions were more clear than I'd anticipated them being, and the fish were spooky. I'd forgotten my PLine. My buddy gave me some of his fluorocarbon line, and I hooked and broke off three fish. It was my fault, for I'm confident that would not have happened had I had my trusty PLine.

With recent upgrades, the quality of PLine's fluorocarbon has improved even more. Never before have knots held so firm, the leader been so resistant to abrasion or held up to such stress.

But the beauty of fluorocarbon lies in its invisible-like quality. Normally, in clear water, anglers downsize the weight of their leader. This equates to more fish being lost due to the sacrifice of stronger line, whereby fish cannot be controlled, thus break off. Because it's clear, just the opposite is the case with fluorocarbon. Rather than downsizing leader weight, you can upsize, because it can't be seen. This means more fish will be hooked, and landed, period.

269. Longer Leader

If you're looking to cover more water with each cast, and present a more natural delivery, try extending the length of your leader. A longer leader will move about more freely during the drift, and on the swing it will sweep and cover more water. Combine this with a small bait, and the presentation gets tossed about in the little currents and carried into food funnels where steelhead often hold.

For salmon that typically hold tight to the bottom when conditions are low and clear, going to a longer leader also works well. Whether back-bouncing, plunking or throwing it out there and letting it soak then moving it around a bit, a long leader allows the bait to be lifted more off the bottom, and flutter around, hopefully drawing the attention of fish.

When using a long leader for steelhead in shallow settings, I'll either go without a drift-bobber, or use the smallest size made, as I don't want the float to carry the bait too high out of the strike zone. For salmon I'll also drop down in drift-bobber sizes, so as not to risk spooking fish that may have been previously hammered on by other anglers.

When using long leaders, avoid the tendency to line fish, or floss them, as it's often called. This is where a long leader is dragged through the mouth of a fish, leading the hook into the fish's mouth, usually hooking it on the outside of the jaw or in the side of the head. To avoid this, the longest leader I'll use is about six feet, not the 10- to 12-foot ones some people opt for. With light terminal gear and proper positioning, six feet of leader is plenty to accomplish what you want. If you desire further separation from the sinker, simply increase the length of your dropper.

270. Lighter Mainline

In low, clear conditions, it may be necessary to downsize your mainline in order to catch fish.

One of the benefits of fishing low water is the ability to downsize your gear, line included. How light you choose to go on your terminal gear is dictated by how well you can manage it, and that directly correlates to the weight of the mainline being used.

Typically, the lighter the line, the lighter you can go on the terminal gear. Too heavy of line results in not being able to cast or manage your terminal gear properly. The benefits of using a light mainline are that it presents options for the use of various lightweight gear and allows you to reach water you might not otherwise be able to with heavier set-ups. A light mainline is also less intrusive, something that can make a big difference when stealth fishing for steelhead or silvers holding in shallow, glass-clear water.

Last, and perhaps most important of all, is that a light mainline creates a very natural presentation due to the decrease in drag. The smaller-diameter line simply does not get caught in currents like line with a larger surface will, but you do have to stay on top of it in order to keep it from getting away from you.

A word of caution, however. If in waters where wild fish are a target of catch-and-release action, be careful not to drop to too light of line. Too light of line not only breaks more easily, but it requires more time to get the fish in. The longer it takes to land a fish, the longer it takes to revive it and the more difficult it is for the fish to fully recover. It's a judgment call, use your best judgment.

271. Lighter Terminal Gear

By downsizing the mainline and matching it to the appropriate rod, it opens opportunities for presenting smaller terminal gear, which can make a difference between catching fish or not, in clear, low-water conditions. This strategy relates more to steelhead than salmon, but can have wide-ranging applications in the right situations.

With a light mainline, smaller lures and baits can be used. At the same time, egg presentations for steelhead can drop down to a size-2 hook versus a 2/0, which will then accommodate a size-14 Corky rather than a size 8. The key is to present a tiny bait, one that fish can see but won't be spooked by.

If drift fishing with light line, the luxury of going with a smaller sinker is also there. The sinker is your control source of how fast the line moves; that is, more weight slows down the presentation; less weight speeds up the drift. How much sinker you choose to go with depends on the water conditions being fished and how far you have to cast to get the terminal gear into the target water.

When it all comes together, the lightweight gear should be in a position where fish can see it. Avoid floating it too high over their heads, and make sure it doesn't speed by too quickly. Then again, some steelhead like a fast swing at the end of the drift, a technique that's easy to accomplish with lighter gear. Timing and positioning are important, as is emulating a natural rate of flow. The more completely these principles are understood and mastered, the better the chances of catching fish on light terminal gear.

272. Longer Poles

When downsizing mainline and terminal gear, it's all for naught unless they match the line and weight ratings of the fishing pole. Today, most rods come with the line and weight class ratings inscribed on them. When buying new rods, pay close attention to these numbers and select models that will fit your specific needs. The better the fit of the rod, the more efficiently you'll be able to master the technique being applied.

It's worth noting that downsizing to a smaller rod does not actually mean the rod has to be "smaller." In fact, with today's

technology, the rods may be bigger, or longer, than models designed for heavier line use. A good example would be a noodle rod or float rod. These rods are constructed in such a way so as to disperse the energy of the fight. Many clear-water anglers opt for 11- and 12-foot-long rods capable of handling line as light as 4-pound test. When fighting a fish, these rods really bend, and that's how they are designed.

With a set-up that light, oftentimes a sinker is not even needed. In fact, some folks are so dialed-in to their lightweight set-ups, they can cast and fish a single egg, nothing else. Talk about the ability to attain a natural drift. Its a prime example of how critical it is to know your gear and it's capabilities, as it can pay off in the form of more fish in the freezer.

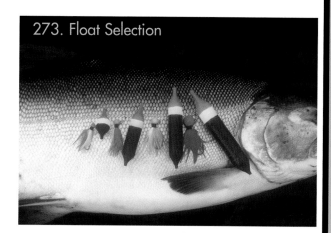

273. Float Selection

With the introduction of float fishing has come a wide range of specialized gear, and nowhere is this more evident than in floats. Floats—or bobbers as some folks still prefer calling them—are more high tech than ever, with aerodynamic and aquatic designs that allow them to ride in precise positions, as well as flinch at the slightest tap.

But rather than focus on float size and style, let's look at color. Personally, I've never found much of a difference in the float colors. I prefer the West Coast Floats due to their design, composition and level of sensitivity. However, there are folks who would disagree with me because these floats are black, and they would argue that the black color of the float spooks fish.

I've caught steelhead on six inches of leader, and silvers on four inches of leader, with the float actually slid down over the swivel so it wouldn't move. That's how shallow the water was I fished, and when coming up for the jigs, the floats didn't seem to bother the fish in the least. Then again, who is to say I wouldn't have caught more on a clear float?

If it adds confidence, then go with a clear float, or perhaps one with the bottom painted blue to mimic the color of the sky. It's one of those things that's hard to test and quantify through logging data and nonjudgmental personal observations. Float color may make a difference, and in this situation, there may be no direct answer, rather than to go with what you believe in.

274. Back-troll Flies

Whether or not you're a die-hard conventional gear fisherman, if you want to catch more fish, it's imperative to diversify. In this case it means crossing over into the world of fly-fishing. But don't worry, you don't have to cast far, in fact, you don't have to cast at all. This form of fly-fishing involves the use of a boat, and back-trolling flies just as you would plugs.

Back-trolling flies for both summer and winter steelhead is very effective in low-water conditions. Why? Because it simulates a natural food source moving downstream. Rather than focus on bright, flashy presentations or scents that appeal to fish, back-trolling a fly gets back to nature, it's meant to match bugs that fish feed on.

A 5- to 7-weight fly rod and a matching WF floating line is all you need to get started. Utilizing a floating line is critical for achieving proper depth. A nine-foot 4X, 3X or 2X tippet is a good choice, and which one you use will be determined by the river and the tenacity of the fish you're after. When fishing a river with wild fish, they'll fight hard, and take me all over, so will go with heavier tippet.

If looking to add even more variance, consider pulling a double-fly set-up, where the top pattern serves as an attractor. Four to five feet should separate the two flies, with the attractor being tied to a six- to eight-inch dropper. Matching the patterns to respective aquatic life in the river being fished is a good rule. In many steelhead streams, a silver-tinsel-bodied sculpin or muddler pattern on a size-10 hook serves as a good attractor and actually produces a large number of hits. Dropping a couple sizes, the trailing fly can be anything you have confidence in, with bead-head patterns and leeches being tough to beat.

Back-troll this set-up just as you would plugs, maybe moving downstream a bit faster in order to more closely simulate a drifting bug. Expand your working base, try new things and you'll catch more fish, even on the fly.

275. Sight-Fishing

While sight-fishing is fun whenever the conditions allow, the challenge reaches its apex in low, clear conditions. The more clear the water, the easier it is to see the fish. But just because it's easier to see them doesn't mean it's easier to catch them. In fact, its quite the contrary.

Fish in low-water conditions often fight for holding space, which means they crowd into the few prime holes or riffles they can find. This leaves them vulnerable and on edge, and they are tough to coerce into biting. The more pressure they receive, the more challenging they become to catch.

One of my first experiences on Alaska's famed steelhead stream, the Situk River, found me staring at schools of 200 and more steelhead. Keep in mind, many of the fish in these schools eclipsed the magic 20-pound mark, but despite long efforts by

myself, my buddies and other anglers, the fish simply would not bite. All the big schools were suspended in slack water. As a general rule, when I see steelhead suspended in dead water, I don't waste time on them; I've never gotten them to bite, not even on the Situk. Same for king salmon. In these cases, I'll seek out smaller schools or single fish to target in faster water. But coho are different, for when suspending in slack water where they will eventually spawn, they will bite.

Low-water sight-fishing can be very challenging and more frustrating than you can imagine. Being so close to trophy fish and not getting them to bite will test your skills and patience. In these conditions, proceed with stealth. Be prepared to pull out all the tricks possible, and note how fish respond to each. If they spook, evaluate why. If they attack a presentation or move quickly to one, mouth it and spit it out, figure out why. The more questions you can answer, the more mysteries you can unlock, the more successful your sight fishing efforts will become.

276. Work Middle Of Currents

Over the years I've had very solid success targeting low-water steelhead in the middle of currents. This is because main currents are deeper, offering a place of refuge, and the broken water at the surface adds more comfort to holding fish. While I've seen salmon moving through and even holding in the middle of fast, deeper main currents, I've had mixed results when targeting them. For salmon, I choose to wait until they move into a deeper hole.

But for steelhead, not only do they feel safe in the middle of currents, but they're often forced there. Bank pressure and boating action will force steelhead to move to the safest place. Clear holes are not an option, unless that's all they have to resort to. And if the fishing pressure is heavy on both banks, as well as from boats, hanging off to the side of the main current leaves the fish too antsy.

For these reasons, it's important to work the deeper, faster-moving center of the main currents. I've even seen this behavior of seeking safety in deeper water by red salmon. Normally, these fish travel in enormous schools, often numbering into the hundreds of thousands. Even in numbers that high, they often spook to deeper water when an angler wades and tries getting too close.

When fishing the middle of currents, you may need to increase the amount of lead being used in order to roll the presentation tight to the bottom, where fish are holding in these conditions. It might even be necessary to upsize the bait offering, so the fish can see it in the deeper, faster-moving water. Assess the situation, calculate where fish should be given all of the conditions and don't overlook those middle slots, places many anglers pass by.

277. Hit Pocket Water

Hitting pocket water paid off for the author in the form of this hatchery winter steelhead.

In low-water situations, fish are forced to hold in what limited habitats are available. These habitats can vary based on the species and time of year, along with other variables such as water temperature, barometric pressure, fishing pressure and so forth. But one of the places salmon and steelhead frequent in low, clear conditions is pocket water.

Pocket water is just that, small pockets of water, normally set off to the side of the main current, where the depth and choppy water attract fish and help them feel safe. For low-water steelhead, pocket water is hard to beat. The same goes for silver salmon, especially in small coastal streams. chinook, or kings, can be found in pockets, but the pockets they prefer are deeper and typically more boiling.

One of the biggest mistakes people make in fishing pocket water is not fishing it. At first glance, the water may look good, but is often dismissed as being too small. A single rock can create a pocket, and a trio of large rocks laying side-by-side is even better. If the gravel on the downstream side is small, whereby easily washing out, a fairly deep hole can be created over the years. Add some choppy, broken water on the surface and the ideal pocket is created.

A prime fishing pocket can be anywhere from a couple feet wide to 10 or so feet long. Then again, they may be five feet wide and only a few feet long. The anatomy of a pocket depends on water flow, the size of the structure—usually rocks—that creates them and the rock composition surrounding the structure. It can change from stream to stream, even from one section of water to another.

Given the low conditions, fishing pocket water is usually a light-tackle affair. You may be able to make a quick pass with plugs, or side-drift the small section. Floating a jig or drifting eggs is also an option. Again, the passes can be very short, but don't let that keep you from fishing pockets, for they can mean the difference between a slow or stellar day.

278. Hit Riffles

Riffles are arguably the best low-water fishing habitat there is. Rifles provide fish, especially steelhead, coho and sockeye, with protection in the form of a broken surface. The faster-moving water, though it does not carry more oxygen than other parts of the river, like many folks believe, does aid in the fish's respiration, which is another reason fish will gravitate to riffles in low water. Angler pressure, if intense, can also cause fish to move into shallow riffles, as can direct sunlight.

Fish have the ability to be camouflaged in very shallow riffles, and it doesn't take much water to hide them. Over the years I've taken steelhead in less than a foot water, silvers in two feet, and chinook in less than four feet of water. Normally, one wouldn't consider fishing such shallow depths for any of these fish, but because the conditions forced them there, fishing them was well worth the time and effort.

Due to their broken surface, heavy, shallow riffles make it nearly impossible to see fish before casting to them. This means that fishing riffles is normally a blind affair. Given that fact, riffles can be fished with quick passes on light tackle, or deliveries can be slowed by adding more weight.

I've pulled 25-pound chinook from riffles on a fast-moving jig, while targeting steelhead, and taken steelhead on a bait I figured to be way too large, that slowly crawled along the bottom intended for springers.

To effectively and consistently catch fish from riffles, a wide range of techniques and gear may be required. If you are confident fish are in a riffle, but the bite is slow in coming, switch to another method. Experiment with various types of terminal gear, speeds of delivery, angles of presentation and anything else that fits with the water being fished. Diversity is the key to consistently taking fish from shallow riffles, and mastering the techniques required will open up many doors, no matter what river you fish.

279. Earth-Tone Clothes

Of the hundreds of seminars I've conducted around the West, only one time has a person asked, "Why are you wearing such bright colors in all of your pictures?" It's a good question, but one I thought would be asked with much more frequency. The answer is, I wear bright clothes because they are more eye-catching than drab-colored clothes. Would I prefer wearing earth-tone colored clothes, you bet, but nature tells the human eye that bright colors are more pleasing, and that's what many magazine editors and TV producers go by. Has wearing bright colors cost me fish? You bet, especially in clear, shallow water.

When working such challenging conditions, make every effort to wear earth-tone, even camouflaged clothes, especially if bank fishing. In addition, when approaching fish, or anywhere fish may be, move slowly so as not to attract attention to yourself. In these shallow conditions, fish are on alert, and will panic at the slightest hint of danger.

Caps and shirt sleeves are the most important areas to hide, followed by the torso. Your head is the highest point of the body, and what fish see first. Arms carry the most movement, and nothing can spook a fish faster than bright sleeves flailing through the air. Next, the torso is also highly visible, making it a good idea to cover that up with a drab shirt or fishing vest.

We were once filming a TV show on red salmon in Alaska. Schools of thousands of fish were filing by. Despite how "dumb" people associate these fish with being, every time I moved to within 15 feet of them, they would shift further out into the current. Mind you, these fish were always on the move, so each one that passed by was fresh, unaware of my presence. But I kept pushing it, wanting to get close to cut the glare on the water so I could see them more clearly. Every time I moved close, they moved out. The camera man suggested I roll down my olive-green shirt sleeves, to cover up my bright-red base layer. I did, the fish started moving where they had been before I spooked them, and we got our TV show in no time.

280. Track Boats

If you're new to a river, or have not fished it much in low-water conditions, proceed with open eyes. That is to say, watch closely where other boats go, how they fish, and where they catch fish. In fact, when they catch a fish, mark exactly where they hooked it. If you see them too late in the battle, and aren't sure exactly where they hooked it, wait, watch them land the fish and observe where their next cast will be. More times than not, the first cast after having landed a fish is made in the same location as the cast that caught that fish; this is especially true in shallow water, where fish may congregate in one small spot.

It's also a good idea to observe what drifts other boaters make, and deduce why they may have gone where they did. Did they go right or left down that riffle, and why? Did they fish while moving through a section of water, or did they push straight through, then drop anchor and start fishing? It doesn't take long to determine if a boater knows what they are doing. Pay attention to the ones who catch fish, and learn.

Even if you know a river well, and where to fish it in normal or high-water conditions, it can be totally different in low water. Many elements undergo change when rivers drop, from where you fish, how you fish, where fish hold and where they move. By learning a low-water fishery, you're broadening your knowledge base, and gaining valuable insight as to how to read low water and interpret where fish may be, thus how to fish it. With such information, you're increasing the ability to take your boat to other rivers and catch more fish under similar circumstances.

281. Observe Bank Anglers

More people bank fish for steelhead than fish from boats. Many of these bank anglers have been fishing the same holes, year after year, and doing quite well. Due to the relatively limited access bank fishermen are restricted to, they are forced to intimately learn a hole if they want to consistently catch fish.

These folks know where fish hold when the water is running at a certain flow, and they know where fish move to when the water drops and turns clear. They know which rock to cast behind between noon and 2:00 p.m. in the middle of the summer, because they know where the sun causes the fish to move to. They are aware that angler pressure will force fish to deviate from their normal route, and more importantly, where their alternate paths and holding zones are. They even know which rock they want to stand on at the start of the morning, where they want to move to at mid-day, and where they should go as the sun drops behind the trees.

The successful bank angler is an educated one, and a great deal can be learned by simply observing one. Some will share their secrets, and even tell how they learned them. When you find kind folks like this, covet the information and honor their requests. If you're not one for social interaction on the water, then sit back, observe and learn. When someone catches fish, note exactly where it came from, what they caught it on and what the conditions were like, including time of day. Opening your eyes, and mind, will no doubt increase your overall fishing skills.

282. Cast And Move

If you're unable to see fish in low water, either due to glare or a choppy surface, one approach to take is cover as much water as possible. This is especially true in the middle of the day, when fish are in a holding pattern. Because fish tend to hold from around mid-morning through later in the afternoon, it's a good idea to go searching for them.

Make your casts and move on, covering as much water as you can. Once fish are found, often there are more to be had, and it's worth spending a little time in that area. If, after 15 minutes you don't catch another fish, move on. Because low-water fishing action can be slow, covering water is often the best approach. The goal is to cover as much water as possible, looking for the biters.

Casting and moving is a good approach if you're short on time. Maybe you only have a few hours to fish, and spending it in hopes of finding a quick hit is an efficient plan. Perhaps you have all day to fish, but still want to cast and move. In this case, pack a lunch and extend the drift. Rather than taking out at the ramp you usually do, continue down to the next one. For bank anglers, rather than parking in one area and waiting for fish, wade your way over as much water as possible; you might even consider driving to another hole or river.

If wanting to cast and move, pick one or two techniques that best fit the conditions and species being targeted and stick with that. Don't spend time trying every approach in every spot you come to, whereby limiting the amount of water you can fish. Covering water and fishing on the move does have its rewards and can be very productive. It's also a good way to see more of the river and enjoy nature's wonders.

283. One-Fish Focus

Focusing efforts on one fish is sometimes the best move.

If seeing fish in low water, it may be worth the time and effort to focus on one fish at a time. This approach can be tedious, time-consuming and truly test your patience, but what you'll learn about fish and how they respond to various approaches will make you a better angler, period. This is especially true with steelhead, where sight-fishing is more applicable than with salmon.

Once a fish is spotted, stealth into casting position and start in. Usually, if the fish is going to bite out of instinctual reaction, it will come on the first few casts. If, after having made several casts with no strike, but the fish is still holding in the same spot,

there's still a chance of catching it. Steelhead are very territorial, and they don't like foreign objects invading their space. This is where you pull out all the stops and make the bite happen.

If drifting eggs by the fish's nose didn't work, start applying scents, to see if that triggers a reaction. Switching to a shrimp tail might be the key, or passing a lure in front of its snout may be what turns it on. Try floating a jig over its head, starting it far enough upstream where the fish can see it coming for a considerable distance. Should none of these produce, go to force-feeding tactics. Slap on a couple ounces of lead and park a bait smack on the fish's nose. Let it twirl and soak in the current, preferably within two inches of the fish's snout.

Oftentimes, when parking a bait on a fish, you'll see the fish begin to grow agitated. Its body movements will increase, it may even start pumping its mouth faster and wider to take in more oxygen. Sometimes they'll pitch onto their sides, venting frustrations. It's about then that they'll usually move up to the bait, eat it and spit it out without you feeling a thing, all in about two seconds. This can happen multiple times, and is one of the most humbling lessons an angler can learn; watching a bite but not feeling it.

If the full shrimp fails to elicit a strike, try going to a small bead or Corky, nothing else on the line. Park it on the fish's nose and let it spin, in hopes of triggering a bite. Force-feeding tactics like this are a test of casting skills, and what you learn from observing the bite and a fish's behavior will improve your knowledge and skills. Change your approaches, be resourceful and above all else be patient, then you'll discover just how rewarding targeting a lone fish can be.

284. Temperature Drops

No matter how low the water is, as soon as there's an outside temperature drop or a cool rain moves through, get out and fish. Often it only takes a degree or two drop in temperature to invigorate fish and get them active. These are good times to be on the water.

One summer we had nearly a week of 100° temperatures at my Oregon home. The water warmed and the fish went off the bite. Then, from the Gulf of Alaska, cool air moved in. The daytime temperatures dropped nearly 30 degrees, and the nighttime temperatures about 20 degrees. Two days of this cool weather was all that was needed, and the bite was on for both steelhead and springers.

Likewise, a blast of rain can spark life in fish, for that surge of fresh water triggers their homing instinct. If a river you fish has other tributaries that feed into it, perhaps their cooler waters may attract fish. I once fished a river in Northern California that was low and warm. After five hours of fishing we had nothing to show for it, then we pulled the boat into where a big, cold, mountain creek entered the river. It looked like Alaska, with both chinook and steelhead in a big school that spanned 20 yards in width, 200 yards long. It ended up being a good day.

Even in cold winter and early spring months, a shot of fresh rain will cause fish to move and become more active. Track weather systems, monitor daily temperature changes and know what tributaries enter a river. By timing your efforts to coincide with a slight drop in water temperature or during the time of a fresh spurt of rain, your low-water fishing success will increase.

One of the hardest things for anglers to do is muster enough energy after a long day on the river to give attention to the boat and gear that was used, or lost. The longer you put these responsibilities off, the harder it is on your gear. The worst part, such neglect can cost you valuable fishing time, even fish.

Even if arriving home late and you know you're not going fishing the next day, there are still tasks to be done before hitting the sack, tasks that will keep gear clean and prolong its life. Granted, most of the tasks can be done the following morning, but not all of them. Get those stinky towels out of the boat, so bacterial growth does not spread. Wash the egg cure residue off the cork rod handles, so they don't become encrusted and give off foul odors. Put leftover baits in the refrigerator so they don't spoil.

These are just a sampling of tasks that can be carried out in order to save time in the long-run. Such efforts will also preserve your gear and make sure you're ready to fish the next time the opportunity arises, and this is critical should you get a hot tip and want to be on the river within an hour or two. The last thing you want to do is give up a hot day of fishing because you failed to tend to responsibilities when you should have. Some of the more time-consuming jobs, like washing down the boat, changing line and retying leaders, may be able to be put-off until next time.

Chapter 7 End-of-the-Day Tips

The point is, fishing success is not solely dependent upon the time you are on the water. A good fisherman recognizes that a great deal of preparation and organization goes in to building success. It's efforts like these that separate the average angler from the elites.

Many anglers dream of being a guide and living the guide's life. But good, hard-working guides that take special care of their gear and are always on top of their game do this line of work as a passion, not to get rich. Most awaken in the middle of the night to prepare gear. Many don't get home until late, then dedicate several hours to cleaning up. I know of many guides who, during the two- to three-month height of their season, average four hours of sleep a night. That kind of dedication is hard on the body and the mind, but it's what they do in order to be successful.

Following are points to consider relating to responsibilities that can be taken at the end of a day on the water in order to increase your overall efficiency the next time out. Some leeway can be taken as to when these tasks get done. The purpose is to raise awareness and spur forethought, so you'll be better prepared with clean, smoothly operating gear the next time you're on the water.

285. Frequent Line Change

Big fish like this one taken by Jerry Haugen, can result in the need for frequent line changes.

How often you change your mainline depends on how much you fish, where you fish and how many fish you catch. I've been on rivers where sharp, bedrock ledges warranted a line change every night we returned to camp. Other rivers may be forgiving, not forcing a line change for weeks.

On the other hand, one, hot fish can fray a line or inflict so many twists a change may be necessary while on the river. In the event that a fish strips all your line, then breaks it off at the reel, you'll obviously be in need of a line change, or replacement as the case may be.

Getting hung-up and losing a considerable amount of line can also impede your fishing, whereby warranting the need for more line. If your spool gets too low, especially on open-face reels, it can be impossible to make long casts and reach the water you want.

Whether fishing off the bank or out of a boat, it's a good idea to have an extra spool of handy, for you never know when a need to change the line will occur. I carry small refill spools in the boat or pack, keeping the big bulk spools at home where the majority of line changes take place.

If your line begins to discolor, change it. If it's been fished in direct sunlight for extended periods, change it more frequently. Sunlight breaks down copolymers and monofilaments, so avoid exposing them to such harsh conditions any more than is necessary.

A good, general rule: If you think the line might need to be changed, change it. If in question of a line's effectiveness, change it. You don't want to risk losing a fish due to bad line, something that's in your control. Besides, the cost of fishing line is negligible compared to other facets of the sport. Of course, the strongest, most abrasion-resistant line you can buy will last the longest and be your best investment.

286. Touch-up Hooks

It's likely the most elementary tip in the entire book, but it's also one of the most overlooked, and that's keeping your hooks sharp. It's true that, today, there are several quality hooks that are needle sharp straight from the package, but they are all vulnerable to dulling with use. It's up to you to keep them sharp.

I'll never forget the first time I fished with Buzz Ramsey. Besides the 20-some rods we had in the boat, and enough tackle to last an entire season, let alone the day, were hook files. In fact, there were four different hook files to be exact, plus several more stashed in tackle boxes.

Buzz's philosophy was to always keep the hook sharp, and he did. Even on the slightest of hangups, where a simple twitch of the rod tip freed the hung gear, Buzz would check the hook. More times than not he'd pass a file over it. "You can't catch fish if your hook's not sharp," was what he shared. Here I was, fishing with the man who is perhaps the most versed salmon and steelhead angler on the planet, and the lesson that stands out in my mind the most from that day, was to keep a sharp hook. Of course, I came away with more wisdom than that, just as I do every time we fish together.

But the point Buzz made was true. No matter how good all of your gear and techniques may be, it's all for nothing if you can't hook the fish. When in a boat, consider keeping at least one file per person handy. It's not a bad idea to have more files than that placed about the boat, so people don't waste time searching for one to use. When fishing off the bank, keeping a file within easy reach, and another as a backup, is a good idea.

What I've found is the more you have to work to find a file, the less likely you are to use it. And if you're not using it, then you're cutting down on your ability to hook and land more fish. In addition to continually checking your hooks while on the river, once you get home, double check them for sharpness. Check the hooks that are tied on the rods or that got used throughout the day—such as plug, lure and jig hooks—as well as any hooks that got tossed aside for retying. It seems like a minor detail, but having sharp hooks is an element of the sport you can monitor, and is certainly not a good excuse for losing fish.

287. Wash Inside Boat

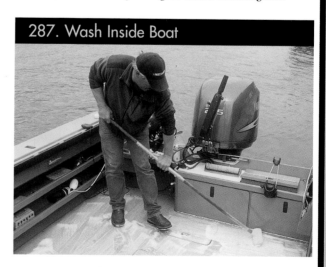

When the day is done, make it a point to wash down the inside of the boat. This is especially important when fishing baits, or when fish have been brought into the boat and come in contact with the floor. Fish slime and bait residues can set like glue in a boat, and harbor loads of harmful bacteria. When on the river the next time, it may be raining or these residues will get wet due to everyday fishing activity. The result is a damp boat that stinks, and keeping these odors from transferring to the baits and other gear is virtually impossible.

Because foreign odors can be so repulsive to the sensitive nose of a fish, it pays to make every effort to eliminate them. Think of it as preventative maintenance. Not only will washing your boat keep it clean for future outings, it will keep it in better condition, prevent rust build-up and extend its overall life.

Use hot water, strong soap, scrub hard and make sure to thoroughly wash every nook and cranny. There are also commercial boat-cleaning products designed to cut through grease, scum, fish slime, dirt and more. Extreme Scents, for example, carries a line of boat-cleaning products called Supreme Marine (www.suprememarine.us), that I've been very happy with.

288. Wash Outside Boat

A buddy and experienced Kenai River guide was having a great season one summer. Then he hit a three-day dry spell where he didn't have a single takedown. He'd not changed a thing, and boats all around him continued catching fish on the same tackle he'd been having success on. Frustrated, he reevaluated every dimension of his approach and could not figure out the reasoning for his instant lack of success.

Then, when securing his boat to the trailer, he noticed a slime build-up on the underside. Once home he took the boat off the trailer and gave it a thorough scrubbing with soap and hot water. The next day, and for the rest of the season, he caught fish every single day. The reason for his brief shutout was likely due to what he surmised to be a virus which was contained on the bottom of his boat, something many people never consider. At the very least, I'm sure the scum line held decaying bacteria which could have easily impacted the bite. Remember, the Kenai is a fairly shallow river, and back-trolling is how this guy fished. Apparently, in addition to laying a scent line with his baits, he was laying a repulsive scent line with the scum build-up on the bottom of his boat.

If regularly on the river with a boat, slime build-up can be a concern. I've talked to several anglers who've experienced the same thing, now they religiously clean the bottom of their boat. Keeping decaying bacteria from infecting a boat is critical, for this revolting scent trail is carried directly to the waters being fished, turning off picky salmon. Hot soap and a scrub brush can save much frustration, as can specialized boat washes, hull cleaners and mildew-stain-removing agents like those made by Supreme Marine.

289. Wash Rods

Fishing with cured baits can be messy, especially if gooey in nature. When done baiting hooks, take a few seconds to thoroughly cleanse your hands prior to making the next cast. This will keep curing residues from contacting and ingraining themselves into reels and more importantly, rod handles.

Keeping your gear clean, rods included, can make a difference in catch rates.

Cork rod handles are bacterial breeding grounds and the more encrusted they become with curing residues such as oils, powders and other chemicals, the more contaminated they grow. The more you handle such things as fish eggs, baitfish and even the fish themselves, the more likely the remnants are to be transferred to rod handles. As these residues age, the formation of unwanted bacteria and foul odors take root, thus impacting the target fish. By keeping rods clean, the chance of transferring repulsive odors to the terminal gear is greatly minimized.

When on the river, keep a wet rag handy, or occasionally dip the handle into the water to keep it clean and prevent unwanted materials from drying on them. Once home, be sure to check the grips to see if they need a scrubbing of hot, soapy water. Not only is having a clean rod and reel good for catching more fish, but it extends the life and functionality of both.

290. Back Off Reel Drags

Believe it or not, one of the most common ways reels are ruined is when they're not being used at all. At the end of the season it's common to give reels a thorough cleaning, maybe even oiling or greasing them as needed. But there's one more thing to do before stowing your reels for an extended period of time, and that's loosening the drag.

Backing off the drag to the point the spool can easily turn with virtually no resistance will help ensure your drag system stays working the next time you want to go fishing. The way a drag operates, generally speaking, is by way of pressure being applied to a specially designed spring. The tighter we crank down the drag, the more pressure is exerted on the spring, the harder it is for a fish to pull out line.

The drag pressure is actually created by the flattening out of a spring, and if that spring has constant pressure applied to it say, for several months while sitting in the garage, it weakens, even when not being used. Prior to storing your reels, even if it's for a couple of weeks, back off the drag. This will extend the life of the drag system and could save you fish. I've seen people lose fish because their drag seized-up due to the very reason we're talking about. Preventative maintenance goes a long way.

291. Wash Towels

Most anglers fishing from a boat or the bank carry a towel along for keeping their hands clean. Like many folks, I make it a point to have several towels in the boat, or backups in the rig when bank fishing. The key is keeping them clean. At the end of each trip, be sure to toss all towels into the washer, even if they were used only one time. Fish slime, blood and bait residues rot and taint towels fairly quickly.

There have been times when I've forgotten to wash my towels, then gone out fishing the next day and they smelled so rank, I didn't want to use them. I routinely go fishing with other folks whose towels smell the same, rank and sour. You know if these odors are offensive to human noses, how bad they must smell to fish. To reuse these dirty towels, then touch the terminal gear, is a surefire way to transfer stench odors fish don't like.

At the end of the day, gather up all towels and throw them in the wash with bleach, or replace them with fresh ones and wash the others later. I actually have multiple towels stacked in the shop, so in a pinch I can grab some clean ones and go. No matter what the cost, use only clean, dry towels at the start of each trip.

292. Wash Ropes

Ropes, such as anchor ropes and bowlines, are handled numerous times a day when on the water. These ropes often lay on the floor of the boat, where they come into contact with fish slime, blood and other dead tissue from baits being used. As the decaying matter rots on the rope, it contaminates it with foul odors, odors that repel salmon and steelhead. For this reason, it's a good idea to do all within your power to keep the ropes clean.

Another way ropes spread foul odors is when they pick up algae, moss and other foreign matter floating downstream. As these things accumulate on the ropes, they are pulled into the boat and left to sit in the bottom. Here they can dry, harden and begin to decay. Over time, the ropes emit a foul smell, a smell you don't want. On hot days these nasty smells can quickly be generated, which warrants cleaning the ropes at day's end.

In order to help keep ropes clean while on the water, consider winding them into a small, clean bucket; this goes for bow and stern anchor ropes. If your pulley system has a locking cleat that's long enough, the rope can often be hung on that, so as to prevent coming in contact with the bottom of the boat. But no matter how you keep them clean while on the river, remember, the ropes contract unwanted materials no matter what you do. In this case, wash them with soap and hot water when you get home, preferably before they dry. Preventing the spread of unwanted odors by way of keeping things clean is an all important piece of that fish-catching puzzle, one that often goes overlooked.

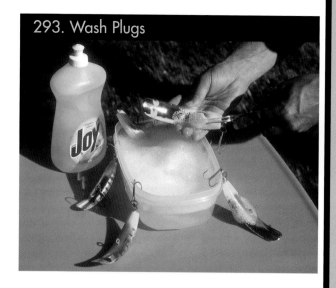

293. Wash Plugs

Whether you're fishing wrapped plugs or not, making the effort to keep them clean is of vital importance. Plugs that have been wrapped contain oil remnants from the fillets, and when drying, these residues solidify on the plug, often producing repulsive odors. At the same time, handling plugs with bare hands leaves human oils behind, something that may also make the difference in whether or not a fish bites.

Prior to placing plugs back in the box at the end of the day, take a few minutes to wash them in hot, soapy water. If you have a sled boat with a hot-water basin built in, these are excellent features, and save time by allowing you to wash plugs as they're used. Simply toss the plugs in the hot-water bin, let them soak, then give them a quick scrub-down with a brush and soap.

If you have to wait until you get home to wash the plugs, a toothbrush and some aggressive scrubbing is often required to fully remove all unwanted build-up. When done, hang the plugs and allow them to air-dry prior to placing back in the tackle box. If you find yourself on the water and not catching fish, this step can explain why your favorite plug may have quit producing.

294. Fuel-Up

Be it a boat or vehicle, it's a good idea to fill up with gas the night before a trip. Be sure tanks are topped off and gas cans full. You never know how long it may take to get fuel in the morning, that is, if you don't forget about it.

I was riding with a buddy one morning, and he forgot to fuel-up the rig. We kept driving, further and further into the country. The mom and pop stations weren't open, and soon we ran out of gas. That worked out great, for the fish.

Not only will fueling-up the night prior to a trip ensure one less thing to worry about getting done, but it will also afford you a few minutes of extra sleep which can be much-needed on those early morning outings.

Even if tanks aren't topped off, it's a good idea to do so, simply because you may end up fishing in a different area than originally planned. Over the years our plans have changed many times, especially when winter steelhead fishing. It's not uncommon to arrive on the river, only to find it blown-out. At the same time, maybe the fish aren't in the river you've been pounding the heck out of. Rather than call it quits, drive to a neighboring river, but make sure you have enough fuel to get there, especially if you're in an area where gas stations are few and far between.

295. Replace All Lost Gear

Replacing lost gear is something that's best done sooner rather than later. This is because the gear we often lose is usually our favorite plug, lure or drift-bobber. The reality, if you don't have your coveted tackle, your confidence level might not be up to where it should be. Likewise, if you go too many trips without replacing lost tackle, you could be surprised on the water one day when you dig into the tackle box and can't find what you're looking for.

One way I ensure I'm never short on prized gear is to always have extra at home. I'll take what I need for the river, but make sure that I have a stash at home to replace what I lose. This is particularly important when getting home late, and leaving early the next morning to fish again. If stores aren't open, it can be frustrating, and not having your favorite gear along is not a favorable way to start the day.

Tackle organization is important when it comes to replacing lost gear, and is something that often goes overlooked. Initially, it's time-consuming but in the end can actually save time, especially if it means delaying or postponing a trip due to a lack of gear. As for the initial costs of investing in more tackle before you actually have to have it, that will all balance out in the end, for you would need to go buy more anyway. Know what gear you have in the tackle box and stowed at home. Make a list of what items you're running short on, so you can pick them up the next time you're in town. Stay on top of the game at all times and you will maximize your fishing time.

296. Replace Leaders

Making sure you always have enough leaders on-hand is important, for the last thing you want to be doing is spending time on the water, tying-up leaders when others around you are catching fish. If you've ever had such a thing happen, it likely won't happen twice.

As with all tackle, keeping things organized and knowing what you have, and don't have, is important. This goes for leaders as well. If you lose a bunch of leaders on the river, make sure to tie up more when you get home, or perhaps the next day. Whenever you choose to do it, just make sure it's before you leave for the next trip.

One approach is to get cozy on a cold, rainy day and tie up all the leaders you can; sometimes this might get you through an entire season. This saves you from having to take time during the season, when the last thing you feel like doing is staying up until the wee hours of the morning to tie leaders.

No matter how you go about it—tying up a high volume of leaders at one time, or replacing them as needed—just make sure it doesn't get away from you. Stay caught up, have the number and variety of leaders tied that you need to suit your fishing needs. Such preparation will ensure that you're ready to fish at a moment's notice. It's much more enjoyable to be fishing when on the water, rather than tying leaders.

297. Cure Eggs

If you're an egg fisherman, we've all been there: You get home late at night, toss the fresh eggs you caught that day into the refrigerator, get busy the following day and forget to cure them. You may get to them a day or two later, but if looking to optimize your egg cure, this is not the way to start.

As the eggs sit there, uncured, their delicate connective tissues continue to break down. The bad thing, you don't realize this is happening until it's too late, that is, when you go to fish them. If you've ever fished eggs that fall apart after the first few casts, or milk out and lose color too quickly, it's not the fault of an inferior cure as is so often thought. More times than not, it's the fact you started with a poor-quality egg. How eggs are handled prior to actually curing them is just as important as the actual curing stage itself.

If on the road, it's best to cure eggs, then freeze them. This prevents having to freeze, thaw, cure and freeze them again, which results in broken-down cell membranes, thus eggs that easily fall apart. Take your cure or cures with you when traveling, as well as bags to cure the eggs in. When traveling, a little forethought can help save your eggs and result in better fishing results down the road.

If curing eggs at home, make sure to have all curing ingredients on-hand prior to heading out fishing. This way, when you get home, all you have to do is throw the eggs in a jar or baggy and start them curing. The last thing an egg fisherman wants to see is his bait falling apart on the first couple of casts, thus wasting valued time on the water. Keeping on top of your eggs and getting them curing as soon as possible will remedy this.

298. Daily Log

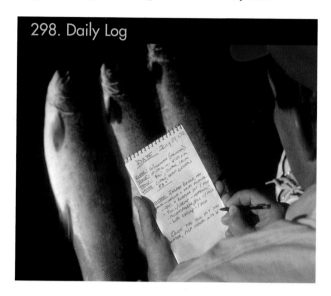

It only takes a few minutes, but can be one of those things that impacts your fishing for years, even decades, to come. It's taking notes at the end of the day, and while it requires a bit of time, it's more than worth it. Being able to draw upon personal observations is invaluable, and serves as a good future reference which can, and will, help you catch more fish.

If you're not into writing long sentences, then keep it simple. Make a listing of highlights you want to touch on and fill in the blanks as you go. Note such things as river levels, water clarity and temperature, barometric pressure, air temperatures, weather conditions, where fish were found in a hole, what they were caught on, what time of day they were caught, what the fishing pressure was like on the water that day and so on. The more detailed you get, the more information you have to reference.

By jotting down simple notes, you'll be able to establish patterns of when and where you catch fish. I once had a seven-year string where I caught my limit of springers from the same hole, on the same bait, standing on the same rock, all on May 22nd. I had a six-year stint where the same results happened with summer steelhead, on July 21st. That string broke due to my wedding the following year, but I did get out on the 20th and managed to limit from the same spot. These are just a couple examples of how note-taking can pay off.

Whether you jot notes in a tablet or on the computer, make sure they are scribed in a place where you can, and will, reference them. All of your time and effort will be for nothing if you don't go back and learn from what you did.

299. Report Tagged Fish

If, during the course of the day, you catch a tagged salmon or steelhead, report it. If it was a tagged wild fish that you let go, jot down the numbers of the tag and call it in to the source listed on the tag itself. If the hatchery fish you kept has a tag in it, pull it out or write down the tag number and contact information.

Reporting tagged information serves several purposes, and the more you can do to help, the better fish and game departments will be able to manage sport fisheries. Tagged fish allow biologists to track them, assess their numbers and calculate such things as how many fish they might be able to put in to a system for anglers. But there's much more to it than that. Tracking tagged fish also helps biologists unlock the mysteries of migration.

We once caught a tagged summer steelhead on an Oregon stream. The tag was a different color than the normal tags of fish in that river. Come to find out, it was not a recycled steelhead from that season, rather one that had been tagged a year prior, in a Washington stream more than 300 miles away. We've also caught fish that have been tagged in one river, turned loose, and showed up in another river a couple months later.

Not only can the information learned from tagged fish help biologists, but it can help anglers, too. What you learn by reporting tagged specimens will aide you in learning about the behavior and migratory tendencies of fish. For instance, if you know more than half of the recycled steelhead move downstream after being rerun—rather than shooting right back up to the hatchery—then you'll know where your time should be spent. However, if studies reveal tagged fish quickly scoot upstream, then you know where to be waiting for them.

Do your part. At the end of the day take a moment to report tagged fish. The more information you share, the more you'll get back, which is a benefit to everyone involved in this great sport.

300. No Such Thing As Luck

As the day winds down and you reflect back on your catch, don't make the mistake of dismissing your success as luck. In our family, L-U-C-K is a four-letter word. We simply don't believe in it and don't use it. Why? Because it doesn't exist. I'm a firm believer that everything happens for a reason, period. There's no chance involved. No luck. It's a matter of being in the right place at the right time, and doing something that caused or allowed a situation to materialize in your favor...or in the case of "bad luck," something turning against you.

Nowhere is this more true than in the fishing world. If you catch a fish, I don't care how big or small it is, it did not happen due to luck. You caught that fish because you put yourself in a situation to, first of all, pursue that fish. Secondly, you evaluated where to fish, not only what river, but what part of the river and more precisely what hole; even where in the hole to make that cast. Third, you determined what you thought was the best presentation to use and the terminal gear you thought would most likely catch a fish.

Once the fish is hooked, the decision-making process does not stop. While fighting a fish a multitude of variables may enter the equation. Do I need to pull anchor and follow this fish downstream? Is it too fast of water to land him in here, or should I pull over? Am I interfering with other angler's water? Can I keep the fish out of the anchor rope? Did I tie good knots? How do I net this thing by myself?

As you can see, there are hundreds of decisions an angler makes during the course of a day's fishing. So, is it "luck" when you land a fish? No. And don't sell yourself into thinking it is. You made all the decisions that led up to the fish being caught, don't sell yourself short.

What it really is, is you learning and applying principles and techniques that allowed you to catch that fish. Even more importantly, it's you transforming into a more complete fisherman. That's what this great sport is all about.

When it comes to consistently catching salmon and steelhead, there's no such thing as luck.

There you have it, 300 tips to help increase your time on the water and make your efforts more efficient. Of course, the primary and/or underlying objective of all these points is to help you catch more fish. While many of the points may have been obvious to seasoned anglers, keep in mind, one of the responsibilities we have is to share information with others, newcomers included, so they can get a taste of what fishing success is all about, helping carry our traditions to future generations. If you are a veteran of the sport, it is my hope that you came away with at least a smattering of new information, something you will at least try in an effort to catch more fish.

While fishing may be an individual sport, we're all in it together. It matters not what age, gender or nationality you are. It makes no difference what job you hold, or even if you have a job. No one of us is more important than the other, and when we're all on the water we are representing everyone—all anglers. With that it mind, it is our duty to do what we can to teach other anglers the difference between right and wrong. It's also our civic responsibility to do what's right, both legally and morally.

The author, left, and videographer Bret Stuart, at the end of a successful day of filming a TV show.

Conclusion

The author's sons and a fish apiece, taken solo; this is what it's all about.

It's up to us to carry on and promote the fisheries we have, so that future generations will take pleasure in living the dreams we have lived. This is where success comes in. The more successful we are—that is, the more fish we catch—the more likely we are to continue fishing. Hence, the more we learn, the better anglers we grow to be. The better anglers we become, the more confidence we have, and with confidence comes sharing what we know.

The processes surrounding fishing are an intricate combination of varied factors. The more tightly we can combine these factors, the closer our relationships will be with one another, and the sport we love.

PLANK COOKING: THE ESSENCE OF NATURAL WOOD

by Scott & Tiffany Haugen

In *Plank Cooking: The Essence of Natural Wood*, globe-trotting authors, Scott & Tiffany Haugen, share some of the world's most exquisite flavors. Thai red curry prawns, Achiote pork roast, pesto couscous stuffed chicken, and caramelized bananas are just a few of the unique recipes brought to life in this fully illustrated, one-of-a-kind book.

In the oven or on a grill, plank cooking is fun and simple. This book outlines how to master the art of plank cooking, from seasoning planks to detailed cooking tips in over 100 easy-to-follow recipes. Though exotic tastes prevail, the ingredients used in *Plank Cooking* are easy to find in most grocery stores. 6 x 9 inches, 152 pages, all-color.

Spiral SB: $19.95

ISBN: 1-57188-332-0
UPC: 0-81127-00164-4

COOKING SALMON & STEELHEAD: EXOTIC RECIPES FROM AROUND THE WORLD

by Scott & Tiffany Haugen

This is not your grandmother's salmon cookbook. The long-time favorites are included and also unique yet easy-to-prepare dishes, like Cabo fish tacos and Tuscan pesto. This cookbook includes: Appetizers, soups & salads, entrees, one-dish meals, exotic tastes, marinades & rubs, outdoor cooking, pastas, stuffed fish, plank cooking, wine selection, scaling and fileting your catch, choosing market fish, cooking tips, and so much more. The Haugens have traveled to and studied cuisines in countries around the world—including the Caribbean, Asia, and Europe—your kitchen is not complete without a copy of *Cooking Salmon & Steelhead*. 6 x 9 inches, 184 pages, all-color.

Spiral SB: $24.95

ISBN: 1-57188-291-X
UPC: 0-81127-00120-0

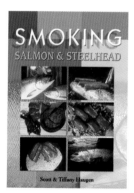

SMOKING SALMON & STEELHEAD

by Scott & Tiffany Haugen

Among the many benefits of fishing is the chance to bring home the occasional salmon for the smoker. But are you tired of using the same old recipe? If so, the Haugens have done all the experimenting for you. The result is this book, filled with 54 wet and dry brine recipes, including: sweet teriyaki, tropical tang, extra hot habenero, sweet & simple, chardonnay splash, spicy sweet, triple pepper, and many, many more. They also share great tips on different smoking woods to use, preparation prior to smoking your fish, cannon smoked salmon, their favorite recipes using smoked salmon, and a section on troubleshooting meant to answer basic questions. If you like smoked salmon, you need this book. 6 x 9 inches, 96 pages, all-color.

Spiral SB: $19.95

ISBN: 1-57188-290-1
UPC: 0-81127-00119-4

COOKING BIG GAME

by Scott & Tiffany Haugen

Ginger Coconut Venison, Cajun Smothered Pork, Orange-Soy Jerky, Planked Bear & Onions; these are just a sampling of the more than 100 classic and imaginative recipes found in this exciting book. Thanks to the subsistence lifestyle they led in Alaska, and their adventures abroad, the Haugens have gained real-life knowledge when it comes to preparing wild game. The result is an eclectic mix of tantalizing and healthy recipes that will transform the way many people view wild game.

Game meat is one of the most nutritious forms of protein, and diversity in preparation greatly impacts the end result. For the Haugen family, wild game is a part of everyday life, whether it's prepared on the stove or grill, in the oven or slow-cooked. When it comes to elk, deer, antelope, moose, bear, wild pig and more, *Cooking Big Game* unveils some of the most enticing, easy-to-follow recipes ever assembled in one book. No matter what your level of cooking experience, this book will introduce you to creative dishes all will enjoy for years to come.

Spiral SB: $19.95

ISBN: 1-57188-407-6
UPC: 0-81127-00241-2

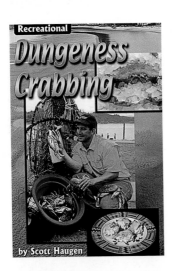

RECREATIONAL DUNGENESS CRABBING
by Scott Haugen

From Alaska to Mexico, Dungeness crabs are pursued for sport and their fine eating quality; *Recreational Dungeness Crabbing* gives you all the information you need to enjoy safe, fun, and productive crabbing. With an emphasis on family, safety, and fun, Haugen covers: natural history of the Dungeness crab; gear; bait; crabbing from a dock or boat; offshore crabbing; raking and dip netting; rod & reel; diving for crabs; crabbing in Oregon and Washington, including hot spots; cleaning and preparing your catch; favorite crab recipes; and more. 6 x 9 inches, 72 pages, full-color.

SB: $12.95

ISBN: 1-57188-288-X
UPC: 0-81127-00109-5

SUMMER STEELHEAD FISHING TECHNIQUES
by Scott Haugen

Scott Haugen is quickly becoming known for his fact-filled, full-color fishing books. This time Haugen explores summer steelhead, including: understanding summer steelhead; reading water; bank, drift, and sight fishing; jigs, plugs, lures, dragging flies, and bait; fishing high, turbid waters; tying your own leaders; egg cures; gathering bait; do-it-yourself sinkers; hatchery and recycling programs; mounting your catch; cleaning and preparation; smoking your catch; and more. 6 x 9 inches, 135 pages.

SB: $15.95

ISBN: 1-57188-295-2
UPC: 0-81127-00125-5

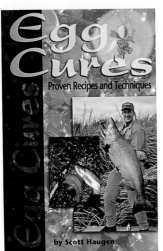

EGG CURES: Proven Recipes & Techniques
by Scott Haugen

Of all the natural baits, many consider eggs to be the best. Before this book, you'd have an easier time getting the secret recipe for Coca-Cola than getting a fisherman to part with his personal egg cure. But now, Scott Haugen has done it for you, he went to the experts—fishermen and fishing guides—to get their favorite egg cures and fishing techniques, plus their secret tricks and tips. The result is this book. These 28 recipes come from anglers who catch fish—read this book and you will too. Guaranteed! 5 1/2 x 8 1/2 inches, 90 pages.

SB: $15.00

ISBN: 1-57188-238-3
UPC: 0-66066-00492-5